SAM RAGAN

SAM RAGAN

North Carolina's Literary Godfather

Lewis Bowling

Kinesiology and Recreation Administration Faculty
North Carolina Central University

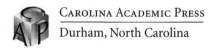

CAROLINA ACADEMIC PRESS
Durham, North Carolina

ISBN   978-1-5310-1705-7
e-ISBN   978-1-5310-1706-4

See catalog.loc.gov for
Library of Congress Cataloging-in-Publication Data.

Carolina Academic Press
700 Kent Street
Durham, North Carolina 27701
Telephone (919) 489-7486
Fax (919) 493-5668
www.cap-press.com

Printed in the United States of America

To my wife, Beth
  Journeys together, quiet times, your laughter,
  The light in your eyes,
  And the pure sounds of a flute—
  I carry them all with me.

To Ollie Lee Bowling IV
  Around the bend in the road,
  The next mountain, the next river, the next ocean,
  Telling us of the wonders beyond,
  Of a man's journey into those wonders.

To Bonnie
  These are the markings that I make—
  The trees now gold that will be green again,
  The slope of land to where the willows grow
  Along a stream that flows to woods
  Where birds now fly.
  I make the markings with my eye.
  For I have not traveled this road before,
  And the markings I make are to remember it by.

Contents

Acknowledgments

L ike Sam Ragan, I am from Granville County, North Carolina. We both grew up in small tobacco farming communities, he in Berea and me in Providence. Berea and Providence are just a few miles apart. For some years now, I have written a history column called *Looking Back* in the *Oxford Public Ledger*. So I have been referring to Sam Ragan, and Thad Stem for that matter, in *Looking Back* with pride, as two writers and poets we are mighty proud to have come from our section of the state. I hope this book does justice to the Berea Bard who did so much for literature in North Carolina.

I would like to thank my wife, Beth Bowling, for her assistance with this book. As with my previous books, she has been my editor, proofreader, sounding board, technology adviser, poem interpreter, and problem solver. Every book I have written, Beth has been right there alongside me. She is the love of my life.

I got my love of reading from my mother, Mary Bowling, who today at the age of 92 can still be seen walking through the aisles of books in the Richard H. Thornton Library in Oxford trying to decide on books to take home. My sister, Bonnie, gives me inspiration every time I see her as she battles a disease that will not let her do some of the things she once did, but she smiles right on through it. My other sisters, Martha and Deborah, and my brother, Lee, have always been there for me also. Two of my sisters, Dale and Phyllis, have passed away but are not forgotten. And my father, O.L. Bowling Jr., was a tobacco farmer just like the Ragan family was in Berea and Johnston County, and although he didn't write poetry, he sure liked to look at "green growing fields."

This is not my first book with Carolina Academic Press, and hopefully not my last. My editor, Ryland Bowman, has guided and helped me all the way through, and I am most appreciative. Linda Lacy at Carolina Academic Press has always been very helpful and encouraging with my books there.

The Sam Ragan Papers are housed in the Southern Historical Collection on the University of North Carolina campus in Chapel Hill, and I want to thank the staff there for their assistance. I also spent time in the Richard H. Thornton Library in Oxford and the Southern Pines Public Library. The Southern Pines Public Library has bound copies of *The Pilot*, which were so useful in seeing Ragan at work as a newspaperman. *The News and Observer* of Raleigh, *The Pilot* in Southern Pines, and the *Oxford Public Ledger* offered many articles about Sam Ragan and articles and columns written by Sam Ragan. In *Pembroke Magazine* and *St. Andrews Review* were many articles and references to Ragan.

I want to thank very sincerely the family of Sam Ragan. Talmadge Ragan and Nancy Ragan, his daughters, and Robin Smith and Eric Smith, his grandchildren, were most helpful. They helped me get to know Ragan as a father, as a grandfather, as a husband, and what he was like away from the office. I turned to them many times, and they always answered me promptly and with informative details. Talmadge even gave me one of Ragan's bow ties, and Nancy and Robin gave me a personal notepad that belonged to Ragan, both gifts I treasure. I also very much enjoyed talking on the phone with Dorothy Ragan Jones, the last surviving sister of Sam Ragan's. What a joy it was to talk with her, and I learned so much more about her beloved brother. Jim Austin and Jerrod Rogers, both family members, were also very helpful.

But to Talmadge, Nancy, and Robin, especially, I could not have written this book without your support and help. You really made me feel like a member of the Ragan family.

Shelby Stephenson, Marsha Warren, and Clyde Edgerton wrote tributes to Ragan for this book. All three of these writers are enshrined in the North Carolina Literary Hall of Fame, and they wanted to honor Sam Ragan and did so very movingly with their words dedicated to a man they admired so much.

Elizabeth Spencer is a legend in the writing community of North Carolina, just like Sam Ragan. I visited Mrs. Spencer in her home in Chapel Hill on several occasions, and she always greeted me with a warm smile and an outstretched hand. She was glad to talk about Sam Ragan, and would always steer my comments about her work away from the conversation. Mrs. Spencer offered me lots of encouragement on this book. And what a pleasure it was to sit next to someone and listen to stories about people she knew, such as William Faulkner, Robert Frost, and, of course, Sam Ragan.

Lois Holt shared her thoughts of "Mr. Ragan" with me and allowed me to use both a poem she wrote and an article she wrote about a man she will never forget. Stephen Smith met with me, as did Glenn Sides. They gave me some real insights into Sam Ragan as a poet and as a newspaperman.

Katrina Denza and Dotty Starling at the Weymouth Center for the Arts and Humanities were very helpful, and the archives at Weymouth yielded papers with good information. Weymouth also has copies of *Southern Accent*, Ragan's longtime literary column, published in *The Pilot* newspaper, and these columns gave me much material for this book. Dotty Starling, Weymouth's Archivist, arranged extra hours so I could have access to these copies, for which I am very thankful. Weymouth also had pictures.

Other individuals who helped me were Charles Blackburn, Christine Ganis, Alice Osborn, Ed Southern, Ted Wojtasik, Dr. John Dempsey, Rebecca Godwin, Faye Dasen, Alan Butler, June Guralnick, Mae Woods Bell, Charles Fiore, Todd Johnson, Howie DeVane, and Marilyn Bridgeman. Charles Blackburn deserves so much credit for making the copies of *Southern Accent* available with ready access at Weymouth. Charles always answered my emails and encouraged me along the way.

Marguerite "Dety" Stem and I visited quite often in her Raleigh apartment before she passed away in 2012. Mrs. Stem was the wife of the writer Thad Stem, and they were good friends to Sam and Marjorie Ragan, so I heard a lot about Sam Ragan before I started writing this book. Mrs. Stem edited one of my previous books, on Alabama and Duke football coach Wallace Wade. She was a tough editor, but I sure wish she had been around to edit this book on Sam Ragan. I know she would have been pleased to see this book published, as she had told me more than once this was a book long overdue.

Governor Jim Hunt talked with me on the phone about Ragan, and offered a blurb for the book. Governor Hunt gave North Carolina such long and distinguished years of service, and one of his best decisions was to appoint Sam Ragan North Carolina Poet Laureate. But he just might be a nicer man than he was a good politician.

My wife and I once attended a church service in Plains, Georgia, given by President Jimmy Carter, and had a picture taken with him and wife Rosalynn. President Carter answered my letter to him about Sam Ragan, and

I must say it was quite a thrill to receive a letter from a former president, especially a man I admire such as President Carter.

Anne Russell is a lady who really offered much information about Ragan, and was a delight to talk to and write to. There can't be a sweeter lady in all of Southern Pines than Jane McPhaul. I met Jane in her home and she told me many things about Ragan. It was a most enjoyable visit.

David Woronoff as publisher continues today to make *The Pilot* newspaper in Southern Pines one of the absolute best newspapers in North Carolina and the nation. *The Pilot,* under David's leadership, was named in 2015, 2016, and 2017 the best community newspaper in the nation by the National Newspaper Association. I talked to David in his office as he sat behind the desk that once belonged to Sam Ragan. All along the way in writing this book, David offered and gave his support.

I talked with Frank Daniels Jr. on the phone a couple of times and he gave me his remembrances of Ragan and offered his support. Daniels is a former publisher of *The News and Observer* of Raleigh and chairman of *The Pilot*. The Daniels family is legendary in North Carolina journalism.

Mark Pace at the Richard H. Thornton Library in Oxford, North Carolina, has helped me with several of my books, and he did so again. Mark is a treasure to Granville County, just as Sam Ragan from Berea is.

If Jane McPhaul is the nicest lady in Southern Pines, Ron Bayes would get the honor for nicest man in Laurinburg, North Carolina. I met with Ron where he was residing in a retirement village and had a delightful conversation with him about Sam Ragan, a man he knew so well and admired so very much. As founder and director of St. Andrews Press and the *St. Andrews Review*, Bayes worked closely with Ragan for many years. A distinguished poet like Ragan, Ron gave me many insights into what made Ragan North Carolina's Literary Godfather.

Forewords by Shelby Stephenson, Marsha Warren, Clyde Edgerton, and Lois Holt

Shelby Stephenson

Shelby Stephenson was born in Benson. He spent many years teaching at UNC-Pembroke and served as the editor of *Pembroke Magazine*. Stephenson has written many books of poetry, and was inducted into the North Carolina Literary Hall of Fame in 2014. In 2015 he was chosen as the North Carolina Poet Laureate and served in that role until 2018. Stephenson knew Sam Ragan well as a friend and fellow poet.

Sam Ragan: Granville County to the World

Sam Ragan wore the literary community like a cloak settling comfortably over the whole wide world. Writers and poets live in his occasional poems to Flannery O'Connor, Robert Frost, William Faulkner, Ibsen, Martin Luther King, Randall Jarrell, Paul Green, O. Henry, Thad Stem, Guy Owen, Yevtushenko, Ronald H. Bayes, and scores of others.

His life and writings deal with recurring subjects: the Depression (Sam was born in 1915), poverty, mules, newspapers, politicians, soldiers, historians, poets and writers. His attitude beams onward, as his life and work evoke living history.

He served as Poet Laureate from 1982–1996. His laureateship was a lifetime appointment.

In 2018 Sam Ragan was inducted into the Cleveland High School Hall of Fame. I was asked to help represent him. I read the poem I wrote for him.

Sam Ragan: In Memoriam (December 31, 1915–May 11, 1996)

How glad I am that my high school helped move your hand toward
journalism and poetry and
democracy with a little "d." Cleveland High School: *This land of ours
is full of schools, schools both*

*great and small; when it comes to praising them, why my school beats
them all.* I'm proud you
graduated from my Johnston County school. I'm sorry your family
lost the farm in Granville, around

Berea, Shake Rag, Stem. You came to Bailey's Crossroads, lived near
Ebenezer Church, among the
Ogburns; your love of words showered acres, snuffling the burning
crosses. Hope was your story,

lyric, svelte. Poverty? You wrote in "That Summer": "A wild turkey
flew out of the woods / And
even if it was out of season / He fed a family for two days. / And it
was better than that mud turtle /

That looked like mud and tasted like mud." I loved to walk into your
office piled high with papers.
You'd peer over them, rise, jingle some change in your pocket and
say, "Well, what do you know?"

"On a scale of one to five, Sam, about minus two," I'd say. Your
vacations you took in your office,
mostly. Sunday mornings? When I'd drive by, I'd see your Buick
parked beside *The Pilot.*

From his early years in Granville County and in the years afterward,
when he became a public figure, an editor and teacher, and promoter of
the arts, his clarity of passion influenced and inspired generations of writers. Sam Ragan's vision for the arts continues to form and shake affirmation in a never-ending song which lingers in the hearts and minds of
human beings everywhere. — *Shelby Stephenson*

Marsha Warren

Marsha Warren was inducted into the North Carolina Literary Hall of Fame in 2018. Warren was Executive Director of the North Carolina Writers Network from 1987 to 1996. In 1991 she was named director of the Paul Green Foundation. Warren has won many awards, including the Sam Ragan Award for Contributions to the Fine Arts, the John Tyler Caldwell Award for the Humanities, and the R. Hunt Parker Memorial Award for Lifetime Contributions to Literature.

When you're asked to write something about Sam Ragan, how do you begin? And where? I think about Sam a lot—he's been vividly in my consciousness since he left us in 1996—that's 23 years ago now. It seems to me that he hasn't evaporated or even faded—he's as vibrant today as he was when he walked among us bow-tied and smiling in his handsome straw hat. I know that's true of everyone who's ever met him; ever been touched by his kindness; ever been privileged to have his counsel and support.

So where does one begin? Is it with his voluminous outpouring of poems; his fierce dedication to solid, truth-telling journalism at *The News and Observer* as managing editor; then, and I love this image—"taking his 1941 manual Royal typewriter with him to Southern Pines," to be publisher and editor at *The Pilot*. How about as the state's first Secretary of Cultural Resources; the first chairman of the North Carolina Arts Council; or as a teacher at North Carolina State University, Sandhills Community College and St. Andrews College? Those accomplishments are all part of his incredible biography on Wikipedia and in numerous other sources. So, I'll just recall the man I knew as Sam Ragan and the nurturing impact he had on the literary community of writers—all of us—beginners to well-published writers.

Sam was our literary godfather, and everyone knew it and we counted on him. I once referred to him in a talk I gave when St. Andrews Press honored Sam for his "lifelong contributions to the literary magazines and small presses of North Carolina," as North Carolina's "Literary Lion"—that nothing ever got past him that would harm literature and that he had the courage to speak clearly to the protection and value of literature. We writers rallied-round Sam when he established the annual Poetry Day at Weymouth—he introduced us and made us feel welcomed and accomplished. In Sam's "Southern Accent" (the nation's longest running literary column) in *The Pilot* he included poems of new writers he'd recently met; railed against lack of funding for the National Endowment for the Arts; scolded communities that banned books; reported on literary events all over the state and much, much more. In 1982, when Sam was named North Carolina Poet Laureate, he continued doing what he'd always done—even more so—but now it was official. I had the good fortune of working closely with Sam while I was director of the North Carolina Writers' Network from 1987–1996—Sam served on my Board of Advisers. But I would have met him as early as 1978 when I became acquainted with the North Carolina literary community—first at the Friday Noon Poets' gatherings at the Red Barron Restaurant in Carrboro and shortly after that at the NC Poetry Society meetings at Weymouth and all over the state and at the North Carolina Writers Conference.

Sam will be remembered for many reasons and one of his most impactful to North Carolina was the support he gave Southern Pines resident Elizabeth "Buffie" Ives (Adlai's sister and long-time friend of Katharine Boyd) as she worked to raise $700,000 to purchase Weymouth, the former home of James and Katharine Boyd—a 215-acre estate, and to form The Friends of Weymouth. With the support of many generous people in the Sandhills and around the state, the Weymouth Center for the Arts & Humanities was incorporated in 1977 and two years later, the Writers-in-Residence program was established. Writers would come to stay in the Boyd's former home and hear echoes of the many literary voices that resounded in the spacious rooms. Sam told us the stories of these great writers who had come to visit the Boyds and to stay and write—he regaled us with the colorful story of Thomas Wolfe's late-night entry into the house through a window, having walked up from the train station, only to be discovered the next morning draped across several sofas—all 6′6″ of him. Sam told us about the times that James Boyd and his best friend, Paul Green, would take turns writing in his study—one reciting, while pacing the room, and the other sitting on the couch inscribing and then trading places. He reminded us about the extraordinary literary legacy North Carolina was fortunate to inherit as a result of Jonathan Daniel's declaration that "Weymouth was the site of the Southern Literary Renaissance." So just as Thomas Wolfe, Sherwood Anderson, F. Scott Fitzgerald, Paul Green, Maxwell Perkins, Lawrence Stallings and John Galsworthy, and maybe even — Sam was never quite sure — William Faulkner came to write, so writers today come to write. Sam knew that as we celebrated the writers who came before us that now we would be expected and charged to become a legacy for the next generations.

Sometime before 1992, Sam got the notion that North Carolina should have a Center for the Book like some other states had, and, as part of that program, we would establish a literary hall of fame. He had in mind a building in downtown Southern Pines about to be vacated, but the cost to bring it to ADA compliance wasn't feasible so James Boyd's former study at Weymouth was selected, and we began our work. After much deliberation and planning, the North Carolina Writers' Network, with the cooperation of the Weymouth Center, help from many writers in the state and financial support from the Department of Cultural Resources, and with Sam at the helm, we were able to set up the North Carolina Literary Hall of Fame in 1996 — it would be Sam's last and greatest gift to the State. Sam died just one week before the first induction ceremony on May 18, 1996 for 15 deceased writers — our strong literary legacy — handpicked by Sam Ragan. We were in touch with David Brinkley (who Sam had given his first newspaper job in Wilmington) and he sent a video tribute for that first induction ceremony on the Weymouth grounds beneath the flowering cherry trees. Sam was inducted the next year.

In 2004 a "Bring Sam Home" campaign was launched to purchase the $25,000 bronze bust of Sam sculpted some years before, in Sam's office at *The Pilot*, by acclaimed sculptor Gretta Bader. In 2005, we celebrated with a "Welcome Sam Home" gala at Weymouth. Sam resides right there in the front entry of Weymouth watching out for all of us — and you can hear him say to us in spirit, as he had in life, "Writing poetry is a journey and the journey counts — not getting there." — *Marsha Warren*

Clyde Edgerton

Clyde Edgerton was born in Durham and graduated from UNC-Chapel Hill. He is a professor at UNC-Wilmington, and wrote his first book, *Raney,* in 1985. Two of his books, *Walking Across Egypt* and *Killer Diller,* have been made into films. Along with being awarded a Guggenheim Fellowship, Edgerton was selected for the North Carolina Award for Literature. He wrote the following about Sam Ragan.

I lived in Pinehurst across from the harness racing track from about summer of 1985 to the summer of 1986. I'd heard of Sam Ragan because he'd sort of blazed the way as North Carolina's first Cultural Secretary and I knew he was a poet. I think I met him through either Shelby Stephenson or Steve Smith, or both of them. There would be literary gatherings here and there and especially at Weymouth Center. I'd come out with my first novel in the spring of '85, and was writing my second, and looked up to him as a sort of state celebrity and poet at the same time. He had a kind of gentlemanly swash-buckling presence — with an ever-present bow tie and a twinkle in his eye and an almost-smile constantly on his face — waiting to break into a smile. He was always ready to laugh, or patiently listen to a story, or tell a story.

He seemed to have no favorites among younger writers — there was a calmness and steadiness and an almost skinny-tall-man-Buddha-like quality about him. I was always happy to see him and I would pop in occasionally to *The Pilot* newspaper office in Southern Pines to say hello to him and Marjorie. He'd welcome me and I'd marvel at the great pile of books and newspapers and slips of paper (and in my memory, the kitchen sink) on his desk. And I was always impressed by the weight and thickness of each *Pilot* newspaper. He was a kind of guiding, literary spirit of Southern Pines and Pinehurst, totally void of any hint of rancor or ill will.

After leaving Southern Pines, I saw him less, of course, but when we did cross paths I always felt his warmth and good will. And his poetry was steady and matter of fact, and so beautifully and almost-stoically non-academic. — *Clyde Edgerton*

Lois Holt

Lois Holt is an award-winning poet and writer. She is a past President of the North Carolina Poetry Society and past Chair of the North Carolina Writers Conference. Holt received the 2009 Sam Ragan Literary Award. She has written many columns for *The Pilot* newspaper in Southern Pines. The one following was written in 2011 about Sam Ragan. It was titled "The People Who Change Our Lives."

It may be just my imagination, but I'm beginning to think that more and more of the men in my life are wearing bow ties.

If I tried to pinpoint it, this subconscious observation started in March when the North Carolina Poetry Society held its annual "Sam Ragan Day" at Weymouth Center. I have seldom missed one and always look forward to seeing my poet friends wearing outlandish, homemade paper bow ties in memory of the honoree.

There was a great deal of excitement about on that second Saturday. But the most noticeable difference was that all the men were wearing real bow ties. My mind went into instant replay.

Both of my parents worked in Erwin Cotton Mill, in Durham, during the Great Depression. My father was a loom fixer, my mother, a weaver.

There were no luxuries and little spare time. But they had finished grade school and could read and write, and each had their fair share of common sense.

My father referenced the Bible for encouragement and inspiration and, for knowledge, a set of Funk and Wagnalls encyclopedias, which he read with the same enthusiasm and earnestness.

One other book, *Great English and American Poems*, was treasured by my mother. By the time I was 6 or 7, I could recite her favorites: "Annabel Lee," Christina Rossetti's "Sonnet," and, forever mine, Alfred Noyes' "The Highwayman."

Somehow, over the years, the encyclopedias and the book vanished. Still, I thought of my mother as being a poet and believed that I might become one.

It would be the early 1960s before I moved to Raleigh and would read a column in *The News and Observer* called *Southern Accent*. I followed it and later submitted a poem to a smaller insert, "Today's N.C. Poem." Shortly after that, I saw an article about a writers' workshop being held at North Carolina State College (now the university). All three were identified with the paper's executive and managing editor, Sam Ragan—someone I had yet to meet.

To this day, I can remember that first evening, my hesitation and then a knowing fascination when I first saw the man sitting at the end of the table. His hair, graying even then, was combed straight back to end at the nape of his neck. And, at his throat, he wore an enormous bow tie.

There were brilliant writers in that class, and all were self-assured and seemed to be old friends. But I wondered how they would call him "Sam" with such familiarity when he was in appearance and manner the embodiment of everything revered as being Southern.

I have never pondered over or questioned the significance of the subsequent events. It was, simply put, a major turning point in my life.

It was with his encouragement that I joined the North Carolina Poetry Society. I accepted his invitation to be a writer-in-residence at Weymouth Center in Southern Pines and membership in the North Carolina Writers Conference.

I became a member of the North Carolina Writers Network and the North Carolina Poetry Council. I went to workshops and countless poetry readings. I studied style and meter. I bought books at book tables. And I read poem after poem.

More than 50 years have passed since that remarkable evening in Raleigh. Have I gone on to achieve fame, fortune and literary acclaim? No. But, I once met a man born with a love for learning and literature who made a mark by knowing his "sense of place."

In March, the editor of this paper portrayed that same silver-haired man and will repeat the celebrated performance at 5 p.m. Friday, May 13, at Weymouth Center. He was strikingly handsome in a sweater vest, long-sleeved white shirt and, of course, a bow tie. And, for a short while, we were both transformed.

Sam Ragan, a bow tie and fedora hat man who this month, on the 15th anniversary of his death, remains beloved by all who knew and were known by him. — *Lois Holt*

Lois Holt also wrote a poem about Sam Ragan:

For Sam Ragan

He is the South
as it was, is and should be,
mint julips and magnolias
textiles and tobacco.
He leans against the gate at #2 Mill
to watch the change of shifts
and listens to the slappin' of looms
tended by one humped
from years of watching the shuttle;
moves on to the Bull City
and the smell of the Bright Leaf,
swearing and swatting at tobacco bugs
on days when even the church fan
won't stir the air.
A little to the south now,
simmering sawdust
and jigsawed stacks of green lumber
set out to age like good wine.
He is the flaunted flame of azalea
on the sun-white of Southport,
the blushing bloom of dogwood
in my beloved Piedmont.
He is Boone, Little Washington
and Chocowinity,
overalls and chewing tobacco
black tie and tails
the dignity of Biltmore.

He is the South
as it was, is and should be.

Introduction

H. L. Mencken, the famed journalist and cultural critic, didn't like to pull his punches. He would rather give you a punch to the gut with everything he could put behind it. And that is what he gave the South in 1917 with his essay "The Sahara of the Bozart." Bozart was a pun on how he thought Southerners pronounced "beaux-arts." As far as he was concerned, the South was as sterile as the Sahara Desert. Mencken singled out the South as the most intellectually and culturally barren region of the country. He claimed that most Southerners' poetry and prose was not worth the paper it was printed on.

To say the least, Southerners tend to defend themselves when attacked. What is known as the Southern Literary Renaissance was the South's response in part to Mencken's diatribe. The 1920s and 1930s saw an invigoration of Southern literature. William Faulkner, Thomas Wolfe, and many others led the way.

In North Carolina, James Boyd, living in a grand house in Southern Pines called Weymouth, wrote the novel, *Drums*, published in 1925, about the American Revolution. Some look at this book as one of the opening salvos against Mencken, certainly it showed that good literature was being produced in the Tar Heel state. Thomas Wolfe would start to put North Carolina on the literary map even more in 1929 with the publication of *Look Homeward, Angel*. In 1930, Robert Penn Warren, Allen Tate, and other writers, all with roots in the Southern United States, united together to write a pro-Southern book, *I'll Take My Stand*.

But literature was being produced in North Carolina well before the Southern Literary Renaissance. One of the first books of poetry printed in North Carolina, if not the first, was James Gay's *Collection of Various Pieces of Poetry*, in 1810. George Moses Horton, a slave in Chatham County, in 1829 wrote *The Hope of Liberty*, a book of poems that is one of the first books by a black author from the South.

Ralph Waldo Emerson, in Massachusetts, published a well-known essay in 1844 called "The Poet." In it Emerson called for America to produce a higher quality poetry than what existed in that time. "The poet has a new thought: he has a whole new experience to unfold; he will tell us how it was with him, and all men will be the richer in his fortune." In 1854, the first anthology of North Carolina poets appeared: *Wood-Notes; or, Carolina Carols: A Collection of North Carolina Poetry*.

Of course, poetry was written in what is now America well before Emerson's essay. Anne Bradstreet, a member of the Massachusetts Bay Colony, came with other English to live in America in 1630. One of Bradstreet's more endearing poems was "To My Dear and Loving Husband." It begins, "If ever two were one, then surely we. If ever man were loved by wife, then thee." Phillis Wheatley, a slave, published her first book of poetry, *Poems on Various Subjects, Religious and Moral*, in 1773.

Perhaps America's greatest poet, Walt Whitman, published his first edition of *Leaves of Grass* in 1855. Whitman wrote that great poets can craft words that will help ease a nation from its troubles and create a better atmosphere for its people.

Even though Sam Ragan used words much more sparingly than Walt Whitman, compared to Whitman's extravagance of rhetoric, I think the two poets had some of the same philosophy. Of course, neither used rhyme as their style; they both thought that rhyme, as a literary device, could limit the meaning behind poems. As Leonard Wheeler wrote to Whitman, in praise of the free verse of Whitman, "O pure heart singer of the human frame divine, whose poesy disdains control of slavish bonds!" They believed a poet's style of writing revealed the human condition, and in much of each man's poetry that was the goal. Like Whitman, Ragan liked to use language that was more open-ended, which both thought would appeal to more people. Ragan believed that a poem should reveal meanings in human experience expressed in precise terms. He thought that too much modern poetry used extravagant and obscure language. Ragan thought poetry reached readers better when concrete words were used instead of abstract words. Using free verse, more like natural speech, Ragan and Whitman thought poetry would be better understood. Ragan believed in writing poetry that was accessible to most readers. He thought poetry should not be a luxury for a privileged few, but a gift for everyone. He once said, "I love the English language too much to waste words."

Robert Frost once said that he saw in free verse "an excessive glorification of freedom over structure." And he made the well-known comment that writing with free verse "was like playing tennis without a net."

Carl Sandburg, in his upper floor study in his majestic home high in the Blue Ridge Mountains of North Carolina, certainly agreed with Ragan that some poetry was too wordy, too abstract. "I say to hell with the new poetry. They don't want to say what it means. They have symbols and abstractions and a code amongst themselves—sometimes I think it's a series of ear wigglings."

Economy of words would not only be found in Ragan's poetry, but also would be a trait he would constantly admonish his reporters at *The News and Observer* in Raleigh and *The Pilot* in Southern Pines to be aware of. Ragan told his reporters to get the most news into the fewest possible words. He challenged reporters to "boil down," to compress their stories.

Sam Ragan's politics permeated his poetry, the reality of his life forged his words, and his family is found in his gentler lines. Just as Ragan's poetry came from his life experiences, Carl Sandburg's did also. Sandburg, whom Ragan knew, once wrote, "Poetry is written out of tumults and paradoxes, terrible reckless struggle and glorious lazy loafing, out of blood, work and war and out of baseball, babies and potato blossoms."

Sam Ragan felt a writer had an obligation to speak to their times. Ragan certainly did this, in his prose, speeches, and poetry. In his *Southern Accent* newspaper columns Ragan praised and critiqued local and national writers, wrote against censorship, supported humanitarian causes, and promoted the state he lived in and loved with all his heart, North Carolina. And poems such as "Notes on the Margins of Our Times," "The Day Kennedy was Shot," "We Shall Overcome," "My Old Mule Is Dead," and "The Depression," among many others, spoke to the times Ragan lived in and experienced.

Economy of words is a constant in a Sam Ragan poem. A book that had a profound effect on Ragan was Edgar Lee Master's *Spoon River Anthology*, in which Masters used free verse poetry. His study of William Butler Yeats influenced Ragan in this regard also. Yeats advocated stripping artificial things from poetry to form a "style like speech. Poetry that is naturally simple, that might exist as the simplest prose, should have instantaneousness of effect."

Read the poems of Sam Ragan. You will see the great gift he had to see and then convey the magic in an ordinary moment. With his poetry and prose, Ragan makes the ordinary seem extraordinary.

Whitman once wrote: "The proof of a poet is that his country absorbs him as affectionately as he has absorbed it." Of course I make no comparison to the country absorbing Whitman as it has to Sam Ragan as a poet, even though two of Ragan's poetry books were nominated for the Pulitzer Prize. But for sure, I can say North Carolina absorbed Sam Ragan as affectionately as he absorbed North Carolina. My goodness, the man loved the Tar Heel state, and his state loved this Southern gentleman.

Betty Smith, a friend of Ragan's who lived much of her life in Chapel Hill, and author of the bestselling book *A Tree Grows In Brooklyn*, once wrote about attributes of writers. What she wrote was a good description of Ragan as a writer, who believed strongly that his prose and poetry came from his experiences from daily living. "A writer is made up of hope, fear, elation, grief, greed, generosity, kindness, cruelty and all the emotions that are common to man. He is by turned bruised and strengthened by the terrific impact of living. But he has that intangible, wonderful something that makes him selectively articulate about all these things and enables him to find the words to write about them and about all the things pulled out of his very life." As you read this book, I think you will see in so many examples that Ragan's prose and poetry were related to events and people he experienced in his "very life."

Slowly in North Carolina a higher quality poetry began to be produced. In 1883, John Henry Boner published *Whispering Pines*. James Boyd, author of *Drums*, also wrote outstanding poetry. John Charles McNeill was a noted poet who was the first winner of the Patterson Cup for Literary Excellence in North Carolina. His book of poems, *Songs Merry and Sad*, was published in 1906. The North Carolina Poetry Society was formed in 1932, and in 1950 the North Carolina Writers Conference was started, in which Ragan played a role in forming. In the 1940s, colleges started to welcome poets to their teaching staffs. Some of these were Randall Jarrell at the Woman's College at the University of North Carolina, now the University of North Carolina at Greensboro, Helen Bevington at Duke, and Charles Edward Eaton at UNC-Chapel Hill.

Bernice Kelly Harris, one of the most noted novelists from North Carolina, spoke about the rise of good literature in the state in 1954.

Southerners do write — probably they must write. It is the way they are: born readers and reciters, great document holders, diary keepers, letter exchangers and savers, history tracers—and, outstaying the rest, great talkers. Children who grow up listening through rewarding stretches of unhurried time, reading in big lonely rooms, are naturally more prone than other children to be entertained from the first by life and to feel free, encouraged, and then in no time compelled, to pass their pleasure on.

Place must have something to do with this fury of writing with which the South is charged. If one thing stands out in these writers, all quite different from another, it is that each feels passionately about Place. And not merely in the historical and prideful meaning of the word, but in the sensory meaning, the breathing world of sight and smell and sound, in its earth and water and sky, its time and its seasons. In being so moved, the Southerners—one could almost indisputably say—are unique in America today.

Sam Ragan echoed some of what Harris spoke about when he once commented on writers from the South.

Place is important to me. I think that it's important to most Southern writers. Malcolm Cowley, one of the best of the literary critics, has said there are three distinguishing characteristics about Southern literature that made it dominant over any other literature in the country, a strong sense of place, the strong sense of family, and a strong oral quality. That Southern writers wrote just like they were talking to you on the front porch or around a fireplace on a winter evening.

North Carolina poetry and prose writing started to grow in the 1930s, 40s, and 50s. Into this era came Sam Ragan, who started his newspaper career in the 1930s. Ragan became very influential in North Carolina journalism in 1941 after being named as state editor of *The News and Observer* in Raleigh, one of the largest and most noted papers in the state. But he really started to influence writing in North Carolina in a big way in 1948 when he first published his *Southern Accent* newspaper column.

Southern Accent would run from 1948 to 1996, 48 years. Ragan's prose was, like his poetry, clear and concise, but also very engaging. Many North Carolina writers had their books publicized by Ragan in this column, and many saw their poems in print for the first time here. Reynolds Price, while still in high school, stayed up all night he was so excited, because he wanted to get a newspaper the next morning knowing he would be seeing his name in *Southern Accent*. It was a rare column when Ragan didn't mention one of the literary magazines in the state or one of the book publishers. Ragan used *Southern Accent* to praise, and in some instances, criticize, North Carolina authors. Writers from around the state, and indeed the country, knew *Southern Accent* would keep them up-to-date on North Carolina literature. *Southern Accent* included literary criticism and social commentary.

As the Director of the North Carolina Arts Council in the late 1960s and early 1970s, Ragan distributed funds to the literary magazines, many of which were getting started and in much need of money. He also doled out money to small presses in the state. During this time, Ragan started the Poetry-in-the-Schools program, which sent writers into public schools for week-long residencies.

While with *The News and Observer* in Raleigh, Ragan published a "poem of the week." Ragan devoted at least two full pages, sometimes more, to literary efforts from around the state each week in *The Pilot*. There would be book reviews, mostly of books of North Carolina authors reviewed by North Carolina authors. Poems, columns, articles, and stories written by North Carolina writers would be on these pages. The book pages in *The Pilot* gave local and state authors a place to publish their poems, to write an article, to get paid for a book review.

Teaching writing was a passion for Ragan, which he did at North Carolina State University, St. Andrews University in Laurinburg, North Carolina, and Sandhills Community College in Pinehurst. Students of Ragan's published more than 50 books of prose and poetry.

For most of his career, Ragan traveled the state, moderating poetry and writing events, such as the annual Writers Roundtable. He made hundreds of speeches about literature and promoted North Carolina literary happenings. He did this in the 1940s, 50s, 60s and 70s, and even more after being chosen as North Carolina Poet Laureate in 1982, a post he held until his death in 1996. As Secretary of Cultural Resources in the early 1970s, he used the position to promote arts throughout the state. He contributed to the formation of the North Carolina Writers Network in 1985.

Ragan was the prime mover behind the establishment of the James and Katharine Boyd estate into what is today the Weymouth Center for the Arts and Humanities in Southern Pines. The writers-in-residence program at Weymouth was started by Ragan, offering writers a refuge to pursue their writing projects. The North Carolina Literary Hall of Fame, housed in the former study of James Boyd in an upstairs room at Weymouth, was the brainchild of Ragan.

Sam Ragan would light up when you called him a newspaperman, and it was as a journalist, editor, and publisher that he made great contributions also. He once said: "Newspaper work has interested me from way back. In newspaper work, you are an observer, and you are on the scene, and you touch everything that's important." As editor of *The News and Observer* in Raleigh and *The Pilot* in Southern Pines, he made his mark in those fields. Stanley Walker was an editor of the *New York Herald Tribune,* and in an essay on "A Good Newspaperman" he wrote about qualities Ragan exhibited. "He knows everything. He is not only handsome, but he has the physical strength which enables him to perform great feats of energy. He can go for nights on end without sleep. He dresses well and talks with charm. Men admire him; women adore him. He hates lies, meanness and sham but keeps his temper. He is loyal to his paper and to what he looks upon as his profession; whether it is a profession or merely a craft, he resents attempts to debase it." Walker didn't have Sam Ragan in mind when he wrote this essay, but Ragan sure would qualify as a shining example of what makes a good newspaperman.

But Sam Ragan didn't just lead the way for North Carolina literature, he fought for arts across North Carolina. I will just give two examples here. While serving as Secretary of what is now the North Carolina Department of Cultural Resources, he convinced the Council of State to pay off a $60,000 debt the North Carolina Symphony owed. Another example is that he was on the founding commission of the North Carolina School of the Arts and was on the first Board of Trustees for the school, which today is called the University of North Carolina School of the Arts, and is located in Winston-Salem.

Even today, more than twenty years after the passing of Ragan, his name resonates with North Carolina writers. Just read the words of Shelby Stephenson, Marsha Warren, Clyde Edgerton, and Lois Holt in this book, who both wrote moving tributes to a man they consider a mentor. An annual event, Sam Ragan Day, is held at Weymouth to celebrate Ragan's legacy, and another annual event, Walking into April Poetry Day, honoring

Ragan, is held at Barton College in Wilson, North Carolina. The Sam and Marjorie Ragan Writing Center is located on the Barton College campus, where workshops and classes to teach the writing profession are held for students and the public year-round.

Sam Ragan is North Carolina's Literary Godfather. To be honest, this is not a title I came up with on my own. In doing research for this book, I kept coming across so many other writers who called Ragan that. He no doubt deserves the title. Rebecca Godwin, the Director of the Sam and Marjorie Ragan Writing Center at Barton College in Wilson, North Carolina, had this to say: "Nurturing writers and helping to create an atmosphere conducive to the arts, Sam Ragan is largely responsible for the thriving literary community this state currently enjoys."

To borrow a line from a Ragan poem, "Birth and death, and in between a little living." Well, Sam Ragan did a lot of living from his first years in rural Granville County to becoming North Carolina Poet Laureate and North Carolina's Literary Godfather.

SAM RAGAN

1

Berea, Granville County,
Tobacco Country, "That summer
when the creeks all dried up"

The Farmer
I have seen sunrise.
I have seen moonrise.
From these fields.
You know the old saying:
A farmer works from sun to sun
A woman's work is never done
And there's a lot of truth in that
I have seen her face grow old and tired
And I ain't what I used to be
But I love to see things grow
There have been some good years
Along with the bad, and there's nothing
Better than looking out over
Green growing fields
There's something about the land
Which gets inside you and it stays
With you the rest of your life
This land has been in my family
For over a hundred years
I sure do hate to lose it.

Growing tobacco, which is what most people did for a living in Granville County, was hard work. But what came from that hard work was a decent living for many of the rural families in this section of North Carolina. And tobacco was rewarding work. Yes, it required long hours. "A farmer works from sun to sun." But all the same, "there's nothing better than looking out over green growing fields."

William and Emma Ragan enjoyed farming. They grew tobacco near the small town of Berea, several miles northwest of Oxford, the county seat of Granville County. Farming tobacco required a lot of help, and so William and Emma had a lot of children. One of their children, a little boy, was born on the very last day of December 1915, New Year's Eve. Sam Ragan would go on to become known as the "Berea Bard" for his great poetry, as evidenced in the poem "The Farmer." He would also become known as the person who perhaps did more to contribute to the growth of literature and the arts than any other in the state of North Carolina. Sam Ragan is "North Carolina's Literary Godfather."

Granville County, North Carolina, is older than the United States of America, having been established in 1746. It was named for Lord John Carteret, England's Earl of Granville. Samuel Benton bought over a thousand acres of this land and named it Oxford Plantation, on account that Benton had visited and possibly even attended Oxford University in England. The town of Oxford was formed from Oxford Plantation, mainly through the efforts of Thomas Littlejohn, and Oxford was incorporated in 1816. Berea, where Sam Ragan grew up, is about eight miles northwest of Oxford.

By 1896, Berea had as many as eight business establishments, among which were several general stores, a blacksmith shop, a post office, and at one time even its own newspaper. The post office was located in Luther Russell's store. Dorsey Oakley brought the mail from Oxford to Berea and Lucious Slaughter delivered the mail around Berea. Berea was once known as Walnut Grove, for its large number of walnut trees in the area. An artesian mineral spring operated in Berea during the early 1900s. A concrete and brick wall still stands where this spring was today. It was a location where people came to drink this medicinal spring water, thinking it would heal diseases and aid all sorts of aches and pains. It was also a nice spot for picnicking and courting. For sure, a young Sam Ragan would have come to this spring during his childhood. Dr. Elijah Meadows was the local doctor in Berea and the surrounding countryside from around 1900 to the early 1920s. The Ragans, of very limited funds, would have only called on Dr. Meadows when absolutely necessary. A one teacher school operated in Berea near where Mt. Zion Baptist Church stands today.

The area around Berea was also known as Shakerag. This name may have originated when country people in that area of North Carolina referred to shake a rag, which meant to "get a move on." Another thought was that there was a lot of moonshine whiskey making going on in that part of Granville County. But it seemed none of the moonshiners ever got caught. When lawmen came calling at the whiskey stills, the moonshiners would "shake a rag" and outrun the lawmen. Another possible reason for the name of Shakerag was that when a person wanted to catch a ride on a train coming through the rural community they would flag the train down by waving a rag. That would be in sections of rural Granville County where there were no train stations. But either way, Berea was also known as Shakerag.

In 1900, Granville County had a population of 23,363, and most of the hard-working people in the region were farmers, mostly of tobacco. Tobacco, or the "golden leaf" as it was called, put money in the pockets of many a family and food on their tables. Oxford and Berea were in the heart of the old tobacco belt, a prime tobacco growing region. Green fields of tobacco could be seen alongside almost every road you traveled on in Granville County, thousands and thousands of acres of the stuff. Berea, in the early 1900s, might as well have been in Durham County, because most of the country roads were nothing more than dirt, and besides, getting to Oxford by horse and wagon took hours. But if you were a tobacco farmer, like Sam Ragan's parents, William and Emma, that tobacco had to be taken off the stalks and bundled up and taken to market to sell, and Oxford was absolutely loaded with great, big tobacco warehouses. There were over ten of these monstrous buildings in and around Oxford, with many longer than a football field. During tobacco market season, around late summer and fall, your nostrils would start to pick up the sweet aroma of cured tobacco more than a mile outside of town as you rode into Oxford. As you got into downtown, that sweet smell would be everywhere. On tobacco sale days, Oxford would be overrun with people, from farmers in town selling their precious leaf, to warehousemen, to auctioneers, to town merchants who employed extra staff to handle the rush, to restaurant owners expecting full tables all day long, to flocks of school children looking eagerly into store windows. After all, something as inconsequential as schools were shut down on these big tobacco market days. And even in hindsight, looking back from today's perspective that was just fine, because tobacco money built Oxford into what it was then, and is now. Farmers spent their money in local stores, paid their school taxes with tobacco money, put that money in local banks. Banks and businesses made money off the hard work of farmers, and farmers kept merchants and "money houses" profitable.

It is doubtful young Sam Ragan would have made the trek into Oxford an awful lot, since his family was all those miles up in Berea, and the only means to connect the two in those times were those dusty, hole strewn dirt roads. During rainy weather it would have been next to impossible. And too, it would take most of a day to make the trip to Oxford and back to Berea, and that was a day that most farmers needed to be in their fields. But for sure, as the 1900s moved forward, Oxford was a busy town with its main income coming from the many tobacco farms that were everywhere in Granville County.

Of course, tobacco work was hard, and there were other problems farmers dealt with. Weather is always a factor, as long periods without rain could wipe away profits, or too much rain could hinder development of the crop and even drown it. Agricultural markets could fluctuate from year to year, the economy could change, other sections of the country could start producing more tobacco, and pests and diseases could ruin crops.

But in the 1910s tobacco yielded good profits for farmers, which meant they had money to put in banks, money to go into Oxford, Berea, Stovall, Creedmoor, Stem, Durham, and other towns and buy clothes, food, and cars, which drove the local economy. Merchants even advertised directly to farmers, with lines such as "Mr. Farmer, We Have the Best Goods in Town."

As a young boy, Sam remembered his father talking in one of the big warehouses in Oxford with a man who had gone to China as a tobacco company representative. The company wanted its men to get close to the Chinese people and to learn their customs and their language. So the tobacco company had a policy of paying their men an extra $500 a year for every 100 words of Chinese they could learn. On the way home to Berea, Sam remembered his daddy laughing about that and telling Sam that his daddy was going to have to learn Chinese.

The 1920s were not as good for tobacco farmers in Granville County. William Ragan felt this change, for sure. For most of his adult life, William Ragan did not own his own land. Therefore he rented land from landowners to farm his tobacco. The 1910 census listed Ragan as a married man living in Walnut Grove Township, Berea, and he was renting. In 1920, when Sam Ragan would have been four years old, William was again listed as a renter. But on February 9 of 1920, William Ragan bought 47 acres of land and paid $705 for it. The land was in Berea, and his property adjoined the lands of Jim Hobgood and Henry N. Thorp. The 47 acres William Ragan bought was from Louvinia Hemis Fuller. A well-known lawyer and politician of Oxford, Archibald Arrington Hicks, attested the sale documents. In 1930 William Ragan is still listed as an owner of his land, but by 1940, after the family had moved from Granville County, and William is listed as living in Wake County, he is back to being listed as a renter. William Ragan, although I didn't find official documentation to prove this, more than likely lost his land or was forced to sell his land in 1930 and that precipitated a Ragan family move out of Granville County.

In the 1920s prices fell for the "golden leaf." Ownership of land by farmers fell; from 1920 to 1930 the number of farmers who owned their land fell from over 42 percent to 36 percent. Tenants, farmers who rented land to raise crops, swelled in the 1920s. William Ragan was a tenant farmer, for the most part, raising tobacco and other crops on other people's land. Along with tending crops, William Ragan worked hard at other jobs, such as working in a lumber yard. He helped to build houses, and also ran a small country store in Berea. In fact, with times always seeming tough and a house full of folks, William Ragan did just about anything that would bring a little money in. William could not read or write, while his wife, Emma, was literate. Hunts in the woods would yield an occasional deer or turkey, while squirrels were shot also when meat was scarce, as it often times was. Fish were caught in local ponds and the Tar River. Emma was also a hard worker, and a very industrious woman. She raised chickens and planted a garden each year for food, mended clothes that needed repairing from farm chores, and provided love to her family.

Farming was a good way to make a living, and farmers in Granville County were proud. Going into what was known as "public work" was looked down on just a bit. People felt sorry for neighbors who had to work with the public. It meant they had failed as a farmer and had to depend upon someone else to provide him with the money to feed and clothe his family. An independence was lost, and neighbors were sorry to see it happen. Berea was a community that was far from any big town, where most everyone was a farmer. It was all they knew for the most part, and even when things got tough, which they often did, very tough, there was a real pride in what they did for a living. And going into "public work" was looked down upon, while farming was looked at as a way of living one took pride in. And for the most part, the Ragans were farmers, no doubt about that.

Sam once recalled talking with an old farmer in Berea about a family who was forced to get jobs in Oxford. "I remember this farmer talking about a man he knew who had a bright future. But this man lost out. Had to give up. Moved into Oxford, and the farmer lost track of him for a while. Then one day the farmer saw him cutting hair, he looked prosperous. Had the first chair, too. His wife had a job in the cotton mill in town. But he didn't look happy."

One habit Sam Ragan developed later in life was to put one of his hands in a pants pocket and jingle his loose change. He would do this sitting or standing. Perhaps this might be a result of his growing up poor, and that this habit might be a reminder to Sam that he had done well, that he had a little money as an adult. Several people who knew him well, when asked about this, came to the same conclusion.

William and Emma Ragan instilled in Sam that one should work hard, care for family, do things right, and respect others. Both of his parents were rather easygoing and tolerated other people's viewpoints, and this was a trait that Sam became known for later in his life. His parents had a great influence on his personality and character.

William Samuel Ragan, Sam's daddy, was born in Granville County, North Carolina, in 1875. William Samuel was the son of William Ragan, who married Elizabeth Slaughter. Samuel Ragan was the father of William, and would have been Sam Ragan's great-grandfather. An unusual thing happened with Samuel, who was born five days apart from his wife, and they died on the same day six hours apart at 75 years of age. Sam Ragan's mother, Emma Long, was born in Franklin County, North Carolina, in 1886. Emma's parents were John Long and Margaret Champion.

William Ragan married Emma Long in 1903, when William was 28 and Emma was 18. This union produced eight children. There were six boys,

William, Sollie, Stephen, Lacy, Melvin, and Sam. There were two girls, Margaret and Dorothy. Sam was the fifth child of his seven siblings.

At the time of the writing of this book, Dorothy was the only surviving child of William and Emma Ragan. I talked to Dorothy on the phone and she talked fondly of her family, how proud she was of Sam, and how happy she was a book was being written about her brother.

Margaret looked like Ava Gardner, according to many people who saw her. Ragan's love for Margaret comes through in his poem about her.

For Margaret

We have shared many things,
Spoken and unspoken,
And memory races over the years
Through the seasons
Of golden falls, flowering springs,
All the green and growing times,
Remembering your laughter,
Your independence, your caring,
Reaching out to others.
I think of you being there
For family and friends.
It was a long time ago,
I wanted to tell you
That you looked like Ava,
But you were better looking.
Now across the years,
Across the long remembering,
I send greetings and wishes
For the best always.

So with those eight children, there were ten mouths to feed for William and Emma Ragan during the early 1900s in rural Granville County. The children were expected to work and perform chores as soon as they could. The boys, at one time or another, all hunted, fished, worked in the tobacco fields, milked the cows, cut firewood, and whatever else needed to be done by young, strong boys. One of the first tasks Sam Ragan would remember was getting up early each morning to put wood in the fireplace in the house and in the wood stove. The girls did much work also, such as washing clothes, helping Emma cook, sewing, canning vegetables, working in the garden, and cleaning the yard and house.

The Ragans lived in a decent house, but there was never a lot of room in the Ragan home of modest size. The 1920 Granville County census showed that William Ragan rented the house. The boys, of necessity, shared rooms. The house sat atop a small hill, which sloped down to the Tar River. A young Sam Ragan spent much time fishing and walking along the banks of the Tar River and on hot days even swimming in it. A good, long vine close to deep water was a great spot for jumping into these waters. The Tar River is 215 miles long, flowing from Person County, North Carolina, into Pamlico Sound in Washington, North Carolina, where it empties into the Atlantic Ocean.

There was hard work required on the farm also. As soon as he was a young boy, Ragan was expected to work the fields, and there were chores around the house. "Everyone had an assignment, something to do, certain responsibilities. I had the responsibility of getting up first and building a fire in the fireplace and in the woodstove in the kitchen and then, if there was somebody in the house visiting, I had to go into that room and build a fire in that fireplace, see that wood was always by the fireplace and by the woodstove. We had a cow. I had five brothers and two sisters, both younger. One brother's job was to milk the cow."

One of the first memories Sam Ragan had was fishing in the Tar River and in a local mill pond with a great-uncle, Richard Ragan, who had served in the Civil War. His great-uncle had served under Robert E. Lee in the Battle of the Wilderness and at Gettysburg. Not only did this great-uncle teach Sam how to catch fish in the river and local ponds, but he regaled Sam with tales of fighting for the Confederacy against the "damn" Yankees. This great-uncle had a very independent streak, and once, during World War I decided to make a statement. There was sugar rationing, and Sam's great-uncle went into the county seat of Granville County, Oxford, and purchased his full quota of five pounds of sugar. Once outside the store, he waited for a crowd to gather, then hurled his bag of sugar against the wall of the store. Sugar dripped to the sidewalk slowly as the assembled crowd wondered just what this man was up to. After all, sugar was a precious commodity during these war years. But Sam's great-uncle figured he had made his statement against rationing, and proudly walked on off to his horse and buggy for his return trip back to rural Berea.

Many years later, upon becoming a poet who was twice nominated for the Pulitzer Prize, Sam Ragan wrote a poem titled "Sugar."

Sugar

It was during the war
And everything was rationed,
But what they talked about the most
Was how hard it was to get sugar.
The man heard the talk over and over,
And he got tired of it.
One day he went into town and bought
All the sugar he was allotted—
Five pounds of it—
And after it had been put into a paper bag
And tied with a string, he went outside,
Waiting until a crowd gathered.
Then he flung the bag of sugar
Against a wall and watched it
Slide down to the ground.
The crowd was outraged,
Said he must be crazy, and somebody
Wanted him arrested, but the policeman
Didn't know what to charge him with,
So he walked away.
"I just wanted to show them," he said,
"That there are things more important than sugar."

One popular pastime in Berea and northern Granville County was cockfighting. Bird fighting was also regularly done across the state line in Virginia along the Dan River. Granville County bordered the Virginia line. Raids were staged in northern Granville County during Sam's childhood for cockfighting, and the young boy heard tales of these local goings-on. Cockfighting went on in many other counties surrounding Granville, such as Person, Vance, Caswell, Warren, and Durham. Cockfighting during the early 1900s was considered a bit more refined than what was called gander-pulling, where a gander or goose was hung by its feet from a tree limb and a horseman would try to pull its head off at the neck as he rode at top speed by the hanging goose. Gander-pulling required some skill, whereas cockfighting was a spectator sport for the most part.

Along with exploring the woods, creeks, and the Tar River in and around Berea, Sam developed a lifelong love of reading and writing. The only book in the Ragan household was the Bible, which Sam enjoyed and read from. Sam started attending school in Berea in 1921. In 1922 Berea High School opened, where the lower grades were held also. There were not many books in this new school, according to Sam in a later recollection, at least not in the first year or two of its existence.

Young Sam Ragan and his family attended Goshen Chapel Church in Berea. He wrote a poem, "Bee Burning," about an experience at Goshen Church. The poem speaks to how maybe sometimes the preacher doesn't always practice what he preaches.

Bee Burning

At Goshen Chapel the bumble bees
Built inside the front door steps
And kept everybody out of church
For two Sundays in a row.
Then the preacher came
And burned them out with a torch.
And after he had burned the bees
He preached a sermon
About burning in hell,
Burning forever and ever.
I thought about the burned bees
Lying on the ground
In that Sunday morning sunlight.
They didn't burn forever,
But they would never fly again.

In 1924, when Sam was nine and it was summer, someone told him there was a woman in Raleigh named Marjorie Beal who would send books to Sam for free if he would just write to her and request them. But he would have to pay for the postage. Even postage money for William and Emma Ragan was hard to come by, with falling tobacco prices, even though they would have loved to have done so. So Sam did some extra work for neighbors and got up enough money to pay for the postage for the letter to send to Marjorie Beal. Sam asked Marjorie Beal to send him three books to Berea. Sam, at the time, was afraid this lady wouldn't know where in the world Berea was. After all, he had never been to Raleigh, the state capital, which was where he was told to address his letter. Under Marjorie Beal's name, Sam wrote State Library. No titles were given by Sam, simply because he didn't really know what to ask for; all he knew was that he wanted to read some books.

A week or so later, three Zane Grey Western books arrived in the name of Sam Ragan. Sam devoured these three books and fell in love with Marjorie Beal. Ms. Beal started sending a list of books that Sam could look at and make his three choices. Little did young Sam know another Marjorie, his future wife, would become the true love of his life. Sam read his three books, and sent them back, as he was told, asking for three more. He wanted to ask for more, but he had been told that was his limit. So, he again read the three books sent to him, and came up with a plan. He had a friend on the adjoining farm in Berea who was not as crazy about sending off to Raleigh for library books as Sam was. The friend agreed to help Sam out, so Sam did some work for this friend's daddy to earn a few extra cents for more postage. Sam gave his buddy the money for the postage and his friend then wrote to Marjorie Beal in Raleigh at the State Library and asked for three books to be sent to him. So, in this way, Sam was able to receive six books to read. Along with more Westerns, Sam got adventure books, some history, some biographies, and some travel books.

This borrowing of books from the State Library and Marjorie Beal went on for several more years. As Sam recalled later in life, "The horizons of Berea and Granville County were greatly expanded by these wonderful books. I continued my experiences with Marjorie Beal until the Depression finally wiped out both private stamp money and public book funds. But that summer when I was nine always will be a memorable one."

Later in life, Ragan wrote a poem called "Two." As he wrote the poem he was thinking about those early years of his life in Berea. "I think that this poem is a composite of several people there: my father, my mother, my grandmother, grandfather, aunts and uncles. I had an aunt who had been widowed. And she had a brother whose wife had died and they just lived together in the house, just those two. And I know too that it was a place right next door to where I lived and I visited there a lot."

Two

In the old house they sit alone—
The rain in the trees
Is hidden by darkness.
And hidden, too, are hoarded griefs
Forgotten now as to why or how.
Still—
Silent faces turn
To a watchful clock,
Crying to time:
Tell me, tell me.

Along with developing his love of reading, outdoor play in and around Berea gave this nature lover much joy. Ragan wrote a poem about those years in Berea later in life.

Crooked Run

We called the creek Crooked Run,
The way it wound in and out
Among the trees,
Never flowing in a straight line,
Taking a turn around the big rocks
And splashing downward
Into the shade of the big oaks
Leaning over the banks.
It wasn't much of a creek.
Sometimes it didn't run at all
But gathered itself into small quiet pools,
Reflecting splinters of sunlight.
Crooked Run was the dividing line—
A place to hide—
And I could hide there for days,
Waiting to be found.

Sam started his schooling in Berea in a rather run down wooden building that had been painted white, but the paint had long ago peeled off and was a "streaked gray" by the time Sam walked in its doors. The first four grades were all taught in the same room. There were few books, and although the teachers did what they could, a great education was not to be had. But Sam worked hard and was a good student, doing what he was told.

A few years later, not only had the love of reading taken hold in Sam, but the love of writing had also. By now he was in the new Berea School, a handsome, big brick building opened in 1922. He always maintained that writing was important to him since when in the seventh grade at Berea School a small "piece" he had written was selected for publication in the local newspaper, the *Oxford Public Ledger*. This was in 1927, so for the next 68 years or so of his life, Sam Ragan would be publishing work of his own. Writing became a way of life from that time forward.

Neil Morgan, who spent part of his early years in Creedmoor, also in Granville County, went on to a prominent writing career himself. Neil was a longtime columnist and editor of the *San Diego Tribune*, working there for over 50 years. Sam Ragan would give Neil his first newspaper job at the *The News and Observer* in Raleigh. Sam and Neil would remain friends for life.

Sam was born in Berea, a town of about a hundred or so on a clear day. I attended school several years later in Creedmoor. Our high school basketball teams competed, and in those days, Berea was a road trip, close to twenty miles each way by back roads, and in those days all Granville County roads were back roads. The journey from Berea to Creedmoor led through Tally Ho, a cross-roads that was the birthplace of James Webb, one of the greats of NASA. It led on through an intersection called Shoo Fly. After all that, Creedmoor, with about 700 people in those days, seemed absolutely metropolitan. Sam left Berea before I lived in Creedmoor. By the time he left Berea, he had already determined to be a writer. That had been settled in the third grade at Berea with an essay about a horse. Neither Sam nor anyone else I've found remembers anything more about the essay. Like all of us, Sam was immediately hooked. He had seen his word set down in stone. He knew it could be done.

So, whether writing became a part of Sam in the third grade or the seventh grade probably doesn't matter much. But for sure, somewhere in those Berea School days of the 1920s in rural Granville County, Sam Ragan developed an aptitude for writing that would lead him on a path to become one of North Carolina's leading newspapermen and poets.

One teacher who Sam enjoyed and learned from was Louise Crews at Berea School. A high school teacher who had a profound influence on Sam in Berea was Ivey Grigg, who graduated from Trinity College in Durham, what is now Duke University. On several trips back to Berea and Berea High School in his later years, Sam recalled his old high school teacher in his *Southern Accent* newspaper column.

> Not long ago we visited the old neighborhood in Granville County in which we grew up and we marveled at the size of the trees, cedars and dogwoods, growing on the grounds of the old Berea High School. Our mind went back to the time we helped plant them. Most of the planting came during the time we would have spent in a Civics class. Schools don't teach the course called Civics any longer, but at Berea it was taught by the school's principal, Ivey F. Grigg, and it was his idea to make the course serve a double purpose. He would get the school grounds beautified and also teach us about the importance of beautification. We learned the textbook, of course, about government at various levels, the structure of government and its processes, how county commissioners are elected and the functions they serve. We read the *Oxford Public Ledger* in class to see what the Granville County Commissioners were doing. But we also learned how to go out into the woods and select young cedars and dogwoods for replanting, and how beautification gave an extra dimension to our lives. Seeing those trees growing at old Berea gave us a greater appreciation of what Mr. Grigg was trying to teach. In the years since every time I have passed those school grounds and looked at those trees I have felt proud. I had a part in planting them.

Ivey Grigg had the conviction that place is important in shaping the character of a people. Mr. Grigg was a school man most of his life. He believed strongly in books, teaching and the classroom, but he also believed there was a lot to be learned by seeing for yourself and doing for yourself and in staying close to the land.

Not everything about going back to where you grew up is pleasant, for sure, as Sam wrote about some time later in life.

Going Home

Going Home is not easy,
It's not a place for going back,
It is always smaller,
Or it's no longer there —
Where apple blossoms bloomed,
And sunlight spattered on the grass,
A concrete cloverleaf now intrudes,
And young songs on the wind
Are now drowned in the roar of cars.
What we lost long ago
Is now lost again.

Sam recalled the Berea of his youth and what he saw some 30 years later on a trip in the late 1950s. It certainly would not be the last trip back to Berea, not even close. The big, two-story Berea High School was still there. Mt. Zion Baptist Church was still there, along with some of the other churches. A couple of the old general stores were there, bringing back fond memories to Sam, now a top man for one of the biggest newspapers in all the state, *The News and Observer* in Raleigh. This man, now in his forties, was earning praise for his work with that big newspaper and for his *Southern Accent* column that so many people in North Carolina read with eagerness each week. As the rural folk in Granville County liked to say, Sam Ragan had got "public work" and had done well, even by their standards. He was starting to be called the "Bard of Berea" in some quarters by this time. But things just didn't seem the same, not like in the 1920s in Berea, when dirt roads took you everywhere, when there were many more mules working the land than tractors, when there were more woods full of trees than the open land he saw now. Sam recalled this visit back home.

I think most of us have experienced it — going back to the place where we were born and brought up. I remember the place where I was born and grew up. The fields were big. The trees were huge. The woods were large. When I went back years later everything was so much smaller. The house where I grew up was a lot smaller. The big oak tree in the yard was not so big. I saw the trees had been cut down or blown down. The huge oak tree which dominated the yard was gone. I don't know if the wind blew it down or if somebody got tired of it and cut it down. I suspect somebody cut it down. And somebody had tried to plant some pitiful little things to replace the trees. They were about two feet tall and they looked scraggly and pathetic. It was hard to accept that. I think we should have a requirement that if you are going to cut down a tree you should have to plant one back right then no matter where you are. I remember an old field there, one which had been allowed to grow back to its nature and, at the time, I could see more pines growing back there. The last time I went back they were pretty-good sized pines.

How wonderful, I thought, to let nature take its course. There's a good stand of pine trees there now. Maybe that's the best thing to do. I want to preserve those memories of long ago; so I write a poem.

Later in his life, Ragan wrote about this topic in a newspaper column of his, *Southern Accent*.

Travelers along the roads of North Carolina can see the hundreds of abandoned farm houses — some empty but still standing, others with roof caved in or covered with kudzu vines — all telling a story of change, of a way of life which has disappeared or nearly gone.

Long ago we had hoped that some of these old farm houses could have been saved, if only to tell how and where people had lived. We once tried to get the State's Division of Archives and History to at least preserve some of the houses in photographs, but there was no money available for the project.

Other writers took note of the change, and we were much interested to see in the recent issue of the *Crucible* in Wilson, that Charles F. Blackburn Jr. had dealt movingly with the theme in a long poem he titled "Saul's Place." It tells the story of change and abandonment.

It is a long poem and we cannot quote it all in this column, but the following extracted portions gives you the full flavor of the message:

Saul's Place

The plow is a memory in the field.
The mule, a memory in a tumbledown barn.
The dwelling is a remnant of desire.
The sky plays its magic lantern show.
The pines at night intrude upon the stars.

New Deal driftwood, rusty tin,
Riding a wave of geology
Under a chinaberry tree.
Saul's house fills up
With possums every winter.
His door is always open
To whatever wants in.

This famous hospitality
Derives from a singular fact—
Saul quit this locality years ago.

Nothing here is up to code.
The power of carpentry
Cannot heal a house
So far past redemption.

It is a haven for hunters.
A place where high school kids drink beer.
When I see that dark house on my
Homeward march, I know home is near.

Did he move on when cotton played out,
Or did his credit desert him first?
When did Saul first begin to doubt
In that field south of the railroad?

Your mind goes, or your health,
Loved ones suffer and decline,
The crop fails, the mule dies,
The rent comes due, or taxes.
Then where the hell are you?

Maybe he knows
(Maybe he knew)
It's not the hardship.
It's our common humanity
That binds us in the end,
That saves us from being
Odd tenants of existence.

I have seen it in all weathers
And know its shape by heart,
Black against the sunset,
Every window ablaze,
More radiant than any cathedral.

Charles Blackburn Jr. worked as a small-town newspaper reporter and editor early in his career, and also was a part owner of a Chapel Hill used and rare bookstore. A frequent contributor to *Our State* magazine, Blackburn is a three-time winner of *Crucible* magazine's short fiction award. His story "Sweet Souls" led to a literary fellowship from the N.C. Arts Council, and he is a past winner of the Sam Ragan Award for Literature. In a phone conversation with Blackburn, he told this author about his poem, "Saul's Place."

Where I grew up in Henderson, N.C., there was about 20 miles of woods and fields back of our house between Henderson and Oxford that we roamed. We were regular woods rats. There was an old abandoned house near the railroad tracks that was known to have once belonged to a man named Saul. Judging from the empty beer cans inside, it had become an occasional refuge for restless teens. This was back in the 1960s. The place finally fell down.

A love of trees and nature would be a life-long passion for Sam Ragan, and his Berea High School teacher, Ivey Grigg, had a huge part in that development. Grigg would have been in his twenties when he taught Sam, and in 1976, at the age of 78, Grigg wrote a book, *Man of the Piedmont: A Profile*. This book was about the unique traits of the man of the Piedmont section of North Carolina, forged in pioneer days and recognizable in 1976, when the book was published by Crabtree Press of Lenoir, North Carolina. Mr. Grigg got in touch with Sam, who by then was owner and publisher of the *Southern Pines Pilot* newspaper, to edit the book. Ragan was happy to help his former teacher.

Paul Green, an author and playwright who may be best known for *The Lost Colony* outdoor drama, was a good friend of Sam Ragan's. Similar to Ivey Grigg, who had such a positive influence on Sam as a high school teacher, Paul Green had such a teacher in Hubbard Fulton Page. I include the following here as another testament to the power of teachers and the friendship of Sam Ragan and Paul Green, two men who influenced the arts in North Carolina as much as any two people. Paul Green attended Buies Creek Academy, now Campbell University, and one of his teachers was Page. Green grew up on a Harnett County farm. Paul Green wrote about Page.

Hubbard Page caused me to forego the plough and finally take up the typewriter as a means of making a living. He taught me the joy of literature. I can still see him as he used to sit on the platform there in the old Kivet Building at Buies Creek and read and talk to us about Hamlet or the Ancient Mariner or read to us with lighted eyes Robert Burns' poems. One Friday at school he made a date for me to come down to his little house there in the edge of Buies Creek the next morning and we would look at some of his poems. I was to bring along some of mine too and we would have a good talking. I arrived early, and we went to it. He brought out all sorts of old pieces of writings from an old trunk there in the harum-scarum room. He was a bachelor and remained so till much later and had little care at the time for the niceties of housekeeping. He read and talked. He read more Burns and a lot of McNeill. The noon hour came on. I got hungry, but he kept at it. Late in the afternoon when the light was failing on his reading, he came to and realized that the day was gone. Finally I timidly got out some of my pieces. He read them and praised them, though actually they were no good. And so I staggered home in the twilight, weak and famished, but happy, and on fire.

Just as Hubbard Page lit a fire in Paul Green, Ivey Grigg helped put Sam Ragan on a path to a great career. Sam Ragan and Paul Green would advance the state of the arts in North Carolina like few others, and their former teachers played a huge role in their lives.

By late in the year of 1930, life in Berea and Granville County was a terrible hardship for the Ragans. Farm income for the Ragans, just like so many other farmers in that region, had declined in the 1920s. There were many reasons for this, among them being falling prices for crop and rising farm costs. Constant use of the same fields depleted the soil of needed nutrients. Also, William Ragan had turned to cutting trees down on his small parcel of land to make money that way, and this led to soil erosion, which yielded less and less food from the garden. Land that he raised tobacco on, at times using other people's land, suffered from soil depletion and erosion also. Working someone else's land to grow tobacco, in exchange for earning some of the profits, as William Ragan did, became on a yearly basis a deal that put him further and further behind. A disease, called Granville Wilt, affected tobacco production in the early 1900s, and it caught hold in several of William Ragan's crops. All of these conditions, plus production exceeding demand, created severe economic strains on tobacco farmers. Tobacco, which sold for 86 cents a pound in 1919, by 1931 was selling for 9 cents per pound.

William and Emma Ragan, growing tobacco in the last couple of years in the 1920s, received less for their cash crop than it cost to produce it. Food and clothing and other basic necessities were barely obtainable. New clothes were no longer possible, as old clothes were kept and sewn back together or patched up. Hunting and fishing for their food took up more and more time.

Losing a chicken was a big loss for the struggling Ragan family. Ragan recalled that day with a poem.

The Day the Hawk Came

On that day in summer
When the hawk came,
The hen's cries signaling his coming
Into the chicken yard,
My mother came running
Flapping an apron.
But the hawk had gone,

Carrying the young chicken
Up and over the distant trees.
The sky was a bright blue.
My mother was crying,
And the hens had gone to hide.

Sam Ragan, by 1930, was 14 years old. He worked the fields with his brothers and father, he hunted for squirrels and other game, fished for food to be put on the table, and did odd jobs whenever he could find them. And there were three other Ragan kids younger than Sam still at home in Berea. By 1930 Sam's older brother, Stephen was 22 years old and working at a saw mill, while Lacy was 19 and had a job as a truck driver. Sollie was 16, Margaret was 11, Melvin was 7, and Dorothy was 3. William Ragan was 53 in 1930 and wife Emma was 43. Also, according to the 1930 Granville County census, two men were boarding with the Ragans at this time. Russell Bonner, 20 years of age, a white man, took a room in the Ragan house in exchange for work, and Pete Thorp, a black man 22 years old, lived in a small building close to the Ragan house.

With little steady income, poor tobacco crops, along with a couple of summers with little rain for the crops, and such a large family, William and Emma started to consider other alternatives, even if that made it necessary to move out of Granville County. Other farmers in the county were doing just that, and quite a few were moving to Johnston County. The sandy land there at the time was thought to grow tobacco more free of diseases, such as the Granville Wilt.

Much later in life, Sam wrote a poem, "That Summer," which recounted some of the anguish his family endured those lean years in their home near the Tar River in Granville County.

That Summer

That summer when the creeks all dried up
Except for a few deep holes
Under the caved out roots of oaks
Now leaning toward the water's edge
The catfish clung to the mud.
But now and then a perch was caught

In the oatsack seine.
Even the Tar was a trickle
And I could walk all the way across
On the rocks, and the place
Where we had swung from limb to water—
Splashing below surface and rising sputtering
Was now no more than moist mud
From which a turtle crawled.

They sat on the porches
And talked of the weather
And Herbert Hoover,
Cursing both, and every son of a bitch
Who had voted for him.
Even if the Baptists saved any souls
Worth the saving
Where in the hell would they find the water
To baptize them.

A wild turkey flew out of the woods
And even if it was out of season
He fed a family for two days.
And it was better than that mud turtle
That looked like mud and tasted like mud…
That summer when it didn't rain.

Of course, farmers had to deal with all kinds of weather. Droughts hit, and then another year perhaps too much rain fell from the skies, and high winds and hurricanes could damage and at times even destroy crops that had been worked on all year. Ragan wrote a poem about too much water and the drowning of a young boy. The following is an excerpt from "The Forgotten."

The Forgotten

That was the summer of much rain
And the crops could not stand
When the wind came.

By lantern light they worked in the fields,
But it was no use.

The streams were overflowing their banks
A boy was drowned when he went too near.
They saw him holding a willow branch.
It bent with him and he was gone,
The water swirling around the willow.
The last thing seen was his hand.

The Ragan family had experienced both the droughts and too much rain Ragan described in "That Summer" and "The Forgotten." They had seen droughts cripple their tobacco, the cash crop, as it was called in those parts. They had fished for catfish and perch and most any other fish that could be caught and taken home for a welcome meal. They had swum those waters of the Tar River to cool off many a scorching day. They had heard grown-ups sit and swear at the Depression and Herbert Hoover and the weather. They had hunted turkeys and not just for a Thanksgiving meal, but any meal.

As mentioned earlier, later in his life, after experiencing success, both professionally and financially, Ragan developed a habit of reaching into his pants pockets and jingling his coins. He would do this at times while talking with someone. A couple people suggested to me this was his way of remembering those hard days of growing up in rural Granville County, when money was so hard to come by for his family and others. Joy Acey would write this poem about Ragan and his habit.

Sam, A Very Rich Man

He stands,
Hand in pocket,
Fingering penny, nickel, dime.
Jingling memories of being poor,
Struggling.
He feels each president's profile.
No reason to begrudge the nickel
For not being a dime.
Each is special, unique,

Just like you.
"Your idea sounds good," he says,
Urging me to try it.
He knows the value of encouragement.

In 1994, Ragan wrote about a gift from his daughter, Talmadge, which recalled the place where he grew up, Berea, in Granville County.

Among the presents our daughter, Talmadge, gave me on my birthday were reproductions of the front and editorial pages of the *Berea Gazette*.

Bill Powell in his *North Carolina Gazetteer* reports on Berea as follows: Berea—Community in Western Granville. Altitude 475. Settled prior to 1870.

We were born at Berea, and it was then and now unincorporated, with three general stores, a post office, a Baptist Church, and a high school.

We didn't know it once had a newspaper until Bill Crews, the Southern Pines attorney whose folks come from those parts, sent me a copy of the *Berea Gazette*, on the front page of which was an overprint of a crowing rooster, the symbol of the Democratic Party at that time. It was an edition from November of 1876, and the editor was celebrating the election of Samuel James Tilden as President of the United States. Of course, history shows that the Republican majority in congress ruled that the votes of South Carolina and some other states were invalid and Rutherford B. Hayes was proclaimed the President. But for a few weeks at least, Tilden was the winner of a majority of the vote and the *Berea Gazette* editor, H.H. Latta, considered it cause for celebration.

In Walnut Grove Township, where Berea was located, Republicans were few and far between in 1876 and long into the 1900s. In the Calvin Coolidge Administration the postmaster at Berea died, and as was the custom of the times, a Republican was to be appointed to fill the vacancy. The GOP searched high and low for a Republican in Walnut Grove Township, and couldn't find one, so they imported one, a Mr. Partin, from Wake County, who served until the post office was shut down. Today Berea is served by the Oxford office as Route 1.

The copies of the *Berea Gazette* which Talmadge obtained through the Public Library—the Thornton Library—at Oxford and gave us were dated May 25 and June 8 in 1878. Under the front page masthead, the publisher proclaimed it as "An Independent Weekly Newspaper: Political, Literary, and Miscellaneous, Fearless and Frank."

A family in Johnston County, the Ogburns, Millard and Alda, offered the Ragans a house and land on which to farm. It would be a tenant farming situation, but it seemed like a better opportunity than those last few years in Granville County, so William and Emma decided to move in late 1930. Pete Thorp, the black man who lived on the Ragan place in Granville County, moved with the Ragans to Johnston County, where he lived in a tobacco pack house at first. Pete got married after a couple of years, and a house was built for the married couple to live in. Pete and his wife continued to work the farm, helping both the Ragan and Ogburn families.

There were many reasons for the Ragan family move to Johnston County in 1930. William and Emma Ragan had a large family to support, and it was becoming increasingly hard to do that in Berea. A tobacco disease, Granville Wilt it was called, was devastating their tobacco crops. The Great Depression's effects were already being felt, and also the Ogburns farmed tobacco, and they knew that William Ragan was a good tobacco man who could possibly help them raise better profit yielding acres of tobacco. And with the move, the labor of the Ragan kids would be of considerable help. Along with all that, the Ogburns were good people who wanted to help another family in need. Perhaps a bigger factor than all of the above, was that possibly William and Emma Ragan lost their farm, or at the least, were forced to sell it because of the hard times they were experiencing.

Later in his life, Ragan must have been thinking of his parents and those hard times growing up in Granville County, when he wrote "The Depression."

The Depression

The depression hit them hard.
George was the first to feel it—
He lost his crop, then his farm,
And the bank came and took

Everything he had left.
He started going from farm to farm,
Looking into smokehouses,
Into flour barrels, going away
Shaking his head, saying
"Can't last much longer."
He came out of his depression
In a couple of years, but didn't
Try to buy another farm.
He started laughing again,
Laughing a lot, laughing hardest
When he saw a banker.

2

The Ogburns, Valedictorian of Cleveland High School, Writer, Editor, Atlantic Christian, *Thoughts While Strolling*, I Smoka Pipe Club

In Johnston County, Millard and Alda Ogburn had four children, two girls, Juanita and Doris, and two boys, James and Hunter. Alda Ogburn was a school teacher when she was a single woman. Mrs. Ogburn loved music, and often held a musical hour in the house. She held strong Presbyterian beliefs and instilled them in her family and the Ragans once they came to live on the Ogburn place. Alda Ogburn had a tremendous influence on Sam Ragan. She saw much promise in the young man, and Sam considered Mrs. Ogburn to be like a second mother.

Shortly after moving into the house that the Ogburns had built for them, it became apparent that more room was needed for Sam and his family. So in the summer of 1931 Sam volunteered to ask the Ogburns if he could live with them. The houses were only a yard apart, so it was a short distance. The Ogburns agreed and Sam moved in. Sam was 15 by then, and he became close to the Ogburn girls, Doris and Juanita.

Sam started attending Cleveland High School in Johnston County once his family arrived at their new home. He was a bus driver there and also excelled academically. Louise Lambert was Sam's English teacher at Cleveland High School, and she influenced him tremendously. By the time of graduation, in May of 1932, Sam was valedictorian of his class. This valedictory speech may have been the first of many public speaking engagements Sam Ragan would give in the years ahead. The Dean of Wake Forest Law School, N.Y. Gulley, addressed the graduating class on "where do we go from here." Superintendent H.B. Marrow presented diplomas. The *Smithfield Herald* newspaper reported, "The Balfoar Company, makers of class jewelry, presented a bronze medal to the member of the senior class who made the best scholastic record during the four high school years. This medal was won by Sam Ragan."

So even though his family had moved to Johnston County and Sam was forced to leave Berea High School and enter a new school, Cleveland High, the young man had done exceptionally well, and adapted to his new environment. He had to leave the house where his family was living on the Ogburn farm because there was not enough room, and go live with the Ogburns in their house. The Ragans were desperately poor when they got to Johnston County, but with the loving care given by the Ogburns, they survived. A local women's club even donated clothes to Sam and his family upon arrival at their new home. After all that, Sam showed the internal drive to achieve that would serve him the rest of his life.

By the time of the move from Granville County to Johnston County, two Ragan sons were out on their own, Stephen and Lacy.

In the spring of 2018, Sam Ragan was inducted posthumously into the Cleveland High School Hall of Fame. Alda Ogburn, the woman who had meant so much to Sam Ragan and his family, passed away in 1947 at the age of 51. Millard Ogburn died in 1950. Sam Ragan would never forget the generosity and loving spirits of these two people who provided a home for his family during those trying years of the early 1930s.

With his fine academic record in high school, Sam was determined to go to college. But he knew his family could not afford to help him financially. So, he headed to South Carolina with $1.50 in his pocket and attended Spartanburg Textile Institute, what became Spartanburg Junior College. Sam had applied for and gotten a job in a cotton mill near the campus, so that was a deciding factor in heading south. He worked from 6 p.m. to 5 a.m. five days a week, 55 hours a week. He went to classes during the day. He knew he had to stick to such an arduous schedule to make college work for him, since although he had the emotional support of his beloved parents, they could do little to nothing to support him with any kind of money.

One very important thing happened while Sam was at Spartanburg. Sam was asked by a local newspaper to cover a basketball game. He accepted this task, went to the game, and called in the story and results by phone to the paper. The paper, which I have been unable to identify, gave Sam a byline and he once said in an interview, "That byline just hooked me for the rest of my life, I'm afraid."

After one year in Spartanburg, Sam enrolled at Atlantic Christian College in Wilson, North Carolina. The origins of what is now Barton College goes back to 1886, and some of the names for this university were Carolina Christian Institute and Carolina Christian College. In 1901, Carolina Christian College obtained Kinsey Seminary in Wilson, and in 1902, the name of Atlantic Christian College first appeared. A four-year curriculum was instituted in 1923. The president of Atlantic Christian College from 1920 to 1949 was Howard Hilley, a former Rhodes Scholar who Sam Ragan admired through his time there in the early to mid-1930s. In 1990, Atlantic Christian College was named Barton College, after one of the founders of the Disciples of Christ denomination, Barton Warren Stone.

The Sam and Marjorie Ragan Writing Center now stands in honor of Sam and his wife Marjorie at 700 Vance Street on the Barton College campus.

Sam entered Atlantic Christian College in 1933. The Great Depression was in full swing, and in North Carolina farm income was less than half of what it had been in 1929. The banking industry was hard hit, therefore credit for farmers compounded what was already a bad situation. By this time, William and Emma Ragan were barely hanging on to their farming way of life. There was mass unemployment all across the state, so other jobs that Sam's daddy had gotten in earlier years, such as working in lumber, were scarce. By 1933, when Sam was entering Atlantic Christian, 27 percent of adults in North Carolina were on relief programs. Textiles took a massive hit, so Sam's plans for a degree from Spartanburg Textile Institute changed, and he decided to come to Atlantic Christian for a double major in English and History. The election of Franklin Delano Roosevelt in the fall of 1932 had given hope to many Americans that better times were ahead, including a young Sam Ragan, who would become a lifelong Democrat.

It wasn't long before Sam made his mark on the Atlantic Christian campus. By his junior year, he had his own column, writing regularly for *The Collegiate* campus newspaper. His column, *Thoughts While Strolling*, appeared in the 1934 issue and was a regular part of the paper thereafter while a student. It was a collection of random thoughts instead of a cohesive narrative, such as his nationally recognized column, *Southern Accent*, which he wrote for 48 years starting in 1948. There were many witty observations, and much of what he liked to write about in 1934, 1935 and 1936 are seen in his later years. Other students on campus started calling Ragan "Shakespeare." In *Thoughts While Strolling*, just as in *Southern Accent* and his later poetry, themes of nature, literature, and humor showed up on a regular basis.

Observations on a downtown street: the public be jammed.
Time means nothing to me, I prefer *Literary Digest*.
Harold Tyre from the side looks like Boris Karloff.
I like to taste the blowing wind when it's thick and raw.
Flowers are hopping out of the ground like rabbits out of a hat.
Speaking of unemployment the average man has 12,000,000,000 brain cells.
Good idea for some to read Master's *Spoon River Anthology*.
"Tobacco Road" is still playing.
The trees are beginning to laugh out loud.
Responsibility causes some people to grow, others to swell.
Words are like clay, with them you can shape the destinies of untold millions.
The girl who won't even neck is nobody's fuel.
Read Dreiser's essay called "Rub-a-dub-dub."
No artificial color can match the green of nature.
Wouldn't it be nice if a person could sleep as well as he can when he has to get up?
Poetry is the words of nameless thought that everybody has but only a few can express.

Along with writing for *The Collegiate*, Ragan wrote poetry while in college. Later in life he recalled, "I write about feelings, and when I attended college I just started sending poems out to some of the little literary magazines. I started when I was 18. My poetry was first published in a magazine called *Moon River*, published in a small town in Illinois, and there were several that I had in a poetry magazine in Chicago. And then I was published in Shenandoah."

Ragan was very active while at Atlantic Christian. He did well academically, attending classes regularly and making excellent grades. Education was deeply important to him, as he knew it was the way to get out of the poverty he had experienced as a youth. He came from a very loving family, they were hard working and responsible people, but were never able to get ahead. Ragan had a good childhood, he had brothers and sisters he loved dearly, and those brothers and sisters had some good times growing up in Berea. But Ragan knew his way out of tough financial times and the Great Depression was to apply himself to his studies at Atlantic Christian and get a good education.

College students need to have some fun, of course, and one club that provided some of that was the Atlantic Christian Pipe Club. Perhaps for the first time of what would become a habit later in his life, Ragan appeared on the front page of a newspaper, *The Collegiate*, in 1935.

PIPE CLUB HOLDS ANNUAL ELECTION
Sam Ragan Elected To Head Organization During Year 1935–36

The article went on to say that Ragan, a junior, had transferred from Spartanburg Textile Institute. The Pipe Club, also known as the I Smoka Pipe Club, while Ragan had been a member, had increased its chapter roll, and added an honorary member, Mr. Ed Stallings, Instructor in Violin at Atlantic Christian. The annual banquet, where Ragan was elected as president, was held at the Wilson Country Club. The Pipe Club received a fan letter from Texarkana, Texas.

Sam Ragan would be a cigarette smoker for most of his life. He was, in fact, what is referred to as a chain smoker. And he didn't particularly like for someone to ask him not to smoke. In one incident, related to me by three people who were there or had heard about it, Ragan, in the 1970s, was at an event to speak. An official saw Ragan light a cigarette and came over and told him no smoking was allowed inside the building. Ragan, with his usual calm demeanor, said nothing in reply, but stood up and walked out of the building and headed toward his car, with all intentions of leaving. The person who had invited Ragan to speak noticed what was happening and rushed out to get him to come back. Ragan came back and continued to smoke his cigarette. In fact, he smoked a couple more that night.

The smoking did catch up with him, as Ragan suffered a collapsed lung and lung cancer later in life. This health scare, along with just knowing he should quit, prompted him to stop smoking cold turkey. He switched to sucking on peppermint candies to help him stop. So many photographs of Ragan show a constant cigarette in his hand, but he showed his will power in being able to stop once he made his mind up to do it.

In March of 1934, when Ragan was a sophomore, P.D. MacLean, managing editor of the *Raleigh Times*, visited Atlantic Christian and spoke about journalism. Ragan never had any journalism courses at Atlantic Christian, but he certainly had an interest, so he attended MacLean's talk. Little did he know by the 1940s he would be an editor himself at the *Raleigh News and Observer* and the *Raleigh Times*.

Certainly, Ragan succeeded in the journalism profession, to say the least, without ever taking journalism classes. He commented on this later in life. "Journalism graduates, I think, come out with a little edge because they've already learned the techniques, what I had to learn by trial and error. But I do think that journalism graduates are missing a great deal because they do not have adequate backgrounds in English and American Literature and in history, especially. I found that getting majors in English and Literature have been invaluable to me."

The Collegiate was the student newspaper on campus and *The Pine Knot* was the yearbook. By 1935, Ragan was the Editor-in-Chief of both. As editor he attended the North Carolina College Press Association Convention held in Raleigh. This training of course helped to prepare Ragan to become one of North Carolina's leading newspapermen in the decades ahead. Especially as editor of *The Collegiate,* Ragan learned to write editorials, assign reporters, decide what news to cover, get advertising, meet deadlines, and other such tasks that would serve him well in his future.

Other activities while at Atlantic Christian for Ragan were joining the Dramatics Club and becoming a charter member of the Vagabonds, a drama club on campus. He was the chaplain of the Sigma Alpha Fraternity, a Critic in the Hesperian Literary Society, on the Entertainment Committee, and was on the Intercollegiate Debating Team.

Georgia Campion was a student at Atlantic Christian during the time Sam Ragan was there, and they got to know each other. Later in her life, Campion recalled some of those memories.

Vivid in memory is an English class I took with Sam. The required 500-word weekly themes are not cherished memories for me, but they did result in our learning the fundamentals of writing. The professor, a tall, large-built Texan, critiqued our papers, using Wooley and Scott's *College Handbook of Composition.*

By sophomore year, the quiet, serious student that I considered Sam to be was becoming a campus leader. We became members of brother-sister Greek organizations.

Sam knew when he came to college that he wanted to be a journalist. This interest led to his editorship of *The Collegiate* and the *Pine Knot,* the college newspaper and yearbook. During junior and senior years, these extra-curricular efforts afforded valuable learning for the aspiring writer. He was also a team debater who relished dissenting viewpoints in both campus and South Atlantic forensic tournaments.

After my family retired to Southern Pines later in life, it was a special joy to renew the Ragan friendship. I read *The Pilot* and Sam's popular column *Southern Accent* weekly. To be remembered, in verse, in the Christmas column was especially touching.

During our careers, we Atlantic Christian College classmates had few opportunities to meet except at homecomings, which the Class of 1936 held every five years for a record 65 years. However, supporting several major projects to benefit the College kept us in touch. We helped to build The Sam and Marjorie Ragan Writing Center, and the Class of 1936 graced the Center lobby with a bronze plaque extolling the distinguished career of our classmate.

When Sam received the Alumnus of the Year recognition in 1990, he was, unfortunately, hospitalized on award day. He asked me to accept the citation for him. One of his books of poetry was off the press that year. I recall quoting from one poem titled "The Measurement of Memories." It was a genuine privilege to remind those present that Sam's poetry measured not only memories of our college days but also his lifetime accomplishments. He was a persuasive and objective writer who inspired many. Sam honored our Alma Mater as few have.

Sam's poetic journey through life ended sixty-four years after he entered college. There is comfort in knowing that his legacy lives on to encourage others. Memories of this gentle, compassionate, and talented classmate and friend are my measured blessings.

There is no doubt that his bachelor's degree from Atlantic Christian, along with his many activities, prepared Sam Ragan well for the future. By the time he graduated in 1936, Ragan knew he wanted to be a newspaperman, and he felt more than up to the challenge. He knew his calling.

As far as I know, Sam Ragan never met Thomas Wolfe, since Wolfe passed away in 1938 when Ragan would have been 23 years of age. Ragan usually considered Wolfe to be the best writer North Carolina produced, and would write about him quite often. But I think Sam Ragan knew his destiny at a fairly young age, at least by the time he was 21, while attending Atlantic Christian College. It reminds me of a similar story related to Thomas Wolfe. In 1923, when he was 23 years old, Wolfe wrote a letter to his friend and former college roommate at the University of North Carolina at Chapel Hill, Albert Coates.

Here I am teaching at New York University, eight hours a week, from February to September, earning $1,800 and getting an ocean of human contact. It might be worse. I'm my own man, and they say the money's mine. I am twenty-three years old, and the spring comes North already, the scent of a prime April is in the air. The day grows warm at noon, soon tar will be spongy on the streets, and the promise of adventure is abroad. I'm young, I'm young, and at least a bit of a poet. Even Freshman Composition may not subdue me. And really, Albert, there are signs and tokens of a growing power within me. Don't laugh, I know you won't, and don't repeat this, but a conviction is upon me that I shall one day do a great and secret thing, only, when I do it, it shall no longer be a secret thing. The desire for extension is strong in me. I must girdle the globe with my silly dreams, no longer will a single plot of earth contain me. Tom Wolfe Room 222 Hotel Albert.

Sam Ragan had those dreams and ambitions as he left college in 1936, and "the desire for extension" was strong in him also, like Wolfe.

A poem written by Ragan caught this feeling, this sense of a "growing power." I think Ragan knew he was his "own man," like Thomas Wolfe.

The One Small Singing

Novelists deal with the time of man—
Birth and death, and in between a little living
That barely breathes and seldom bleeds.
And poets too, but rarely find
The shining moment
Or the one small singing
Of every man.

"Birth and death, and in between a little living." Sam Ragan certainly
did a little living between his birth and death, and he found that "one small
singing" in himself to share with others. Just like Thomas Wolfe.

3

Newspaperman, Marjorie,
The City of a Million Azaleas,
"I Saw God"

Ragan's first job after graduating from Atlantic Christian was a tempo-
rary one at a newspaper in Lumberton. The *Lumberton Post* editor, Mr.
Wiggins, was taking a three week leave of absence, and he was pretty much
a one-man staff. Sam heard about the opening and hitchhiked to Lumberton. Not sure such a young man right out of college could run the paper
in his absence, Mr. Wiggins finally asked Sam what church he was raised
in. Sam told him he was a Presbyterian, and that pleased Mr. Wiggins as he
had been a Presbyterian elder for 35 years. So he told Sam that he would
give him a chance. He offered Sam $7 a week, plus any commissions he
might earn from selling ads for the paper. People in and around Lumberton, in the depths of the Great Depression, just didn't have much money to
buy ads, so the commissions for Sam were not very good. Sam did a good
job with the *Lumberton Post* in his three weeks. He worked hard, and some
of the experiences he went through with this small newspaper helped to
prepare him for newspaper work in the future.

Later in life, Ragan recalled those days in Lumberton. "I sold advertising. I went to the courthouse and got the news there and covered the police
station and town hall. Everything from writing personals to death notices
to police reports, everything. So I learned by doing."

His next job was in Hemp, North Carolina, in Moore County. Hemp is
now known as Robbins. Stacy Brewer owned a newspaper in Hemp called

the *Plain Dealer*. It was a new paper, and things were tough. It was 1936, and the Depression went on. In 1943 the name of the town was changed to Robbins to honor Karl Robbins, a wealthy manufacturer who donated money to the town to make many improvements, such as a water treatment plant and a waste disposal plant. Another person to come out of Robbins was John Edwards, a United Stated Senator who ran for President and grew up in Robbins.

Brewer had founded the newspaper *The Pilot* in Vass, before moving it to Southern Pines, where it is today. Little did Sam know in 1936 that one day he would own *The Pilot* himself. But Brewer hired Sam as editor, at only 21 years of age. This must have made Sam one of the youngest editors of a newspaper in America. Making money from this new startup newspaper during these terrible times was hard to do. At the end of the week, Brewer would count any cash left over after the printing company was paid, and decide how much he could pay Sam. It wasn't much more than the seven dollars a week he received at the *Lumberton Post*. But Sam was working and happy to be fully employed, and he spent more than a year working for Stacy Brewer at the *Plain Dealer*.

One lifelong friendship developed for Sam while in Hemp. Sam met Clifton Blue during that time. Blue had moved to Aberdeen after merging *The Captain,* which he had started in Vass, with the *Sandhill Citizen.* Sam was having trouble with the printer at the *Plain Dealer* so Sam called Blue. Blue had just gotten his paper out in Aberdeen and he told Sam to bring the *Plain Dealer* over to Aberdeen. But when Sam arrived, he found that Blue was having some trouble with the one linotype machine he had. But together, the two men worked late into the night to get the type set and the paper printed on an old flat-bed press. That first encounter with Blue showed Sam how he was willing to go the extra mile to help a friend out, and Sam would never forget it.

Not only did Sam learn much from his job as editor of the *Plain Dealer* in Hemp, but he met someone who he would spend the next 60 years with. By chance, the *Plain Dealer* printed its paper in Hamlet, at the printing press of the *News-Messenger*. So one day, Sam was taking the papers to Hamlet to get printed, but also to gather some facts about a bank robbery in nearby Candor.

M.T. McGaskill was a cashier at the Bank of Candor that day in 1937. He recalled the robbery, "I was there at the cage when he and a companion walked in. He was dressed in a neat brown suit. His hat was at a rakish angle. His shirt collar was spotless. He asked me to change a $10 bill. I reached to take it from his hand. I never got that $10 bill. A gun was in his other hand. I wasn't surprised when Bill Payne stuck a gun in my face. I had been expecting a visit from him a long time, ever since he escaped from Caledonia Prison Farm. For months I had been practicing what I would do if Payne, the man everybody in North Carolina dreaded, should walk in and throw a gun on me. But he had me."

Bill Payne had been robbing banks since 1921, when he robbed his first in Mount Airy. He was caught and served 3 years for that, getting out in 1924. But in 1926 he struck again in Orange County, North Carolina, was caught and put in prison. He escaped and shortly after, with help from others, robbed the Bank of Norman in Richmond County. Payne and his men fled to Tennessee and got into a gun battle with local police near Knoxville, in the small town of Newport. The gang was caught and returned to Richmond County in North Carolina. Payne was sentenced to 10 years in prison. He was put in the state prison camp in Bladen County. On July 7 of 1930, Payne and a buddy escaped. Payne was caught in Indiana in 1931 and brought back to North Carolina. But prison life just didn't suit Bill Payne and his cohort by this time, Wash Turner. In 1934, Payne and Turner escaped, then were caught six months later. They were sent to the Caledonia Prison Farm in Halifax County. But as stated before, Payne and Turner looked at prison as kind of a place to rest for a while, then bust out. On February 15, 1937, they left Caledonia Prison Farm after a good night's rest and a hearty breakfast. They stole a laundry truck on the prison grounds and took off. By this time, national news organizations were picking up on these two crooks, who just could not be contained in prisons. Payne and Turner were partial to bank robberies, so they did some more of those.

One day near Asheville, a state trooper, George C. Penn, from Carthage, saw them and gave chase. In the shootout that ensued, Penn was killed. At this point, a federal fugitive from justice warrant was issued for Payne and Turner. The FBI Director, J. Edgar Hoover, even included Payne and Turner on his eight most wanted list in America. Eventually, Payne and

Turner were sitting in a car in Sanford. The next thing they knew they were surrounded by FBI agents and local police. They surrendered. They were tried and convicted to die in the gas chamber and put in Central Prison in Raleigh. On July 1, 1938, Payne and Turner were executed.

Probably the only good thing that came out of Payne's and Turner's crime wave was that Sam Ragan and Marjorie Usher met for the very first time that day in 1937, when both of them ended up on a sidewalk in Hamlet expecting to possibly see Payne and Turner drive through after robbing the bank in Candor. Marjorie was working for the *Hamlet News-Messenger*. A crowd had gathered, but the bank robbers did not come through Hamlet that day, or if they did, they were not noticed. So even though Sam had been bringing the *Plain Dealer* from Hemp to Hamlet to get it printed, he had not met Marjorie until that day on the sidewalk waiting for the notorious bank robbers.

Lula Frances McCall, who was the daughter of Francis Bragg McCall and Ella Bell, was born in 1890 in Bladen County. Lula graduated from Littleton College in Littleton, North Carolina, in 1912. Lula used this fine education to teach in public schools, at Littleton College, and worked for the United States Government in Washington, D.C. In 1915 Lula married James Braxton Usher in the Mount Olive Methodist Church. James Usher was born in 1885 in South Carolina and was a graduate of Wofford College in South Carolina. James was the General Manager of Z.V. Pate Enterprises in Laurel Hill, North Carolina. Sadly, James Usher passed away in 1918, a little more than three years after James and Lula were married. James died of the terrible flu epidemic that came to much of America during that period. Rose Usher was born on May 16, 1916, to James and Lula, but did not survive birth. But on March 31, 1917, Marjorie Lois Usher was born.

While only eleven years old, Marjorie wrote a story for the *Charlotte Observer's* Young People's Page and earned a byline. She also got paid for the story, one dollar. It was a short story about a boy who ran away from home to join a circus. Just as in 1927, when the *Oxford Public Ledger* printed a story of Sam Ragan's, Marjorie Usher was now smitten with writing. As Marjorie recalled later in life, "there was never anything else I wanted to do but write for money."

Marjorie was among the first women graduates of the UNC School of Journalism in 1937. Her first job after graduation was with the *News-Messenger* of Hamlet. Later she worked as a reporter for the *Laurinburg Ex-*

change, the *Kannapolis Daily Independent*, and the *Wallace Enterprise*. She then became editor of the *Onslow County Record* in Jacksonville, making Marjorie Usher one of the first female editors of a newspaper in North Carolina. Later she worked for the *Wilmington Evening News*.

Sam Ragan's next job after leaving the *Plain Dealer* in Hemp was as a sports editor at the *Concord Herald Observer*, which was a morning newspaper. This was early in 1938. That job didn't last too long before a staff meeting was called one day. Zack Roberts and Ray King, owners of the *Herald Observer*, told everyone that the newspaper had been sold to the afternoon competitor, the *Concord Tribune*. The next morning's issue would be the last. But right after the meeting, the owners of the *Herald Observer* pulled Sam aside and told him that Talbert Patrick, the publisher of the *Goldsboro News-Argus*, wanted him to report for duty the next afternoon.

Two hours before the staff meeting, Sam had been the only person working at the *Herald Observer* when Mr. Patrick had dropped by, with the rest on lunch break. Sam showed him around the offices and they talked. Apparently, Mr. Patrick had been impressed by the young man and decided on the spot to bring him to his newspaper in Goldsboro. Sam had been polite and articulate, as he was known to be throughout his life, and this impressed Mr. Patrick. His new job at the *News-Argus* was going to pay him $18 a week, a $2 raise from his job at the *Herald Observer*.

But Sam and his co-workers at the *Herald Observer* were determined to make the last issue of the paper the best ever, and so they worked deep into the night. Later on, Sam recalled that last issue. "It was a sad time, but there was also something else in the air—a determination to make that last issue the best one ever published. When the paper was finally put to bed and the first copies had rolled from the press I was packed and ready to go. Scott Summers and Sam Cheek took me to the bus, and when I left I carried a copy of the paper with me. It was the last edition, but it was a good one."

Very early in the morning, Sam caught a bus to Charlotte, then another bus to Laurinburg, where he had a layover. So he was able to see Marjorie Usher, who he had been seeing ever since that first day when they met in Hamlet. Marjorie was by now working for the *Laurinburg Exchange*. He got back on the bus and reached Goldsboro at 4 p.m.

Sam had heard about his new boss, the editor of the *News-Argus*, Henry Belk. Belk was well-known around the state for his good work in Goldsboro, including his thoughtful editorials. James Butler, the *News-Argus* Farm Editor, took a liking to Sam, and offered to rent him a room in his house. Butler also introduced Sam to the rest of the staff. Along with many responsibilities, Sam was told he would be covering sports, like he did in Concord. That turned out to be fine with Sam, who really liked baseball, and Goldsboro was in the old Coastal Plains League. Mule Shirley was the manager of Goldsboro, and Mule and Sam developed a good friendship. Sam enjoyed being outside, so sitting in the sunshine and covering a baseball game to him was considered pleasant work. On occasion, Sam traveled with the team to such towns as Snow Hill, Ayden, Kinston, and Wilson. Watching Peahead Walker, the player-manager for Snow Hill and who later coached the Wake Forest football team, strut around was a sight that Sam always remembered with fondness.

During these first years on the job at different newspapers, Ragan performed, at one point or the other, almost every job required to produce a newspaper. He was a copy man, an ad man, a reporter, an editor, he wrote editorials, he assigned reporters to cover certain events, wrote obituaries, and so on. At *The Pilot,* even in his later years, he would walk through the printing area, the offices, and the hallways and pitch in wherever he thought he was needed. He would even throw papers in his car and distribute them to stores and newspaper machines on occasion.

Sam Ragan, in these early years of being a newspaperman, was going through some of what Ernest Hemingway did. Hemingway's first job after high school was working as a reporter for the *Kansas City Star.* In a letter to his father, Hemingway wrote:

> It's exhausting having to write a half column story remembering to use good style, perfect style in fact, and get all the facts and in the correct order, make it have snap and wallop and write it in fifteen minutes, five sentences at a time to catch an edition as it goes to press. To take a story over the phone and get everything exact, rush over to a typewriter and write it a page at a time while ten other typewriters are going and the boss is hollerin at some one and a boy snatches the pages from your machine as fast as you write them.

Henry Belk and Sam Ragan would remain lifelong friends. Ragan credited Belk with teaching him as much about newspaper work as anyone.

Belk told Sam to go out and cover a Sunday morning sermon by a Goldsboro preacher, which made Sam wonder why. Later, Belk explained to him that news can be anything which interests people, and that there is an infinite variety of news. What people do, what they think, and what they feel is news. Once, after Sam had reported on a tornado in Wayne County, Belk asked Sam to stay behind after all the rest of the staff had left after a meeting. In the little newsroom of no more than three desks, Belk talked to Sam, who at this time was only 23 years of age, for about two hours. Sam mostly listened. Belk was pleased with Sam's work, and gave him a piece of advice that Sam would many times later in life recall and put to good use. "Write with wonder," Belk told him. "Write as if you are seeing something for the first time, and you want everyone else to see it the same way, with eyes of wonder."

Some other events that Sam covered while in Goldsboro with the *News-Argus* were liquor still raids that he went on with the sheriff and his deputies, and a night raid of a house of prostitution. Once on a particularly hot day in July, Sam wrote about a man frying an egg on a Goldsboro sidewalk.

While Sam Ragan was working in Goldsboro, Marjorie Usher was working for the *Kannapolis Daily Independent,* and later the *Onslow County Record* in Jacksonville, so they continued their romance that had started back during that bank robbery in 1937. She also worked at one time with the *Wallace Enterprise.* While at the *Onslow County Record,* Marjorie was promoted to editor, thus becoming one of the very first female editors of a newspaper in North Carolina. They once attended a dance in Rocky Mount, and on the way back, Sam ran out of gas in his car. It was dark, and the road had little traffic. There was nothing they could do until someone came by and went and got enough gas for them to get home.

One day in 1938 Marjorie drove to Faison to visit an aunt, and after that visit drove over to Goldsboro to visit with Sam. On a Sunday afternoon Sam drove Marjorie around and stopped on a hill where there was a beautiful view of the countryside. Sam asked Marjorie to marry him, and she accepted. So Goldsboro was a special place for Sam Ragan in more ways than one.

The Wilmington *Morning Star* offered Sam the job as sports editor at $25 a week, which was a $7 a week raise from what he was making at the *News-Argus* in Goldsboro. Al Dickson was the managing editor at the

Morning Star and was a big influence on Sam. In a *Southern Accent* column while at *The Pilot* in Southern Pines, Sam recalled those days in Wilmington working for Dickson.

> He was a true newspaperman in the fullest sense of the word. To him it was a calling, as well as an art, a craft, a profession. It was our [Sam always wrote of himself in the third person in *Southern Accent*] privilege to work with him years ago. Often after we had put the paper to bed around 2 o'clock in the morning we would go to an all-night café around the corner and there stay until the sun came up. There were always "night people" there, and we would listen to their stories, and Al took a special delight in them. I remember Harry Hayden, an old newspaperman who had worked with John Dos Passos and H.L. Mencken. Harry had a lot to talk about, and with him, you didn't have to listen, he would talk anyway. Then there were truck drivers, fishermen, night watchmen, and a policeman or two who worked the night shift. There were other times we remember — forays to the beach, long talk sessions in which the famed Dickson wit was in full sway, roaming wide, keen and hilarious. He was a man who could cut through the fog of semantics, of sham and pretense, and sum up a situation in one quick phrase. [Sam's writings and poetry would reflect some of this in the future] He could be devastatingly witty in his comments, but there was never malice in what he had to say. Even in retirement a subscriber to *The Pilot*, he would frequently call to comment upon something in the paper.

David Brinkley was hired while Sam was sports editor and was running the night desk at the *Wilmington Morning Star*. From Wilmington, Brinkley started work at the *Morning Star* while still attending New Hanover High School. Brinkley worked for NBC and ABC as a newscaster in a career lasting over 50 years. From 1956 to 1970 he co-anchored NBC's top-rated nightly news program, *The Huntley-Brinkley Report*, and in the 1980s and 90s was host of the Sunday *This Week with David Brinkley* program.

"Sam was the first poet I ever knew," Brinkley once said. "We used to go out to a Greek all-night café and talk for hours. Sam taught me the good half of what I know, the useful half." Of the young sports reporter, Sam said of Brinkley, "What he didn't know instinctively, you only had to tell him once. He knew what to cover and how to get news and how to write it. His natural talent was evident from the start, and he could turn out a prodigious amount of news copy. David would interview someone and get the essence of the man's personality as well as what he said in a concise and tightly written story."

Brinkley did not have the best relationship with his mother. But he overcame that. "Mama seemed to love babies, dogs, and her flower garden, but nothing or no one else. When I could no longer stand to be at home, I went to the public library. I had a better relationship with the librarian than with my mother."

Sam Ragan could see that Brinkley knew how to write news, and report on it. For one of his first assignments, Brinkley made quite a splash. A local woman called the *Wilmington Star* to report how, 40 years earlier, her grandfather had brought a 60-year-old century plant home from Mexico. She said the plant was going to bloom for the only time in 100 years that very night. The fire department set up floodlights and a big crowd turned out to watch the event. Brinkley was sent by Sam to cover the event, even though it wasn't exactly a sporting event. Brinkley gave a colorful account of what happened when the promised blooming did not occur, "I arrived to find a wonderful scene. Popsicle vendors working the crowd, the fire department's emergency floodlights, their diesel engines roaring, lighting up the block and the gingerbready front porch where the Mexican agave sat in a large pot looking like not much. The owner of the plant told me 'I will never trust a Mexican again.' Brinkley's story was picked up by the Associated Press. Newspapers carried the story across the country. This young man was on his way.

David Brinkley, and Sam Ragan to a degree, influenced the literary and journalistic careers of David Brinkley's sons. Alan Brinkley wrote *Voices of Protest*, which won a National Book Award. Alan also wrote other books and had a distinguished teaching career at Harvard and Columbia. Alan's brother, Joel, was a reporter and editor for *The New York Times,* and another brother, John, is a writer for *Forbes* at the time this book went to publication.

David Brinkley's long career led to a positive influence over many journalists and broadcasters, and Brinkley's influence on others, to a large degree, was prompted by what he learned from his days at the *Wilmington Morning Star* and the many hours he spent with Sam Ragan. One example of this was the career of Jack Perkins, a former NBC News reporter and host of the A&E television program "Biography." Perkins worked for "The Huntley-Brinkley Report," the nightly news program that David Brinkley and Chet Huntley did for NBC. Perkins worked closely with Brinkley. The influence of Sam Ragan can clearly be seen in what Perkins once said about working with David Brinkley. "What Brinkley taught me was a master class in how TV news should be written. Say less, mean more. If a story is dramatic, you don't have to tell it dramatically. Be simple. Direct."

One story Sam covered while sports editor in Wilmington was an appearance by the heavyweight professional boxer, Tony Galento. Sam wrote about that experience.

They called him "Two Ton" Tony Galento, and he came within an inch of knocking my head off. That was back in the days when I was sports editor of the Wilmington Morning Star and Tony Galento had passed his greatest moment of glory. That was on the night of June 28, 1939, in Yankee Stadium when Galento came within seconds of becoming the world heavyweight champion. He floored Joe Louis, the "Brown Bomber" with a powerful left. Louis staggered up in time to avoid the knockout count and went on to win the fight. Tony Galento fought for 15 years. At his fighting trim he weighed 235 pounds and most of it on his five feet, nine inch frame was in his fists and belly. He trained on big black cigars and all the beer he could find. In fact, he had the look of a beer barrel. When Galento came to Wilmington he was refereeing wrestling matches. We got a call the afternoon Galento came to town and a press conference was set up in his hotel room. We went over and were ushered in and when I put out my hand to Two Ton Tony he swung on me with that left hand which looked like a ham. It swished past my chin, and Tony roared with laughter. He then gave me a bear hug and we sat talking for an hour. He was downing one beer after another. I thought about that a few days ago when I read that Tony Galento had died in Livingston, N.J., at the age of 69. He was not your classic fighter and he never won the championship, but he certainly enlivened the American fight scene as much as anyone else who has put on the gloves.

Ragan wrote about some other experiences while he worked in Wilmington.

Wilmington was a colorful city. Marjorie and I were married while I worked there. I was courting her while she worked as editor of the *Onslow Record* in Jacksonville, and I would get up early on Saturday morning and catch the bus for the 50-mile ride to Jacksonville.

After Marjorie and I were married she went to work on the Wilmington paper — *The Evening News*, where John Marshall was the managing editor. Her hours as a reporter on the News were 7 a.m. to 5 p.m. My hours on the *Morning Star* were 1 p.m. to 2 a.m. In the early days of marriage we didn't see much of each other, but we did have supper together at the New York Café and usually spent the weekends at the beach. The cost of living was low, and we were able to have a furnished apartment in town and a cottage on the sound. I had been given a $2.50 a week raise from my $25 starting pay at the *Star* when I left the *Goldsboro News-Argus*.

Al Dickson was the managing editor at the *Star* and he was a joy to work with. I was the sports editor and the only reporter on the morning newspaper. I spent the afternoon covering a downtown beat, and started placing telephone calls to the sheriff and other major officials as soon as I returned to the office. By the time of the first edition deadline of 11 p.m. I would write an average of 45 news stories, and add to that with police reports for the final edition at 2 a.m.

Another reporter had been on the staff of the *Richmond Times-Dispatch* and the *Baltimore Sun*, where he had worked with H.L. Mencken. The only problem was he fell off the wagon about every other week, and he would disappear. Once he was sent to Wrightsville Beach to cover the final banquet of a convention (I believe it was the N.C. Bar Association). On the way to the beach hotel he stopped by the yacht basin. It was the cocktail hour and he was invited aboard. He passed out, was tossed onto a bunk, and the yacht set sail the next day at dawn, with the reporter still sleeping it off. About three weeks later Al Dickson got a telegram from Jacksonville, Fla., asking that money be wired to him so that he could come home. It was, and he came back to work — at least until he paid off his bus fare.

Lamont Smith was the editor of both the *Star* and the *News*, and the editorials reflected a desire that each newspaper be a bit different. He still wore the crewcut he had acquired at The Citadel, and he spent most of the days drinking beer in a downtown tavern. When I was interviewed for the job at the *Star*, Lamont took me to the tavern and ordered beer. We talked about nearly everything but the job, and then we shook hands on it. He asked me to pay for the beer and I did.

Despite his foibles, Lamont had a strong sense of justice. He almost single-handedly saved a man from the electric chair by hiring a same make and model of a car to prove the defendant could not have driven from Wilmington to Asheville to commit the murder he was convicted of doing. The man's execution was stayed at the last minute and he was later released on a full pardon.

The editor who brought the *Star-News* into prominence was Alfred Granberry Dickson, who spent more than 40 years at the papers. He was a warm and witty editor who didn't let that deter him from taking on such formidable foes as the Ku Klux Klan, or public officials who were playing fast and loose with public money. Al won national awards for his editorials and he more than anyone else was responsible for ending the intimidating influence of the Klan in the southeastern area of North Carolina. Al was one of the leaders who spearheaded the movement to establish the University of North Carolina at Wilmington.

There was more variety to the news to cover in Wilmington. There was the usual share of murder and mayhem, as well as fires, hurricanes and other disasters, but also there was news of shipping, ocean-going commerce, the nearby beaches, and a historic city which wasn't reluctant to be playful.

Later in life, Ragan wrote a poem about Wilmington.

The City on the River
The river moves,
Inward with the tide,
Downward with the upland flow
Of water, and the city moves
From the water's edge,

Moving outward
With the huge bearded oaks,
The tall long-needled pines,
Marching and sauntering with history,
A large and looming list
Of historic names and events.

This is the city which sent
Thousands of now familiar names
To settle the north and west,
The river was their highway.

Here are the lilting winds and breezes
From the nearby sea,
Always the inviting sea,
The sounds and the beaches
Giving their color to the town
Which grew into a city—
A city which always seems to know itself.

History is made from memories,
And there are memories
Of a girl chasing a butterfly
Down the bluff to the river,
And the all-night care
With a fistful of silences, and
Long talkative hours when secrets
Are told of town, family, friends,
Events recalled in low-voiced pride,
At first hesitant, and then
As firm and cheerful as the sunrise
At Wrightsville where they often
Fish all night long.
Night people are different from day people.

In the beginning, old Wilmington
Had a fascination for the new.
In New Hanover it first was New Carthage,
Then New Liverpool, and New Town,

But Spencer Compton would be pleased
With the final decision—his namesake,
And what it has become,
A blend of the old and the new.

The city of a million azaleas,
Giving their bright colors to a colorful past,
Perfumed and putting on a pretty face,
And those of you have been part of it
Carry with them always
A thousand memories...
A thousand memories
Of a place, a time, a people.

Also in Wilmington, Ragan started a tradition. One afternoon in late December, Sam met with Jimmy Wade, who was the Wilmington City Commissioner in charge of public works. Wade complained about the problem of picking up discarded Christmas trees, and what to do with them after they were picked up. Sam suggested the city should hold a burning of the Christmas trees, that this was a custom in some European countries and was done in some parts of the South. Wade liked the idea and it was done for the first time in Wilmington a couple of weeks later. The trees were brought to a park, lit into a bonfire, and people gathered around and sang and danced. This tradition went on in Wilmington for many years, stopped for a couple of years, and then was revived. By the time Sam Ragan started this tradition in Wilmington, he had been promoted from sports editor to city editor of the *Wilmington Morning Star*.

A poem Ragan would write in the future was about an incident while with the *Wilmington Morning Star*.

I Saw God

At the old Star-News building
People could walk in off the street.
They often did late at night,
And this man walked in and said,
"I just saw God."
He looked around the newsroom,

And saw I was alone.
I didn't say anything.
"He was standing right there,
Looking in the window of Belk-Williams...
Just like you and me."
The man pointed a finger at me—
"Write it down," he said.
"I saw God."

On August 19 of 1939, Sam and Marjorie were married. Before the wedding, Phebe Harland held a shower for Marjorie at the Woman's Club in Jacksonville. The clubhouse was adorned with bowls of pink and yellow dahlias and yellow marigolds. Upon arrival guests were given sheets of paper in the shape of bells on which they wrote advice to the bride-elect. The sheets of paper were then tied together with green ribbon and given to Marjorie.

On the day of the wedding, Sam received a light-hearted telegram from a friend, who called himself "The Office Cat." This person quoted Proverbs, "It is better to dwell upon the house tops alone than with a quarrelsome woman," and Kipling, "Until men are made like angels with hammer and chisel and pen, we'll work for ourselves and a woman forever and ever amen."

Despite this little jab, Sam Ragan and Marjorie Usher got married that afternoon, at 5 p.m. in Laurel Hill at Laurel Hill Methodist Church. The Reverend E.H. Measemer presided. Baskets of pink myrtle flanked the altar, and Tchaikovsky's Andante Cantabile was played.

The newly married couple received lots of gifts from family and friends. Among the gifts were a table lamp, sheets, a towel set, a serving tray, pillow cases, candle holders, a bridge set, a satin gown, an electric iron, a porcelain vase, crystal goblets, a table cloth, and a book titled *Conversation at Midnight*.

Marjorie got a job with the *Wilmington Evening News*; so Sam worked for the *Wilmington Morning Star*, the morning paper, and Marjorie worked for the afternoon paper. They got a furnished apartment for $25 a month and another small place for only $10 a month in Wrightsville Beach. They had a car. "Those were wonderful times," Sam recalled later in life.

Marjorie remembered when she knew Sam was the one for her. "I knew he was the one when he read to me his poetry on the vine-shaded porch at my home in the small town of Laurel Hill. I was 20; he was 21." It seems that poetry not only would bring Sam Ragan many professional honors, but also a wife whom he loved dearly all of his life.

Right after the wedding, the Ragans got on a mail boat on the mainland for a honeymoon on Ocracoke Island. It was a three-hour ride across the sound. Upon nearing the island, Sam and Marjorie noticed a big crowd of people waiting anxiously for the mail boat's arrival. Upon asking the boat captain, he learned that the people knew that this was the day of delivery of the Sears Roebuck Catalog. So after going to the nearby post office and waiting for the mail to be sorted, that throng of folks happily went home with a catalog tucked under their arms. In a *Southern Accent* column in 1993, Sam recalled some of the nostalgia for the Sears Roebuck Catalog, and that day in 1939 when they traveled on that mail boat with the Sears Roebuck Catalog.

> That "big book" was a prized possession in rural homes all across America, and in isolated places like Ocracoke Island, it was truly treasured. Most of the South's rural poor couldn't afford to order much from the catalog, but they could look at it and dream and silently wish to be blessed with something from the book. There wasn't much that wasn't offered in the Sears Roebuck Catalog—everything from socks and 10-penny nails to entire houses.

Not only did Sam and Marjorie meet during a bank robbery, but on their wedding honeymoon Sam was robbed. A man demanded money from Sam, said he had a gun, and Sam gave the robber what cash he had on him. The newlywed had to borrow money to get back home. The money, of course, was repaid.

There was an Associated Press article about the robbery under the headline, "Honeymooning Ragans Robbed, Police Aid."

> Sam Ragan, honeymooning reporter of the *Star News* (formerly of the *News Argus*) and his bride of a night spent their first day of married life penniless and hungry, and it required the combined efforts of three police departments to provide them with provender.

The Ragans were robbed on their nuptial night. Sam's frantic SOS to Wilmington was delayed and when finally received it was too late to wire money. A telephone call to the Fayetteville Hotel revealed that the Ragans had checked out and headed north with nothing to give but love.

State police located the couple approaching Varina. Mayor Tom Cooper of Wilmington called the police chief at Varina and arranged for the hungry honeymooners to be supplied with cash.

Ragan was married at Laurel Hill Saturday to Miss Marjorie Usher, editor of the *Onslow County Record*, Jacksonville.

Ragan recalled his days working in Wilmington later in *Southern Accent*.

Marjorie and I were married while I worked there. I was courting her while she worked as editor of the *Onslow Record* in Jacksonville, and I would get up early on Saturday morning and catch the bus for the 50-mile ride to Jacksonville.

One Saturday we spotted a news item in the *Morning Star* which stated that Gene Austin would be performing at Southport that night and we both said in union "Let's go," and we did. It had been years since anyone had heard of the old-time ragtime piano player, who was the composer of the classic song "My Blue Heaven." Gene Austin was in top form and after the performance he invited us to join him and his wife for a snack and coffee. It was a delightful two hours of talk and reminiscing, a moment in time which we treasure.

After Marjorie and I were married she went to work on the Wilmington paper—the *Evening News*, where John Marshall was the managing editor. Her hours as a reporter on the *News* were 7 a.m. to 5 p.m. My hours on the *Morning Star* were 1 p.m. to 2 a.m. I can remember getting off work at 2 a.m. and walking out of the building in the dark hours of early morning. I enjoyed the mixed smells of flowers and the ocean.

In the early days of marriage we didn't see much of each other, but we did have supper together at the New York Café and usually spent the weekends at the beach. The cost of living was low and we were able to have a furnished apartment in town and a cottage on the sound. I had been given a $2.50 a week raise from my $25 starting pay at the *Morning Star* when I left the *Goldsboro News-Argus*.

It wasn't long after the wedding that Sam thought he should consider an offer from a long way away. The *San Antonio Evening News* offered him the job of assistant city editor, and Sam accepted. Despite his love of North Carolina, Sam felt he owed it to Marjorie and himself to explore this new opportunity and accepted the position. During his short time in San Antonio, Ragan met a newly appointed lieutenant-colonel who was in charge of public relations at Fort Sam Houston. The man was Dwight Eisenhower. It was the first of several men Ragan would meet who either were Presidents of the United States or would become one. Ragan met Jimmy Carter on several occasions, and once introduced Ronald Reagan after Reagan had been elected governor of California. It was at an Associated Press Managing Editors convention in San Diego. Ragan had been elected President of the AP Managing Editors Association. Ragan, the newspaperman, shared a table with the future President during lunch. In 1974, Ragan served as one of Gerald Ford's hosts when President Ford came to Pinehurst to dedicate the opening of the World Golf Hall of Fame.

I wrote to President Carter in 2018 when writing this book, asking him if he could comment on Sam Ragan. Ragan kept a picture of him shaking President Carter's hand. My wife and I had attended a Sunday School lesson taught by President Carter at Maranatha Baptist Church in Plains, Georgia, a few years before, when we had our picture taken with President Carter and former First lady Rosalynn Carter. A few weeks after sending the letter to President Carter, I received a handwritten reply, telling me that he certainly did remember Sam Ragan, and that he even remembered when Ragan, along with about a dozen other newspapermen, had been received by him at a reception at the White House. I had sent one of my favorite Ragan poems, "The Farmer," to President Carter, and he commented in his reply that he really liked the poem, that it reminded him of some farms and farmers in the Plains area when he was a young peanut farmer himself.

Only a few months after arrival in Texas, however, Sam received a telegram that would change his life, and give him his first long term job. *The News and Observer* in Raleigh offered Sam its state editorship in 1941. Sam said yes and, at 26 years of age, had a leadership position with one of the top newspapers in all of the South.

4

The News and Observer, Josephus Daniels, James Boyd, Nancy, "The very special you"

Ragan recalled getting a job with *The News and Observer.* "Josephus Daniels asked if I was interested. Of course, *The News and Observer* was then, and now, regarded as the newspaper in North Carolina. It would be the sort of thing that anyone would jump at. I wired right back, 'I'll be there in two weeks.' I went to *The News and Observer* just before Pearl Harbor in October of 1941 and stayed there until January 1, 1969, except for when I was away serving in the Pacific Theater as an enlisted man in the Army. I served in the Signal Corps and military intelligence. I went back to *The News and Observer* after the war and was named Managing Editor in 1948 and then Executive Editor of both *The News and Observer* and the *Raleigh Times* in 1957. I held that job until I came to *The Pilot.*"

The News and Observer traces its roots to *The Sentinel,* which was founded in 1865. After *The Sentinel* went out of business, the owners of the *Raleigh Observer* bought *The Sentinel.* After a few years, Samuel Ashe, the owner of the *Raleigh News* bought the *Raleigh Observer.* Ashe combined the two newspapers in 1880, making it *The News and Observer.* In 1894 Josephus Daniels bought the newspaper. *The News and Observer* would be run by the Daniels family until 1995, when it was sold to the McClatchy Company for $373 million.

Josephus Daniels was born in 1862. He was appointed by President Woodrow Wilson to be Secretary of the Navy during World War I. Daniels hired Franklin D. Roosevelt, the future president, as his Assistant Secretary of the Navy. Daniels and Roosevelt would become lifelong friends and confidantes. Roosevelt, after being elected President in 1932, appointed Daniels as his Ambassador to Mexico from 1933 to 1941. Daniels ran *The News and Observer* until his death in 1948 and made it a strong advocate for the Democratic Party. After Josephus Daniels passed away, the four sons of Josephus assumed control, Jonathan, Frank, Josephus Jr., and Worth. Jonathan was editor from 1933 to 1941 and from 1948 to 1968, and Frank was president and publisher, and later chairman of the board. During Jonathan's leadership of *The News and Observer*, the *Raleigh Times* was bought, in 1955. Claude Sitton served as editor in chief from 1971 to 1990. Sitton won the Pulitzer Prize in 1983 for commentary for his columns on the editorial page.

Sam Ragan would get to know Josephus Daniels well after coming to *The News and Observer* as state editor in 1941, although Ragan would forge a much longer relationship with Jonathan Daniels. Sam wrote about Josephus Daniels after his passing in 1948.

Franklin D. Roosevelt called him "Chief," but thousands of Tar Heels spoke of him simply as Josephus. For 54 years Josephus Daniels ran *The News and Observer* as editor and publisher. Over those years in countless homes throughout North Carolina people would open their newspaper with the words, "Let's see what Josephus says." And Josephus Daniels did not hesitate to speak out if he thought special interests were getting special favors in the seats of government, or if he thought the people of his beloved state were not receiving the education, the health care, the good roads, or other things he thought they deserved. He truly saw *The News and Observer* as the "tocsin," a good old-fashioned word which means an alarm bell, and he was not reluctant to name names and cite circumstances if he thought a warning bell should be sounded. He had been influential in the Democratic nomination of Woodrow Wilson for President in 1912 and Wilson chose him to be Secretary of the Navy in his cabinet. It was in that post where he won considerable acclaim for his skill and leadership during World War I. Young Franklin D. Roosevelt served as an undersecretary with Daniels and later when FDR became President he appointed Daniels as Ambassador to Mexico, a post he held until he resigned in 1941 and returned to Raleigh to resume his duties as editor of "The Old Reliable." Josephus Daniels also wrote books, relating his experiences as an editor, as Navy Secretary, as Ambassador, but those books were more than personal reminiscences but reports and insights into the times in which he lived. He had a lifelong devotion to the Democratic Party. Josephus Daniels, in his broad-brimmed, flat crown Quaker-style hat, his black suit, white starched shirt and black string bowtie was a familiar figure in high places in the state and nation. He was writing editorials and working on another book up until a few days before he died. In his last will and testament, he said, "I advise and enjoin those who direct the paper in the tomorrows never to advocate any cause for personal profit or preferment. I would wish it always to be 'the tocsin' and devote itself to the policies of equality and justice to the underprivileged. If the paper should at any time be the voice of self-interest or become the spokesman of privilege or selfishness it would be untrue to its history." The sons of Josephus Daniels—Josephus Jr., Worth, Jonathan, and Frank—chose those words for the masthead of *The News and Observer* and they are there today.

Josephus Daniels was born in the Civil War year of 1862 (he died in 1948) and he had bought the N&O at a bankruptcy sale in 1894 and he saw the Raleigh newspaper grow into the top ranks in the state and to earn the title of "The Old Reliable."

My ties with the N&O go back to 1941 when I joined the staff as state editor. I worked closely with Josephus Daniels, who returned late that year to the paper after serving as Ambassador to Mexico. My eldest daughter, Nancy, was born on May 18, and she received a hand-written note from Josephus Daniels the next day after her birth.

He worked up until his death in 1948, writing editorials and a column with stub pencils which others had discarded. He took seriously what a reader had told him to do—"Joe-See-For-Us." He called his column "The Rhamkatte Roaster" and he really roasted many public figures who took stands with which he disagreed. An ardent dry, he castigated those who favored liquor sales, and he wrote about the ABC system, and he said ABC stood for "Alcohol Brutalizes Consumers."

Josephus was once quoted as saying, "What the Good Lord lets happen I'm not ashamed to print." *The News and Observer* for many years followed that policy.

When I became State Editor the N&O claimed 54 North Carolina counties, primarily Eastern North Carolina, as their prime coverage area, and I set about covering those 54 counties with the same thoroughness as the city editor covered Raleigh. Within a couple of years there were few things happening in those 54 counties that the N&O didn't know about, and it printed it.

Very early in my time at the N&O I remember being chided by Josephus Daniels for once referring to a 72-year old man as "elderly."

The man had been hit by a car on Fayetteville Street and I had written a headline which said simply, "Elderly Man Hit By Car." The next day I was called to Mr. Daniel's office and the man, who was not hurt by the encounter with the car, was loudly protesting the reference to him as being elderly.

Mr. Daniels heard him out and then told me, "I don't think we should call this boy elderly."

At the time Josephus Daniels was 84 years old.

It was not long after Ragan accepted the job at *The News and Observer* when Japan bombed Pearl Harbor and World War II started for America. So war news and activities on the home front dominated news coverage for this new state editor in Raleigh.

The town of Southern Pines would one day figure in the legacy of Sam Ragan. In 1941, James Boyd bought *The Pilot*, the newspaper in Southern Pines. Boyd said upon purchasing *The Pilot*: "In taking over *The Pilot* no changes are contemplated. We will try to keep this a good paper. We will try to make a little money for all concerned. Wherever there seems to be an occasion to use our influence for the public good we will try to do it. And we will treat everybody alike." That quotation would grace the pages of *The Pilot* for years to come.

Boyd came from a wealthy family, and eventually moved to Southern Pines to live. Boyd's grandfather, James Boyd Sr., a Pennsylvania coal magnate, had purchased more than 1,500 acres of land in Southern Pines set in a forest of virgin longleaf pines. The estate was named Weymouth, because it reminded Boyd of Weymouth, England. Weymouth served as a winter retreat for the Boyd family for many years. Boyd Sr. was married to Louisa Yeomans Boyd.

In 1909, fire damaged 900 acres of Boyd Sr.'s land. Boyd had the land carefully restored, showing his concern for the natural environment. The *Southern Pines Tourist* reported in 1910, "The work that is being done is but a restoration, a going back to the state of nature, a repair of the ravages of the elements."

James Boyd, the grandson of James Boyd Sr., served in World War I and returned in frail health. He decided he wanted to live in Southern Pines and he and wife Katharine Lamont had a grand house built. This house is now the Weymouth Center for the Arts and Humanities. Boyd once said of the estate and land surrounding the house, "This is really the most beautiful country I know. It has a certain wildness without being desolate... solitude without loneliness."

Boyd graduated from Princeton and served in World War I as an officer in the United States Army Ambulance Service. He was an avid fox hunter and master of the Moore County Hounds after moving to Southern Pines. Boyd became a writer, publishing what some consider to be the best novel written about the Revolutionary War, *Drums. Drums* was published in 1925. Another book by Boyd, *Roll River*, along with *Drums,* is recognized as a major development in the historical novel as a category. Boyd wrote other well-received books, poems, and many short stories and essays. Many famous authors visited Boyd and his wife, Katharine, at Weymouth, such as Thomas Wolfe, Paul Green, Sherwood Anderson, and William Faulkner. Once, Katharine came downstairs very early one morning to find a man with extremely long legs sleeping on her couch. The six-foot, six-inch Wolfe had caught a train down from New York City, and on his way home to Asheville, his hometown, had let himself in during the overnight hours and went to sleep. Wolfe became a good friend of the Boyds and a frequent visitor.

Katharine Boyd once expressed her desire that her estate become "a place where writers and artists could gather and work, where men and women could explore new thought, and where sparks of creativity could be struck as they had when it was her home." Today Weymouth certainly serves that purpose, and the Boyds would be happy to see how Weymouth has and is helping so many writers and artists in their craft.

In 1941, Boyd published an essay in *Story* magazine, and wrote a little about what Southern Pines was like at that time.

> In my town, Southern Pines, there are twenty-six hundred people. The railroad runs down the main street but it is not as bad as you might think. On each side of it there are magnolias and shrubs put out by the Chamber of Commerce and then a fairly wide street and a sidewalk with sycamores and store fronts. Down the hill on the other side of the tracks the old houses are big and easy among big trees and further on down is the creek and on both sides of it the Negro section. The little houses are pretty there, too, now. On this side of the tracks, up the hill, the new houses are spruced and suburban U.S. No. 1 runs through. That is the town.

This was the opening paragraph to "A Man in Town," an article about the famous author Sherwood Anderson visiting Southern Pines and Weymouth. Boyd would pass away in 1944 at age 55, in Princeton, New Jersey, where he had traveled for a speaking engagement.

James Boyd was a friend of Jonathan Daniels, and on a visit to *The News and Observer* offices in Raleigh in 1941, Ragan met Boyd and talked with him, mostly about Boyd's book, *Drums*, which Ragan had read and enjoyed immensely. Ragan would eventually move to Southern Pines and become good friends with Boyd's widow, Katharine. For sure, Boyd was a huge influence on Ragan, who also had read Boyd's poetry. In fact, a poem Boyd wrote, called "Sonnet," was a predictor of the poetry Sam Ragan would one day write. An excerpt follows.

> If poets are not listened to, the blame
> Is theirs. They speak unclearly, and are lost
> In their own psychic maze and the intricate game
> Of words. In a twisted world what matters most
> Is simple statement, open to the least
> Of men. No precious patterns hold the ear.
> Now to be heard the poet must speak plainly.

Each word must be inevitable, urgent, pure,
If people are to hear, above the roar,
The voice of those who know what speech is for.

Sam Ragan would one day become known for the lean wording of his poetry, words that came directly at the reader. Ragan liked to often say, "A poet can say in a few words what a novelist says in 100,000 words." Ragan once referenced James Boyd's poem, "Sonnet," as a poem he admired and learned from.

Clyde Hoey was the governor of North Carolina in 1941 when Sam Ragan arrived in Raleigh to start his job with *The News and Observer*. Ragan knew that getting to know Governor Hoey would help him better share state news with the readers of *The News and Observer*. Ragan heard that Governor Hoey had a daily habit of leaving his office every morning at 10 a.m. and walking down Fayetteville Street to Brantley's Drug Store for his morning dope. A dope was what many called a soft drink at the time, a Pepsi or a Coca-Cola. Ragan would often wait on Governor Hoey and walk with him down to Brantley's Drug Store and talk with him on the way. Governor Hoey was a talkative person and seemed to enjoy these walking chats with the newly installed State Editor of *The News and Observer*.

The year 1941 was important for the publication of a book called *The Mind of the South*. It was a book that was written by W.J. Cash, and the book deeply interested Sam Ragan. The chapter that most interested Ragan was Cash's chapter on Southern literature, an interest Ragan shared with Cash. *The Mind of the South* would have a huge influence on Ragan. Cash noted the Southern Literary Renaissance, and the work of such writers as Thomas Wolfe and Paul Green, and others whose works disclaimed H.L. Mencken and his words against Southern culture and the lack of good writers in the South, published back in 1917 and mentioned earlier in this book. Cash in his book of 1941 wrote, "the multiplication of Southern writers would go on at such a pace until in 1939 the South actually produced more books of measurable importance than any other section of the country, until anybody who fired off a gun in the region was practically certain to kill an author." Sadly, shortly after publication of *The Mind of the South*, Cash hanged himself, possibly suffering from depression. Cash, during the primary period of writing the book, lived in Shelby, North Carolina.

There was joyous news for the Ragans in 1943, as they had their first child, Nancy. Nancy would eventually give Sam and Marjorie two grand-children, Robin and Eric, whom they both loved dearly. Nancy has lived an exciting life, becoming a Buddhist after meeting the Dalai Lama in India. Being named Nancy Ragan, especially in the 1980s when President Ronald Reagan and First Lady Nancy Reagan occupied the White House, was not easy, so Nancy adopted the name of Rita. She has lived in New York City, and as a hobby stiches art in the miniature. Nancy was admitted into the University of Georgia at fifteen, got married later and had Robin and Eric, then became a single mother. She lived in Vancouver, where she did design work for the *Vancouver Courier*, and became a drummer for a pair of punk rock bands. She managed The Dishrags, a well-known band in Canada. She once lived on a houseboat on the Cape Fear River in North Carolina. She moved back to New York City and lived in an apartment on the Upper West Side, walking distance to Central Park, and ate sumptuous meals at the Peacock Alley in the Waldorf-Astoria.

"Sam thought of Mom as an adventurer, a lover of life who saw the world with the tenacious curiosity of a child," says Robin. "He thought her brave to go after what she wanted and found her optimistic spirit conta-gious. I believe they were kindred spirits."

Later in life, Nancy recalled some memories of Sam Ragan as her father.

I will always remember how he would read books to me, holding me in his lap. My favorite was *Alice in Wonderland*. When I was very young, he would on occasion take me with him to work at *The News and Observer* offices. I had free run of the place, and everyone was real nice to me. I would sit under his desk and read books and draw on the unending supply of paper there.

My first movie was when Daddy took me to see *The Wizard of Oz*. I was only four, and when the flying monkeys came on I was so scared I ran out of the theater. He caught me and held me tight, and told me he would not let any monkeys ever get me. The next day, he bought the book for me and read it to me, and explained the book to me.

During tobacco harvest season, Daddy would take me to his par-ent's house and all of the Ragan family would help out. I especially loved Grandma Emma's Southern style cooking, she even let me make the corn pone patties.

At home, Daddy had a sweet tooth. The refrigerator was always stocked with ice cream, and he would stuff drawers in the kitchen with moon pies and oatmeal cream cookies.

And he was one terrible driver! We would be riding somewhere and Talmadge and I would be in the back seat and he would see something and turn all the way around and point to it so we could look, and the car would be weaving all over the road.

In a poem entitled "Nancy" Sam Ragan wrote of his first child.

Nancy

You talked about bluebirds
When you were three—
And the bright bluebird
Winging into the sunlight
Always seems a part of you.
There was that song,
"Nancy With the Laughing Face,"
Which brightened dark days of long ago,
And other sights and sounds
Flood the memories
Of someone very special.
It has been a wonderful journey,
And it's the journey that counts,
Not the getting there.
Here at home the dogwood is in bloom,
And across the miles I am proud
That others share my pride in you—
The very special you.

But along with the good news of a beautiful baby daughter, Sam got one of the rites of passages that most writers experience, a rejection letter. In 1943, a letter arrived from a big publishing house, Harcourt and Brace, from New York.

Dear Mr. Ragan,

I am sorry that we can't make a publication offer for your novel, *Here's to the Land*. It interested us a great deal, and we gave it a very careful reading. But in spite of our admiration for many individual scenes, we weren't fired with that kind of enthusiasm that is needed to launch a novel successfully.

Sincerely, Lambert Davis

This rejection surely hurt the 28-year-old Sam Ragan. He would never write a novel, although he would go on to write books of non-fiction and books of prize winning poetry. But the Great American Novel was not to be for this young state editor of the *The News and Observer*.

The year 1943 also was when Sam Ragan was drafted into the United States Army.

5

In a Field Hospital on Okinawa

O n his draft card, Ragan was listed as living on South 5th Street in Wilmington and working for the *Wilmington Star*. He had registered with the Selective Service in October of 1940. His registration card in 1940 listed him as being six feet tall and weighing 158 pounds, with gray eyes, brown hair, and a ruddy complexion. He registered at the Custom House in Wilmington.

Ragan would spend most of his three years in the service in the Signal Corps, military intelligence. He saw some things that stayed with him the rest of his life. Often when asked about his experiences, he would look down at the floor and shake his head slowly, the memories of those times making him not want to think about it or reflect too much. But he opened up at times. His grandson, Eric Smith, remembers times late at night in the Ragan house in Southern Pines, where Sam talked to him about World War II. Eric recalled that Sam and some others on a patrol boat in the Pacific came to an island where they discovered about half a dozen Japanese officers bodies in a cave, who had apparently committed suicide.

Ragan was stationed for some time in Fort Ord, California, near Monterey, California. On the first Sunday in Monterey, Ragan had some time and walked into the little town on the bay. Upon entering Monterey, Ragan noticed a festive air about town with people gaily dressed. He followed the crowds of people to the wharves where the fishing boats were docked. He found out it was a day of blessing for the tuna fleet as the fishermen prepared for a new fishing season. People were getting on the boats, so Sam joined in, and found that everyone was eating food from the boats, so he joined right in. While stationed there, Ragan came back to the wharves several more times when he had some free time. In 1945, John Steinbeck's *Cannery Row* was published, where he wrote about the street in Monterey lined with sardine canneries, where Sam Ragan had walked many times and been so intrigued. Ragan purchased the book as soon as he could and read it with special interest. He later recalled that as he read the book he felt he knew the characters, such as Mack, Doc, and Dora. Ragan from that point in World War II became a lifelong reader of John Steinbeck, enjoying most everything the man wrote, including novels, stories, and travel pieces, but *Cannery Row* remained his favorite work by Steinbeck.

Ragan took his basic training in Missouri at Fort Leonard Wood, then was sent to Fort Ord in Monterey, California, and then to Hawaii. In Hawaii he was stationed on Oahu with a Signal Corps battalion and stayed in Schofield Barracks, 25 miles in the mountains above Honolulu. He was attached to the 10th Army headquarters. Most of his duty on Oahu was manning the message center. Hawaii was operating in the aftermath of Pearl Harbor, so things were on edge. Ragan was given a secret security clearance because of the information he saw and passed along to others.

In the Pacific he was in the Philippines, and then Okinawa. At Okinawa Japanese planes raided the area where Sam was stationed, and a bomb was dropped. A piece of shrapnel cut one of Sam's arms, although it didn't lodge itself in the arm. But he was bleeding badly enough that an officer insisted he go to a field hospital. The officer also knew that Sam had had a painful attack of a kidney stone just a couple days before the bombing. There was a terrible rainstorm going on during the bombing. The field hospital was very close to the front lines. Sam was put on a cot in a tent, and the cots were crowded up next to each other. There were soldiers suffering horribly, many in agonizing pain from the bombing. There was a man lying next to Sam on another cot. The medical staff didn't expect him to survive the night. There was a bullet lodged near his heart. And because of the war conditions in the area, the dying man could not be flown out for the type of surgery that might save his life. Making him as comfortable as possible was about all that could be done. Another wounded man lying close to Sam kept asking Sam, "What happened? What happened?" Sam's reply to this man was that he couldn't tell him because he was not there with him when it happened. Years later, Sam wrote a poem about this occasion, as he lay in that field hospital on Okinawa, bleeding from his arm, with dying and severely wounded men all around him.

In a Field Hospital on Okinawa

No, no, no, no, no, no —
It did not happen that way.
I was sitting there,
I heard him cry out,
I thought the shell had got me too,
And there were more of them,
Falling, falling, falling…
The ten yards were ten miles.
I wanted to go there —
Did I go?
Did I go there,
Did I go there,
When he cried out?

One good experience from World War II was that Sam got to see Irving Berlin. Sam was on Luzon in the Pacific when Berlin came with a group of soldier performers. A makeshift theater was set up. Sam and the other soldiers sat on the ground in front of a stage that had been hurriedly put together in a coconut grove. Twice during the show, it was interrupted by air raid alerts with Japanese planes flying low over the beach area just beyond where the show was taking place. Each time the lights had to be quickly put out.

But the show would just start up again, and everyone had a good time. Berlin sang some old songs from World War I. Sam even got a chance to talk briefly with Berlin after the show, and he always remembered that occasion, a respite from the horrors of war.

Another good thing to come out of the war was Sam reading Bill Mauldin's cartoons. He spent so much of his time in service "island hopping in the Pacific" as he called it. He was on the go so much that he rarely got his hands on the newspaper *Stars and Stripes*. But on the rare occasions when he did, Sam enjoyed Mauldin's Willie and Joe characters in his cartoons.

After the war, Mauldin became one of the most well-known writers of cartoon editorials in the country. While with the *The News and Observer*, Sam bought Mauldin's cartoon for the paper. Sam once arranged for Mauldin to speak in Raleigh and picked him up at the airport. They became good friends. Ragan would later write a poem about cartoonists, with Bill Mauldin in mind.

The Cartoonists

He admired the cartoonists
On the editorial pages,
And he talked about them
As if they were old, admired friends,
Calling their names—
Herblock, Mauldin…
"They can say so much," he said.
"One little line
Tells it all."

Ragan also recalled listening to Tokyo Rose while stationed in the Pacific. He commented on whether the propaganda from Tokyo Rose had its designed effect of demoralizing American troops. "As far as we could tell those radio broadcasts had no demoralizing effect on anyone. In fact, many of the GI's enjoyed the broadcasts, especially the old American records, and laughed heartily at most of the statements."

While in the war, Ragan recalled a popular activity he observed. "When I served in the Army in the Philippines cockfighting was a favorite sport among the natives. Young Filipinos would walk around with a rooster under an arm, just in case they encountered someone else with a fighting cock, whereupon a fight would be arranged on the spot and often would take place in the middle of a dirt road while a crowd gathered to cheer one or the other on and perhaps make a bet or two on the outcome."

On April 12, 1945, President Franklin Delano Roosevelt passed away. Sam Ragan graduated from high school in 1932, the year FDR was elected, and was in college when FDR was inaugurated. He listened to the inaugural address on the radio and was inspired by the "new deal" for America that FDR called for. Ragan remembered hearing the awful news of FDR's passing.

I was on the Task Force flagship just off Okinawa when the news came of FDR's death. I can recall in detail where I was and what I was doing. In looking over the shoulder of a radio man in the Message Center I read the words which Mrs. Roosevelt had dispatched to two of her sons serving with the same Task Force 68. What Mrs. Roosevelt said was:

"Pa slipped away today."

That was all, but the sons and all of us knew what she meant. A few minutes later I joined the chow line and relayed the word that Roosevelt had died.

My wife, Marjorie, was working on the major Washington newspaper at the time, and she wrote me in detail about the teary-eyed faces on the streets of our nation's capital as the word spread. She was present at the White House when Harry Truman, the Vice-President, was sworn in as FDR's successor and she said it was a somber event.

On April 18, 1945, Ernie Pyle was shot and killed during the Battle of Okinawa. Pyle was a war correspondent who won the Pulitzer Prize in 1944 for his coverage of infantry soldiers. The very day before Pyle was killed, Sam Ragan met and talked to him. Sam remembered that day,

I had seen him the night before when he came aboard the *Eldorado*, the command ship of the task force invading Okinawa. I chatted briefly with Ernie. He was a quiet man and looked weary. He had gone through the war in Europe, and was now covering the last stages of the war in the Pacific. He didn't have to go with the small group that went on the island. The island was supposed to have been cleared of enemy troops by then, and he went along for the ride and a short walk in the sun. But the walk was brief. From a hidden and by-passed machine gun nest there came a burst of gunfire and Ernie Pyle was dead. There were five bullet holes in his helmet.

On a ship far out in the Pacific Ocean while in service, Ragan saw a butterfly and wrote the following poem later in life, around 1990. Ragan loved to see butterflies, admired their beauty, and would write several poems about them. Ragan's youngest daughter, Talmadge, inspired him to write "Two Butterflies."

It was during a stay in the hospital for Sam and Marjorie. Marjorie was sick, and Sam was getting radiation treatments for the lung cancer that would eventually take his life. Talmadge flew in from Los Angeles, where she was living, for an extended visit and to take Sam to treatments. Sam and Marjorie were in the same hospital. Sam did not want Marjorie to know about the radiation treatments, so he had a note put on Marjorie's door, reminding the staff to not mention to Marjorie that he was a patient. Sam would put on a coat and bow tie when he visited Marjorie, so she would think he was coming from work. He would stay just a few minutes and go back to his room. Sam and Talmadge kept noticing the same butterfly outside his hospital room window each day. The butterfly always seemed like it wanted to come in, and Sam and Talmadge took it as a good sign. Ragan wrote "Two Butterflies" because the butterfly outside his hospital room reminded him of the butterfly he saw on that ship in the Pacific Ocean during World War II. "Two Butterflies" was written during a very challenging time of his life but being with Talmadge and talking with her gave him strength, just as seeing beautiful butterflies did.

Two Butterflies

I keep thinking of that butterfly
I saw skimming the waves
In the Pacific more than 200 miles from any land,
More than 45 years ago.
He or she was large, bright blue and
Beautiful. I keep remembering
How beautiful she looked in the sunlight.

A few days ago another butterfly
Kept returning to the same place
On the large windowpane,
Fluttering its large yellow wings,
Bright in the sunlight.

I think of these two butterflies —
So long ago, so far apart,

Their lives so short—
Who live only to be beautiful—
Isn't that enough?

Ragan recalled the end of the war later in life in a *Southern Accent* column.

On August 6, 1945, when the atomic bomb was dropped by U.S. forces on the Japanese city of Hiroshima I was on Okinawa, a part of Japan's island chain, and preparing for an invasion of the main islands.

The news first came in a brief bulletin in the 10th Army Message center, but by the time the second atomic bomb was dropped on Nagasaki three days later we had learned a lot more about this powerful weapon.

That second bomb brought an offer to surrender from the Japanese and then all of us on Okinawa waited with bated breath as Washington took its time in replying to Japan on the surrender offer. When surrender was accepted, the island of Okinawa exploded with celebrations. Anti-aircraft gunfire lit up the sky, and a major running across an open field with a bottle of liquor held high had it shattered in his hand by falling flak. The colonel who headed our small intelligence unit rushed into the Quonset hut and started pawing in a pile of papers in a corner. He pulled out a full bottle of bourbon and we all toasted peace at last.

It was an indescribable feeling. None of us thought about Hiroshima or Nagasaki, but we all knew that it was the atomic bomb which brought peace to the world and probably saved at least one million lives, both American and Japanese.

Our small intelligence unit had been working with realities, such as landing on a narrow beach and climbing a bare 40-foot cliff and the knowledge that the Japanese army would battle to the death to save their home land. Surrender was unthinkable for them, it would disgrace them, their country and their emperor. An invasion of Kyushu would be like Iwo Jima and Peleliu a thousandfold over. The war, we concluded, could go on two more years. President Harry Truman was right in his decision, and we know we are alive now because the bomb was dropped.

Ragan met Ralph Whitfield in Okinawa. Ralph developed the nickname of Slick because of his poker-playing skills. Ragan and Slick became life-long friends. After the war, Sam and Marjorie set Slick up with Marguerite Lipscomb, who was related to the Ragans, and Slick and Marguerite eventually married.

Later in life, Ragan wrote the poem "Postwar" about the end of the Civil War. But Ragan must have been thinking about coming home to Marjorie and three-year-old daughter Nancy, and all there was to do once he got home from World War II, similar to the Civil War soldier in "Postwar."

Postwar

He came home from Petersburg,
Footing it down the road with three others
Who fell off by the way,
He going the last miles alone.
The chimney's smoke quickened his steps.
She was waiting in the doorway
And ran down the path to meet him.
Not much was said:
They walked back together
And he took off his hat and stood a moment
Before going in to supper.

He cleaned the spring,
And there were three places in the fence to mend.
A new ground was cleared,
And after the plowing was done,
Along the road he planted a row of cedars.

Ragan would have probably agreed with Ulysses Grant when he said, "I advocate war only as a means to peace." That is evident in Ragan's poem "Notes on the Margins of Our Times," which includes stanzas about the Vietnam War. An excerpt follows.

And in the Mekong Delta
The captain speaks matter-of-factly:
We had to destroy it
To save it.

The soldier squats in the jungle dark,
Holding his rifle in one hand.
Charlie's out there —
I don't know Charlie,
And Charlie doesn't know me,
But we're going to kill each other.

While her husband was serving in World War II, Marjorie was looking after their daughter, Nancy. She also took a job with the *Washington Times-Herald*, where she covered politics mostly. The *Times-Herald* would later become the *Washington Post*. Marjorie became one of the first women to cover the United States Senate and was present when Harry Truman was sworn in as President after Franklin Roosevelt's death in 1945.

After the war ended, Marjorie returned to Raleigh and became news director of WRAL Radio, becoming the first woman in the state to hold such a position. Marjorie Usher Ragan was really a pathbreaker in women's journalism in North Carolina. Later in her life, she was the state publicity director and editor for PTA Magazine in North Carolina and worked with the North Carolina State University News Bureau. She reviewed books for publications, and later in life served as associate editor of *The Pilot* newspaper in Southern Pines, working alongside Sam.

She was also a noted book reviewer. She believed in being judicious in using words, like her husband. In a review of a book written by well-known author Robert Ruark, Marjorie Ragan put this judicious use of words to practice. Here is her review in its entirety of the Ruark novel, *Something of Value*. "*Something of Value* isn't."

One of her greatest thrills in life, she once said, was "getting my teeth into a good news story, digging out the facts, and writing the story." Her former journalism professor at the University of North Carolina, Chapel Hill, Oscar Coffin, once called her "a damn good newspaperman."

Sam Ragan talked about Marjorie in an interview later in his life.

During the war, she went to Washington and worked for a newspaper there, covered the United States Senate. When she came back to Raleigh, she worked as news director for a radio station. She had her own news bureau there. She worked as public relations director at N.C. State University. Then when she came to *The Pilot*, she was associate editor. She's at one end of the building, and I'm in the other. We had two children, and she stopped work when they were growing up. She's one of the brightest people I ever knew. I suppose she's had more influence on my life than any other one person. She's one of the best read people you will encounter anywhere in the country. She still reads about five or six books a week. I say she's an authority on so many subjects that I have to consult her. She does not write poetry, but she has a great appreciation for it. She is my best critic.

Marjorie was also a lover of roses and grew prize roses. She was elected as president of the Raleigh Rose Society and even wrote a book about roses.

Sam Ragan ended his army service in 1946, and he knew what he wanted to do. Josephus Daniels had told him that he had a job back with *The News and Observer* in Raleigh when the war ended. Daniels was impressed with his young state editor. For Sam there was some real comfort in knowing that after the war ended, he had a good job to go back to. He had a wife and now three-year-old daughter to support, and he felt very lucky to be working again for one of the leading newspapers in the entire South. Newspaper work was what he wanted to do with his life, and he was good at it.

Officially released from the army on January 13, 1946, Sam was awarded a disability pension, and also was eligible for vocational rehabilitation and hospitalization. He was suffering from severe vertigo, caused by his war experiences, accompanied by some hearing loss.

6

The Ahoskie Case, *Southern Accent,*
Talmadge, "The Girl in the Green Bathing Suit"

S am also still dreamed of being a novelist. After having *Here's to the Land* rejected in 1943 before entering World War II, he submitted the same book with some revisions to Houghton Mifflin in New York. He got another rejection delivered to his then home on Watauga Street in Raleigh in early 1946.

> Dear Mr. Ragan,
>
> We read *Here's to the Land* with a great deal of interest but unfortunately we were unable to accept it for placement on our publishing list. Although we feel that the background and characters are handled extremely well, the story and its theme has the misfortune of being dated at the present time. We hope that you will let us see anything you may do in the future in the writing field as we are more than interested in your work.
>
> Joyce Hartman

In 1947 Ragan received a lot of national press and attention over the "Ahoskie Case." Harvey Jones, a black man who lived on a farm about seven miles outside of Ahoskie, North Carolina, drew the winning ticket for a new Cadillac car, valued at $3,200. Harvey lived with his wife and one child in his father's house on a ten acre farm. They had chicken coops with 50 hens, one horse, and they grew mostly peanuts and corn on the land. Harvey was 23 years of age and a World War II veteran.

The winning ticket for Harvey was drawn at the Ahoskie Kiwanis Festival in June. When Kiwanis officials and Sheriff Charlie Parker realized that a black man was the winner, Sheriff Parker drove to Harvey's house and told him that the ticket he had paid $1 for was only for white people. A man had sold Harvey and a few other black people tickets not knowing they were to be sold only to white people. So Sheriff Parker gave Harvey his $1 ticket fee back to him and left. In comments later, Harvey said, "Sheriff Parker told me I had the lucky number but I couldn't win the car because it wasn't for colored people."

Over in Raleigh, Sam Ragan heard about this injustice. He broke the story first, with several articles appearing in *The News and Observer*. The articles by Ragan were picked up by the major press wires around the country and newspapers wrote editorials about the incident in Ahoskie. Even several European newspapers carried the story on page one. Senator Carl Hatch of New Mexico read about it and threatened to talk about the incident on the Senate floor. The nationwide publicity that Ragan's reporting generated prompted the Ahoskie Kiwanis Club to offer Harvey Jones his new car. Jones asked if he could have the money equivalent of the new Cadillac. They agreed and presented Harvey a check for $3,200.

In an Associated Press interview, Sam talked about the incident. "I handled the story lightly instead of indignantly, stressing the idea that Jones had been lucky in the drawing and unlucky when he didn't get the car but that he was being philosophical about it. I had an idea that after the story got out into print it would bring repercussions and get something started and it did." The AP went on to state in the same article, "The American press, rising to a situation as it can, roused the public as it can, over the Ahoskie Case. A Negro was denied the car for which he held the winning ticket in a Kiwanis lottery in the North Carolina town. Sam Ragan, State Editor of the *Raleigh News and Observer*, got wind of the story, dug it out, and printed it. The press association picked it up and the wires vibrated with an instant response to an injustice anybody could understand."

In 1948 Ragan started a column called *Southern Accent* in *The News and Observer*. Little did he know at the time that this column would run until 1996, when he would pass away. The column ran for 48 years, making it the longest running column of its type in America. It would be a literary column for the most part, touting and praising North Carolina authors mostly, but also writing about authors from around the country. *Southern Accent* also contained information about the arts in general, and bits of humor. Ragan gave many well-known authors around the state their first publication in his column. For example, he published a poem of Reynolds Price when Price was still in high school. Price said that he was so excited that he couldn't sleep the night before he knew the column was coming out. Both established writers and people wanting to become writers would send Ragan books, poems, short stories, and essays hoping Ragan would publish their work in *Southern Accent*. And he often did.

In August of 1948, in one of his first *Southern Accent* columns, he wrote about Betty Smith.

The old adage that "hope springs eternal in the human breast" has been the theme of many major novels and stories. Betty Smith has used the theme in her two novels of the Brooklyn saga. The title of her second novel, *Tomorrow Will Be Better*, is a paraphrase of those words by Pope. Several critics took occasion to make the inevitable comparison of the new novel with the widely popular *A Tree Grows in Brooklyn*, and in the comparison the second novel comes off second best. One critic said that in *A Tree Grows in Brooklyn* the reader could identify himself with and feel sympathy for Francie Nolan, but in *Tomorrow Will Be Better* there is little identification with Margy Shannon or sympathy for her. There probably will be more novels from the material which Betty Smith has selected as her own. The two so far have dwelt on the theme of hope, and no doubt the others will follow the same pattern—for it is true that for the Nolans and the Shannons there is "no other medicine but only hope."

Frank Slaughter, by quite a coincidence, was born in Berea, just like Sam Ragan. It may be that no more successful authors ever lived in the same such small community in North Carolina. Slaughter would go on to sell more than 60 million of his books, mostly novels. Slaughter was born in 1908, seven years before Ragan. Slaughter graduated from Oxford High School and then from Trinity College, now Duke University, at the age of 17. He then got a medical degree from Johns Hopkins. He became a physician in Jacksonville, Florida, and started writing his novels in the 1930s while still practicing medicine. Several of his books became films, including *Doctors' Wives,* made into a 1971 film of the same name starring Dyan Cannon and Gene Hackman. As might be expected with both spending part of their early lives in a small community such as Berea, Ragan and Slaughter were cousins. Sam's grandfather, William Ragan, married Elizabeth Slaughter. In 1949, Ragan wrote about Slaughter in *Southern Accent* in *The News and Observer.*

> Dr. Frank G. Slaughter paused long enough while in route to his home in Jacksonville, Florida, a few nights ago to relay the information that he plans soon to write a sequel to *In a Dark Garden,* the historical novel that has sold over a million copies and is being reprinted in several foreign languages. The sequel will have an Eastern North Carolina setting, mostly around Wilmington and the Cape Fear area, and will deal with the Reconstruction era. Dr. Slaughter, who grew up in Granville County, was home to visit his mother, a patient at Duke Hospital. He is at work now on a book concerning medicine in the Renaissance and the novel is scheduled for publication in the fall. Dr. Slaughter's first novel, *That None Should Die,* is being reissued by Doubleday in the spring.

In 1948, Ragan was promoted to Managing Editor of *The News and Observer.* Not only was he obviously doing a good job at *The News and Observer,* but he continued to write for other publications when time was available. In May of 1949, he wrote an article in *The Progressive,* a magazine published in Madison, Wisconsin. Ragan wrote about North Carolina Governor Kerr Scott. He was paid $15 for the article.

In a nod to Ragan's growing respect among newspaper people in the state, the North Carolina Associated Press News Council was formed in 1950, and Ragan was elected its first president. More than twenty of the major newspapers in the state were members of this new organization. Among the papers were the *Raleigh News and Observer, Charlotte Observer, Durham Herald,* and *Asheville Citizen Times.* One resolution the new organization passed at its first meeting was to oppose off the record press conferences.

Thad Stem was from Oxford, about eight miles from Berea in Granville County. Sam Ragan and Thad Stem, despite their close proximity, didn't know each other while growing up in Granville County, but they became the best of friends once they started their literary careers. Stem would go on to write many books of fiction, non-fiction, and poetry, and thousands of newspaper and magazine articles and columns, and is now enshrined in the North Carolina Literary Hall of Fame. Sam and Thad often corresponded, and I will include quite a few examples of their letters in this book. In December 1950, Thad, who was born on Front Street in his parent's house in Oxford and lived there his entire life, wrote to Sam. (Thad's father was Thad Stem Sr., who was the very first captain in the history of Duke basketball, and later served as mayor of Oxford.)

Every man ought to have a good wife and a good pocket knife. You have the good wife. I told you at the steak parlor in Raleigh that I want you to have a good knife. I am enclosing one under separate cover that I have whetted in advance. This is not a Christmas present and entails no return. It is just a love offering. Pocket knives have afforded me a lot of pleasure, and too, I feel lonesome without a good one in my jeans.

Your column is getting a wide and favorable coverage. Friends of mine throughout the state have sent clippings to me. *Southern Accent* is excellent. We look forward to them eagerly each Sunday. You are gaining adherents all the time.

I was very much amazed that Faulkner won the Nobel Prize. I am happy that a Southern man could win.

Even in 1950, H.L. Mencken's criticism of writers from the South and Southern culture still stung. In an essay in 1917, Mencken, perhaps the best-known newspaper columnist in the entire nation, had called the South "The Sahara of the Bozart." Mencken wrote that after James Branch Cabell had been counted one could not find a single Southern prose writer who could actually write. Mencken went on, writing that the South was "almost as sterile, artistically, intellectually, culturally, as the Sahara Desert." Mencken's diatribe attracted wide attention in Dixie, even a decade or so after it was published, and I'm sure Thad Stem was thinking about

Mencken when he wrote Ragan about Mississippi's William Faulkner winning the 1949 Nobel Prize for Literature.

The Southern Literary Renaissance followed Mencken's criticism, so Mencken actually contributed to the rise of Southern literature through his biting words. The Southern Literary Renaissance was the reinvigoration of American Southern literature that many historians say began in the 1920s and 1930s. William Faulkner, Tennessee Williams, Robert Penn Warren, Thomas Wolfe, and James Boyd were among others who led this advance.

Elizabeth Spencer, the nationally acclaimed novelist who was born in Mississippi and has lived in Chapel Hill since 1986, once said of this Southern renaissance, "There used to be almost a tangible tension between the movement of what might be called American civilization and the more static aspect of things in the South." Spencer attributes the burst of literary creativity in the South to the "tangible tension" and to the desire to depict a waning way of life, to "get it all down," before the modern world assimilated it. She mentioned Southerners' "Proustian sense of time," in which "the past is never gone."

Sam Ragan often cited the acceptance speech of William Faulkner when he won the Nobel Prize for Literature as an example of the importance of writing. Ragan, who would teach many writing classes at colleges and universities, read the speech to his students and discussed the speech's meaning. An excerpt from the Faulkner speech follows.

I believe that man will not merely endure: he will prevail. He is immortal, not because he alone among creatures has an inexhaustible voice but because he has a soul, a spirit, capable of compassion and sacrifice and endurance. The poet's, the writer's, duty is to write about these things. It is his privilege to help man endure by lifting his heart, by reminding him of the courage and honor and hope and pride and compassion and pity and sacrifice which have been the glory of his past. The poet's voice need not merely be the record of man, it can be one of the props, the pillars to help him endure and prevail.

Ragan wrote of William Faulkner in a poem.

The Human Heart

He spoke for himself,
But William Faulkner spoke
For all writers when he said
That, deep down, they wrote
About the same thing.
That thing, he said, is
The human heart in conflict
With itself.

Ragan's *Southern Accent* column continued to be noticed around the state. In 1950 Dillard Gardner, who was Librarian of the North Carolina Supreme Court Library, wrote to Sam voicing his hearty support. Phyllis Peacock wrote to Ragan also. Peacock was a legendary teacher at Raleigh Broughton High School, and she taught and greatly influenced three famed writers, Reynolds Price, Anne Tyler, and Armistead Maupin.

Your Sunday column interested me as usual. Keep up the crusade for intelligible, readable writing. There is far too little of it. With every good wish and a God's-speed in your efforts to encourage translucent writing that ripples and sparkles in the sun. — *Dillard Gardner*

Despising flattery, I never wrote a fan letter in my life, but in the interests of truth I ought to say that I turn to "Southern Accent" first. — *Phyllis Peacock*

Another baby girl was born to Sam and Marjorie in 1951. Talmadge Ragan was named after her dad, Samuel Talmadge Ragan. Talmadge would go on to graduate from the University of North Carolina at Chapel Hill. She was an actress in *The Lost Colony* outdoor drama in Manteo for several years, and produced commercials in New York City. She has been a writer and speechwriter. Moving to Los Angeles, Talmadge was active in the television and film industry. She married Worth Keeter, and they founded Blue Kiss Media, a film and commercial production company. Talmadge has been the voice for many audiobooks. Her father wrote a poem about her, and called it "Talmadge."

Talmadge

I have not written a birthday poem
For you before, but I have thought of many.
So many running together
In memories of sun and sea,
Blue moon and blue skies,
Summer nights and the fragrance of flowers,
Journeys together, quiet times, your laughter,
The way you walk, the way you talk,
The light in your eyes,
And the pure sounds of a flute—
I carry them all with me
In a memory of you and your face,
I write now on your birthday,
Remembering,
I write of love—
And wonder.

Along with helping to run *The News and Observer* and writing his growing in popularity *Southern Accent* newspaper column and raising a family, Sam continued writing for other publications. *The People's Choice* magazine out of New York City paid him $75 for a 600-word article about his fellow Berea friend and cousin, Frank Slaughter, who by this time, in 1951, had achieved national acclaim. Sam concentrated on Slaughter's book, *The Road to Bithynia*, which was a Biblical novel.

But his work as Managing Editor for *The News and Observer* kept Ragan busy and paid the bills. In 1952, Kenneth Royall, from North Carolina, who was Secretary of War under President Harry Truman, was upset with *The News and Observer*. At the time Royall was a partner in a prestigious New York City law firm. Royall, a Democrat, saw that *The News and Observer* wrote "Mrs. Royall was one of the Washington women [author's note: when Royall served in the Truman Administration] who got a mink coat at wholesale back in the period which made mink coats the Republican symbol for official Washington." Royall said that the statement was untrue, and that he nor Mrs. Royall ever purchased a mink coat while in Washington. Royall demanded that *The News and Observer* admit its mistake and apologize to his wife.

Sam Ragan replied to Royall in a most cordial way, as you would expect from a man who was called by so many people who knew him a "Southern gentleman." Ragan told Royall he would certainly do what was right and proper but referred Royall to a statement he had been quoted as saying that he "had bought his wife three mink coats in the last fifteen years through wholesalers." So he let Royall know that any correction *The News and Observer* printed would also have to include Royall's quote.

The 1950s was a good time for Sam Ragan. He had a beautiful wife, Marjorie, who he loved dearly, and two daughters, Nancy and Talmadge. The family enjoyed living in Raleigh, and Sam loved his job as managing editor with *The News and Observer*. By 1960, he would be promoted to executive editor, so obviously the Daniels family, who owned and published the paper, were pleased with his work. His *Southern Accent* column was getting noticed around the state and other parts of the country, and he was writing articles for magazines and other publications. He was becoming a well-known newspaperman in North Carolina and was one of the leaders in the state literary scene.

In an interview, Ragan talked about the function of a good newspaper, and *The News and Observer* during the 1950s.

What people do, what they say, what they think, is what goes into a good newspaper. I think that a good newspaper is going to have a good editorial page. An editorial should be provocative and get people to think. I think that you should make your paper open to the expressions and opinions of others. I don't ask people to agree with me on editorials, but I do hope that they will think about it and respond to it. I think we have an obligation to look over the shoulder of public officials. If we think they're doing right, doing something good, say so. But if they're doing something wrong, or something that you don't approve of, you say that too.

In the 1950s *The News and Observer*, while I was there, got very much involved in the Willis Smith-Frank Graham senatorial campaign. We supported Frank Graham. On the night that Frank Graham was defeated in the second primary, Jonathan Daniels, who was then editor, had the vision to see something while we were waiting for the election return to come in. He saw a little piece on the AP wire about the invasion of South Korea by North Korea. The beginning of the Korean War came on that very same day. Jonathan saw that this was something very important and significant, and he wrote an editorial about that to go in the next day's paper. I give that as an example of how newspapers should stay on top of things, and Jonathan Daniels was one of the best at that kind of thing.

I remember being at a national editor's convention in Chicago right after Eisenhower was elected in 1952. McCarthyism was going on, the Korean War, the economy in North Carolina, what was happening in local counties and small towns in our coverage area, we tried to inform our readers about all that was going on. It's a huge responsibility, and we took that responsibility very seriously. At that time we reported in *The News and Observer* all the bills that were introduced in the state legislature. I thought one of the greatest compliments that *The News and Observer* ever got was when Gregg Cherry was governor. He had made an appointment to a state office. This man asked the Governor, "What do you expect me to do?" Governor Cherry said, "I want you to do your job and don't do anything that you don't want to read about on the front page of *The News and Observer* the next morning." That's about as good a compliment, I think, that you could pay to a newspaper.

The News and Observer was in the forefront on civil liberties in the fifties and sixties. I was completely in accord with that. We were way out ahead of everybody else in championing civil rights.

The Lost Colony, the outdoor drama written by Paul Green performed on the Outer Banks of North Carolina, became almost an annual event for Ragan. He absolutely loved the play, and attended the show dozens of times through the years. His daughter, Talmadge, acted in the drama. Ragan not only loved literature, but arts in general, such as plays, drama, dancing, singing, music, and lectures. He also sat on *The Lost Colony* Board of Directors for a number of years. In 1951, he used part of a *Southern Accent* column to praise *The Lost Colony*.

Paul Green's *The Lost Colony*, which tells the story of the first colonists which Sir Walter Raleigh sent to the New World in 1587, is now on its way into its 11th season. Primarily, credit for the success of this symphonic drama is due to the creative imagination of Paul Green—the way in which he combined three arts of the stage to evoke the story and the spirit of the lost colony. Drama, music, and ballet all have their part in the production. But the theater itself bestows a benediction that has beckoned thousands. The show goes on where the Lost Colony lived and enacted its real drama. Year after year in the quietude of the audience there is implicit recognition of the blending of truth and drama.

Even as early as 1951, Ragan used *Southern Accent* as a platform to showcase North Carolina authors. "September Signs of Carolina," submitted to him by Mary Medley of Wadesboro, caught Sam's eye.

The black grape has its sugar stored—
The scuppernong its luscious flavor.
While lands their yearly fruitage hoard,
The apple blends its acid savor.
Ultra, radiant, sunlight spills
Its sparkling, potent, chartreuse liquor
Upon the drowsy fields and hills
To lure their yielding quicker.
Bees eye the stickweed for late honey.
The harvest makes in the flushing noon.
Short-lived are the useful hours, sunny.
For a cool, night wind brushes the moon.

Ragan usually used *Southern Accent* to praise writers, but he could review a writer critically if he thought circumstances warranted it. In the same column in 1951, William Styron got praise and Randall Jarrell got scolded just a bit.

Young William Styron, whose first novel, *Lie Down in Darkness,* was published last week, is being hailed in early reviews of his book as a writer of great talent. Robert Mason says in the Norfolk *Virginian-Pilot:* "As a craftsman and artist, William Styron at the age of 26 bears risk of the word genius." It was at Duke University, under the guidance of Dr. William Blackburn, that Styron started writing short stories and received encouragement to become a writer. He spent about three years writing *Lie Down in Darkness*. That it was three years well spent most readers will readily agree.

In 1948 when Randall Jarrell's book of poems, *Losses*, was published I commented that on the strength of that volume Mr. Jarrell should be classed as one of America's leading poets writing at that time. After reading his latest book of poems, *The Seven-League Crutches*, I am forced to revise downward my earlier estimate. It just doesn't measure up to *Losses*. In fact, I am a little confused about the whole work, which includes 28 poems grouped under three headings: "Europe," "Children," and "Once Upon a Time." The theme of these poems, as I understand it, concerns the fundamental brotherhood of men. But the execution of the poems does not live up to the conception. There is originality in phrases and expression, but the language of *The Seven-League Crutches* is jerky, unsure and much in the manner of marionettes performing in a fog. Written in a metallic, mechanistic style, from which emotion has been squeezed, these poems convey but little feeling or understanding. Frequently there are clear lines of poetry, but in the summing up the picture becomes clouded. Mr. Jarrell, an associate professor of English at Woman's College in Greensboro, is currently on leave of absence at Princeton where he is a resident fellow in creative writing and a lecturer in the Princeton seminars in literary criticism.

Nature and what Ragan saw as he drove around the state also made its way onto the pages of *Southern Accent*, as in this from 1953.

April, I think, is the finest time of the year to ride through North Carolina. There are the new plowed fields and far off across the flat fertile land the first green of spring. Maybe a man and a mule with a plow, though there are not as many men and mules as there used to be. But there's sure to be a tractor moving faster than a mule and turning more furrows and leaving a larger cloud of dust behind the man riding across the land.

Around houses and along the roadside there are many flowers. Azaleas have become very popular. And there are apple blossoms in the air. Where the road runs through bottom land thousands of flowers rise from the dark soil.

And everywhere are dogwood blossoms. The matchless white blossoms fairly jump from the dark woods. There are millions of them and when one experiences the sight of dogwood in bloom in April one can be proud that North Carolina chose this blossom for its state flower.

Another way Ragan used *Southern Accent* was to write about people in the arts he knew or admired. Eugene O'Neill passed away in 1953. A critique of William Faulkner and mention of James Street follows the O'Neill piece and was written in 1954. James Street moved to North Carolina, and among other works, was known for his Southern historical novels which explored classic Southern issues of race and honor. Street died of a heart attack while in Chapel Hill to present awards in radio broadcasting in 1954. He had stopped by in Raleigh to visit with Sam Ragan just a couple of days before his death.

Eugene O'Neill died the other day, and news of his death was curiously like something from another era. For O'Neill had gone out of fashion in recent years. Critics wrote disparagingly of his talent, and his last staged play, *The Iceman Cometh*, created little stir in the world of the drama.

O'Neill was not essentially a dramatist. In reading his plays one gets the feeling that they were not written primarily to be staged but as literature. O'Neill chose that form for literary expression rather than the form of the novel or the narrative poem. That is not to say that there was no drama in O'Neill's plays. They had the pitch and the power of great drama, but it was the drama found in great novels or tightly compact short stories or poems. If he is to be compared to any other contemporary in the field of writing, perhaps he comes closest to the vein of Robinson Jeffers. There is the same starkness and nakedness of human emotion in *The Roan Stallion* as in *Desire Under the Elms*, for instance. The same spirit of pessimism, sometimes of doom, pervades their work.

The playwright O'Neill commanded great respect and attention in his day, not as much from the theater-going public as from the teachers of drama, the critics of the 20s and early 30s, and students in colleges who, on reading O'Neill, felt perhaps for the first time the real power of writing.

O'Neill the playwright may be forgotten, but O'Neill the writer will long live in literature.

Faulkner's books are remarkable works of craftsmanship. But they are difficult to read. Sentences that run as long as 17 pages do not readily invite readership. For the reader who sticks with it, however, there is a reward. Faulkner is one of the world's greatest writers today.

In any writing, the purpose of which is to convey meaning to someone else, there is no substitute for clarity. Yet a reader who stays with Faulkner has nothing but admiration for the completeness of his style, the sure command he has at all times of his theme, and the way he weaves the tangled skein of his story into a complete whole. He never leaves any dangling threads.

James Street's unexpected passing was a shock to the state which he had adopted. The Mississippi born writer had endeared himself to North Carolinians and in more ways than one.

A few days before he died Street came by to see me on his way to a television show about his Holiday magazine article on the South. We talked about William Faulkner, about public appearances, and a dozen other things. Street admired Faulkner, as a man and as a writer. It is significant, I think, that a few minutes before he collapsed at that Chapel Hill meeting that he made the remark to a radio commentator "I have wished all my life to write one line as good as anything Faulkner has written."

North Carolina was benefitted by James Street's stay in the state, and the lives of so many of us were enriched by his having passed this way.

An annual tradition of Ragan's in *Southern Accent* was his Christmas poem each December. These poems were eagerly anticipated around the state, with friends and writers hoping to get mentioned. The poems were lengthy, running hundreds of words longer than his poems he would publish in his books to come. He used the poems to celebrate one of his favorite times of the year, to say hello to friends, to review the past year, and to offer some encouragement. His 1954 Christmas poem follows, excerpted because of length.

Tis the day after Christmas—the end's drawing near
For our Christmas wishes, and Happy New Year.
With a jingle of bells, and songs very loud,
Merry Christmas to clans from McAnn to McLeod.
To Elks and their ilk in all of the lodges,
We add greetings to all, and to Governor Hodges.
For school teachers everywhere, pats on the back,
And a holiday season of hitting the sack.
For T.G. Stem we can be terse,
We wish him another book of his own verse.
For Chapel Hill football fans, more winning times,
Less "Gently, Sweet Afton" on bell tower chimes.
Greetings to Daniels—Frank, Jonathan, Joe—
To Russ Grumman, Miss Cobb, and Dr. Clarence Poe.
Especially greetings to folks here in Raleigh—
To Clyde Smith, Mrs. Peacock, a fresh sprig of holly.
An Orange Bowl victory for Duke's great Blue Devils
And safety to everyone after their revels.
To Smithfield's Miss Gardner and more Smithfield hams,
You just can't beat Smithfield for turning out gams.
To June West and other "Southern Accent" contributors,
To Ike London and the other newspaper distributors,
To people in purple and all beauty queens'
To children who acted nativity scenes.
To Bill Sharpe and Sally, we hope that "The State"
Of your health is as good as you good people rate.
To Burke Davis, Walt Spearman, and Bernadette Hoyle,
The pleasure to readers is worth all your toil.
Our best bow to poets like Charles Edward Eaton,
And the Oriental Allen's whose first name is Seaton.
For the poem you sent us we'll tune up a harp,
And say thank you, your honor, to Judge Susie Sharp.
To Frances Gray Patton and other good writers,
To soldiers and sailors and Camp Lejeune fighters.
And to all those for whose names we can't find a rhyme
We'll greet you in person, some other time.
And so Merry Christmas to all, cultured and pagan,
From the two kids, Sam and Marjorie Ragan.

"A Christmas Night," a poem by Ragan, sends a message of what Christmas, to some degree, should be about, helping those in need. It is about seeing an old man in a thin jacket out at night, a cold night with ice on the grounds and roads, carrying wood and Christmas presents to someone in need, probably alone. The old man waved and smiled at the passing car. The sight gave the driver of the car, and I want to think it was Ragan, a warm feeling as he drove away. Ragan would say many times that most of his poems came from his life's experiences, taken from "fragments of living."

A Christmas Night

It was a cold night
And there was ice on the road,
Our car started to slide
As it moved up the small hill,
And the headlights caught the old man
In a thin jacket
Pushing a cart filled with sticks.
There were some bundles and a package
Piled on top, and the old man
Grinned and waved at us
As he pushed the cart
Into the yard of the little house
Where a single light shone.
The tires gripped the road
And we drove on into the darkness,
But suddenly it was warm.

Arthur Abernethy was the first Poet Laureate of North Carolina. In 1953, Governor Umstead appointed James Larkin Pearson as Poet Laureate of North Carolina. Pearson would serve as Poet Laureate for almost 30 years, until 1982, when Sam Ragan would take Pearson's place as Poet Laureate after Pearson passed away. Pearson was born in a cabin in 1879 on Berry's Mountain in Wilkes County, North Carolina. His education was very limited, but he taught himself through reading as much as he could. In 1910, he began publishing a newsletter, the *Fool Killer*, which grew to a circulation of 50,000 around the country. The paper was meant, according to Pearson, "to make a fellow laugh right big and to cram a truth down his throat while his mouth was open." Upton Sinclair wrote about Pearson and his poetry in *The New York Times,* and they published his most well-known poem, "Fifty Acres." This poem was about his farm in Wilkes County. He wrote several books of poetry, including *Fifty Acres and Other Selected Poems, Plowed Ground: Humorous* and *Dialect Poems, Early Harvest: The First Experimental Poems of a Self-Taught Farm Boy,* and *My Fingers and My Toes.* Pearson passed away at the age of 102 and is buried in the Moravian Falls Cemetery in Wilkes County.

The News and Observer moved into a new building in 1956 in Raleigh. Ragan wrote about the move in *Southern Accent.*

There's always a twinge and a tear, I suppose, in leaving a place where one has long lived. Physical surroundings have a way of seeping through one, taking a hold that is hard to shake off. That is true, I know, of a newspaper office where one has worked over the years, long hours of watching clocks in the fight to meet deadlines, of watching men feel their way over a typewriter keyboard to tell the never-ending tale of man's triumphs and tragedies.

Newspaper people, despite popular notion, are a sentimental lot. They like to re-hash the good stories of long ago, to recall with loving pride that time when the words came just right to tell the story of a drama of the human heart. For news is a thing alive, a pulsing, beating thing that never really dies. And once a man has held it in his hands, really held it and knew it, it never leaves him.

In the news room of a morning paper, as the clock's hands sweep on toward the time when the presses must roar out with the printed word for breakfast, there is always a consciousness of time, of words and time. From across the nation, the state, the city, the world come words to be shaped into news. Men working with the raw material that comes over the telegraph, the telephone, or in the quiet talk of a man on a street corner, fashion it into news. The one purpose is to tell it completely, clearly, and vividly, so that the man who reads it on the morrow will understand his time, his place, and his people.

The building where this is done becomes a part of this nightly drama. It absorbs something of the spirit of the task. Yet it remains brick and stone and steel and windows through which come the lights of the city, and the sound of night sirens. It is a part of the news drama, but the men who work there are not conscious of it until they leave it.

Such awareness came this week as *The News and Observer* moved into new clean quarters around the corner from its Martin Street home of almost 50 years. Everyone, from the oldest to the youngest of what Josephus Daniels lovingly referred to as "The News and Observer family," has looked forward to the move into the more spacious, more comfortable home facing the park on McDowell Street. Yet, in the moving, there is a wisp of nostalgia for the old place, and, if not a tear, at least a last long look at the cobwebs in the corner.

Guy Owen was born in Bladen County, North Carolina, in 1925. He grew up on a tobacco farm like Sam Ragan. His childhood in the Cape Fear region of the state, during the Great Depression, working on the farm, and working in his father's country store, gave him much of his material that he wrote about later in life in his novels and poems. In 1965, he published *The Ballad of the Flim-Flam Man*, and a movie was made from this book in 1967 called *The Flim-Flam Man*, starring George C. Scott and Michael Sarazin. Owen's 1970 novel, *Journey for Joedel*, was nominated for a Pulitzer Prize. His poetry collection, *The White Stallion and Other Poems*, won the Roanoke-Chowan Award for Poetry. Owen also taught at several colleges and universities.

In 1958, while teaching at Stetson University in Florida, Owen founded *Impetus*, a journal which developed into what is now *Southern Poetry Review*. Sam Ragan and Guy Owen formed a friendship that lasted from the 1950s to 1981, when Owen passed away at the age of 56. One of the first places Owen had his poetry published was in Ragan's *Southern Accent*. The following letter was written to Ragan from Owen in 1958 from Stetson University in Florida. The second letter was written in 1959.

At the end of the year the new Athenaeum Press is planning to publish a first volume of poems by me, *Cape Fear Country and Other Poems*. Since the poems are real "tar heel" poems, I am anxious that they reach a tar heel audience. I suspect that my name is almost completely unknown in the very area I write most about. It is for that reason that I write you. I wonder if you could reprint one or two of the enclosed poems in your *Southern Accent* column? I have read your column for a number of years. Last year you reprinted a poem by my good friend John. F. West. If you cannot squeeze in one of my poems, I would appreciate a brief mention of my book. I shall send you a copy when it comes out.

※

I'm sending you a copy of *Impetus*, a poetry magazine I started last year. I think you might be interested, it contains the works of three N.C. poets — O.B. Hardison (a poet of some promise), Wade Wellman (Manly's young son), and one of my own poems. I have a writing grant for this summer. I will spend this time working on a second volume of poems. I also am working on a book of short stories dealing with my section of "Cape Fear Country." I would like to interest Blair Publishers in one of my books about North Carolina. Random House has had one of my novels for months now. They don't seem to know what to do with it — but I'm prepared for the worst! Thank you for using my poems in your column. Thanks to you the book of poems did much better in N.C. than we expected.

Sam Ragan's stature among newspapermen and writers all around North Carolina was firmly established by the mid-1950s. Writers from around the state were sending him short stories and poems and other things they had written, hoping Ragan would mention them, or better yet, publish their work in *Southern Accent*. He was the Managing Editor of one of the largest circulation newspapers in the state, *The News and Observer*, which was also recognized as a leading newspaper in the South. By 1958 he would be promoted to Executive Editor of both the *News and Observer* and *the Raleigh Times*. The *News and Observer* had purchased the *Raleigh Times*, Raleigh's afternoon newspaper, in 1955. He was one of the founders of the North Carolina Literary Forum, which was first held in 1956. That year's program was themed "The Southern Literary Renaissance," and on the panel were Ragan, Jonathan Daniels, Paul Green, Frances Gray Patton, and Wilma Dykeman. In 1958 Sam moderated a discussion, "A Writer's Responsibility to His Times," that featured Doris Betts, Fred Ross, and Harry Golden. Ragan was part of the Literary Forum again in 1959 with John Ehle, Burke Davis, and Inglis Fletcher.

Invitations to speak came quite frequently for Ragan. One which he particularly enjoyed was an invitation to his former home county of Granville. The Beta Club of Oxford High School listened to him talk about good books they should read. Ragan used the occasion to visit where he grew up, in nearby Berea.

Random House sent Ragan a copy of William Styron's book *Set This House on Fire*, because of Ragan's belief in the young writer, as Ragan wrote about Styron many times in *Southern Accent* in the 1950s when Styron was getting established as a writer. An editor at Random House wrote Ragan a note along with the book, "Both William Styron Sr. and William Styron Jr. wish to express sincere thanks for your prophetic vision of what William Jr.'s future as a writer would be."

A big event that further solidified Ragan's respected status in the newspaper industry, in North Carolina and the nation, happened in November of 1958. Ragan was elected treasurer of the Associated Press Managing Editors Association at a convention in Indiana. In an address at the convention, Ragan foresaw the demise of newspapers that was to come.

> Economic pressures of publishing will reduce the number of the nation's newspapers in the next 30 to 40 years. Newspapers should resist the psychology of big business likely to accompany the trend to monopoly. To weather the rising costs of production and the competition of other mediums, newspapers must cultivate a personal contact with the readers. In many respects, today's newspaper is becoming too impersonal and aloof. There is less and less identity of the reader with his newspaper. Too often we leave out the vital story of people and the how and why of their struggles in a sometimes imperfect world. It is almost certain that 30 to 40 years from now there will be fewer newspapers, and even more monopoly.

How prophetic this has turned out to be.

Charlie Craven came to work at *The News and Observer* in the 1950s. Craven and Ragan would be friends from that time until Craven passed away in 1983. Ragan would recall his good friend in *Southern Accent* after he learned of Craven's death.

Charlie Craven's job application intrigued me from the start. He had written me at *The News and Observer* from the University of Missouri School of Journalism, where he was working on a master's degree after graduating with a degree in journalism from UNC at Chapel Hill. He wrote that he was doing his master's thesis on Josephus Daniels, the long-time publisher of *The News and Observer*, and wanted permission to use the newspaper's library for research.

I wrote him back that we would be glad to let him use the library, and soon came another letter saying that he would like a part-time job while doing his research. When he was told that such a job might be arranged he wrote again that he really needed a full-time job. By this time I was hooked and I put his application on file for the next job opening. That came within a few months, but by that time Charlie had left Missouri and was at work on the *Star-News* of Wilmington, where his parents then lived. But Charlie came on to *The News and Observer* where his talents as a reporter and as a writer soon became evident.

That was the beginning of a friendship which lasted until his death a few days ago. Over a period of 31 years Charles Craven became famous as a columnist on *The News and Observer* and he carved out a special niche for himself in North Carolina journalism.

Charlie was best known for his stories about the street people of Raleigh. Soon after he came to *The News and Observer* he started writing some off-beat stories about goings-on on Martin Street and they wound up with his by-line on the back page. I thought they should be in column form and suggested that they be carried under the title of "Byways of the News." The column became one of the most popular features ever published in *The News and Observer*, and in 1956, Orville Campbell and his Colonial Press of Chapel Hill published a collection of the columns under the title of "Charlie Craven's Kind of People." Bill Ballard did the illustrations, and an autographing party was held at Rusty's, the beer joint and pool hall made famous in Craven's pieces. Martin Street was swarming with people that night and Craven was the genial celebrity.

Charlie had read a great deal. His own style of writing was closer to the hard, lean prose of Ernest Hemingway than to that of another writer he admired, Thomas Wolfe, also a native of Asheville. His sentences were often pointed and sharp, but there also was a gentle quality to much of what he wrote. There were not many wasted words in his prose.

Some months ago Charlie and his wife, Sylvia, whom he met while both were on the N & O staff, came for a visit with us in Southern Pines. We shared stories, some of them hilarious, about those good days together at *The News and Observer.*

There was a special quality in Charles Craven as a writer and as a person. He will be greatly missed.

Ragan, even in 1958, could see the economic struggles of newspapers to come, how big companies would buy up newspapers, and how other "mediums," as he called it, would hurt newspaper's bottom lines. For sure, Ragan, while working at *The News and Observer,* and in the years to come running *The Pilot* in Southern Pines, would definitely do his best to keep a personal relationship with his readers, covering their struggles and accomplishments, publishing their letters to the editor, and having an open-door policy to his office. Often readers would come in without notice and come into his office and talk, and Ragan would take the time to listen and talk with them.

Ragan believed strongly in magazines containing a lot of material from its local base. He would take *Carolina Quarterly* to task a couple of times in the future about not having much from North Carolina writers. In 1958, he did the same with *The South Atlantic Quarterly,* which is published in Durham. Ragan mentioned the magazine in *Southern Accent,* stating that the magazine contained little material on its region. W.B. Hamilton, the Managing Editor of *The South Atlantic Quarterly,* wrote a letter to Ragan, agreeing with him. Ragan is given credit by some for changing this problem, because in the years to come, there was more coverage of Southern material. In the letter to Ragan, Hamilton was most cordial.

I have seen the paragraph in your column last week pointing out, and by implication deploring, the fact that *The South Atlantic Quarterly* contains little material on its region. I have noticed that myself, and I, too, heartily deplore it. You will pardon my asking help in remedying the lack of Southern material. Could you nominate me a sound reporter who could do a good job, *New Yorker* fashion, on the 1958 Indian Uprising at Maxton? Or someone who could report on the industrialization of the South? Or the development of higher education? Or the press? Or, leaving out polemics, the racial situation? We are deeply interested in reporting and commenting upon Southern literature and political economy, but we are also interested in seeing to it that the intellectual life of the South is not provincial. When I say I would welcome help from you, I am most sincere.

In his response, Ragan, as one would expect, was also very cordial. He wrote Hamilton and offered several possible writers who could do a good job writing about the South and the issues it faced. In fact, some articles that appeared in *The South Atlantic Quarterly* in future years were written by writers Ragan recommended.

Continuing his own writing career, even while helping to run one of the biggest newspapers in the state, Ragan, in 1957, wrote an article in a magazine about traveling in North Carolina.

The traveler in a hurry in North Carolina can stick to the highways but he who would know the land will take the byways.

The paving of more than 12,000 miles of secondary roads over from 1950 to 1954 opened up to travel hundreds of areas.

From the long coastline that dips and turns with hundreds of bays, sounds and inlets to the Great Smokies, 600 miles away, where peaks tower higher than anywhere else east of the Rockies, the traveler is finding long hidden delights in vistas and views. He is finding the little villages where time all but stood still, and he is finding a feel of the countryside he did not know before.

For to know the feel of the land one needs to travel those little-known roads, out from the towns, out where the corn rows run down to the edge of the road. He needs to travel casually and leisurely to feel and know the sweep and spill of the land, a growing greenness of crop and tree, the somnolence of swamps where dark waters weave around cypress knees, and then the sudden lift, the rise, and sunlight in a quiet valley.

And there are the little towns and places too small even to boast the title of village, with names to bemuse the wayfarer. There is Calabash and Crooked Run, Day Book and Dundarrach, Harmony and Honey Hill, Snow Camp and Shake Rag, Sandymush, Grapevine, Big Laurel and Bandana, Trust and Balm, Tusquitee, Tomahawk, Sugar and Scotty, Walnut Cove and Whynot.

These are the people that make up a heavy percentage of North Carolina's four million and more people. They refer to their new paved roads as "Scott roads" in honor of Governor, now U.S. Senator, W. Kerr Scott under whose administration a two-hundred-million-dollar bond issue was voted and put to work on building and paving the great network of roads across the state. Governor Scott saw his road program as something that would bring rural and urban North Carolina closer together. It has done that. It has brought the countryman to town in quick comfort. But it has also sent thousands of Tar Heels and visitors to the country. The Sunday afternoon driver is no longer a casual traveler, but an explorer. He is finding a land, his land, which he did not know before.

Ragan, with his many speaking engagements and activities which took him to all parts of North Carolina, enjoyed the drives through small towns and the countryside. He enjoyed looking at farmers in the fields as he passed by, flowers blooming, tobacco fields being harvested, children playing in the yard, mailmen doing their job, drug stores in small towns with locals enjoying a hot dog, a wave from strangers, how the change of seasons changed the appearance of places he had traveled through months before, the smell of tobacco in big warehouses as he passed through a town. He commented on his drives and travels around the state quite often in *Southern Accent*.

Doris Betts was born in Statesville, North Carolina. She received the Putnam Book Prize in 1954, at the age of 22, for her first book, *The Gentle Insurrection and Other Stories. Beasts of the Southern Wild and Other Stories* was published in 1973 and nominated for a National Book Award. She would go on to write many books of short stories and novels and teach at the University of North Carolina. Her characters in her books dealt with events in the South to a large degree. Religion was a common theme. Her novel, *Souls Raised From the Dead*, was named by *The New York Times* as one of the 20 best books of 1994.

Betts and Sam Ragan developed a warm relationship in the 1950s. As with so many aspiring authors, Betts looked to Ragan as someone who could further her career, and as a dear friend. Ragan was always more than happy to do what he could for writers, especially those from North Carolina. Below is a letter to Ragan from Doris Betts in 1958.

Thad Stem told me there had recently been a contest in his town for the biggest bitch extant but he had been unable to nominate since his candidate lived in Sanford and was unknown to the Oxford gentry. I cooled him off soundly. Not for the bitch, of course, but for the unmitigated insult of suggesting I am unknown, even in benighted Oxford.

Besides, as Bernadette [Bernadette Hoyle, who wrote *Tar Heel Writers I Know*, among other books] is about to immortalize me in print in her forthcoming tome, Thad and I and you may safely assume that I have at last arrived and can begin calling myself a real honest-to-pete writer.

Finished first draft of the short novel last week, and monumental tasks of getting some shape and sense into it lie ahead. There's an added rush—Random House is reading a collection now, with an enthusiasm so lukewarm that it approaches the temperature of ice water, and the only way I can sell that fictional stepchild is by rushing into their hands a real live novel before everyone around the table has had a chance to say: NO. My position, legally, is tenuous because I can't sell a novel unless I sell the collection because my release from Putnam's had more strings than a marionette so all this is undercover and full of posturings. What will happen, I fear, is that Random House will respectfully decline both stories and novel and there I will be, crestfallen, with a whole stack of manuscripts suitable for scratch paper.

Harry [Harry Golden] writes me that Sandburg [Carl Sandburg] has asked him to do a biography. I bought Harry's *Only in America* and enjoyed it, and thought the several bone-serious pieces, "Public Right" and "Private Privilege," superb. Just bought and read, too, Mary McCarthy's *Groves of Academe*. Have two other of her books and am full of admiration.

I forgot I hadn't told you the name of the short novel, so far it's *The Learn'd Astronomer* a la Whitman, and I shouldn't be at all surprised if someone somewhere called it an apologia for Christianity, which surprises us all. Enough said. [The novel eventually was named *The Astronomer and Other Stories.*]

I am knee deep in Virginia Woolf and Katherine Mansfield. New book Blair is publishing *The Hatteras Man* is interesting.

Bill Blackburn [William Blackburn taught English and Writing classes at Duke for 45 years, mentoring writers such as William Styron, Mac Hyman, and Fred Chappell, among others] came through yesterday en route to Duke; we always enjoy seeing him and he had all sorts of literary gossip. The Guggenheim [Betts won a Guggenheim Fellowship in 1958] has brought some interesting feelers from publishers. I am very busy and very happy and have recaptured the feeling that I shall live to be a hundred and write a lot of things.

Carl Sandburg was born in Illinois but lived the last 22 years of his life in North Carolina, at Connemara, a 246-acre farm in Flat Rock. Sandburg won three Pulitzer Prizes, two for his poetry and one for a biography of Abraham Lincoln. His *Chicago Poems, The People, Yes, Rootabaga Stories, Complete Poems,* and *Abraham Lincoln: The Prairie Years and The War Years* are some of his notable works. Sandburg was a most remarkable man, not only being awarded a Pulitzer for poetry and biography but was also a noted folk singer. After moving to Connemara in 1945, he continued to write while his wife, Lilian, raised champion dairy goats. Sandburg passed away at Connemara in 1967. Sandburg is now enshrined in the North Carolina Literary Hall of Fame, along with his good friend, Sam Ragan.

Ragan got to know Sandburg in the 1950s, and worked with Henry Belk, his old editor at the *Goldsboro News-Argus,* to hold a Carl Sandburg Day in 1958 to honor this writer who was known around America. Ragan wrote a column in early 1958 about Sandburg's 80th birthday that year, and from that came the effort to honor the famed author. Sam Ragan commented on this event later in life.

I talked with Henry Belk and Jonathan Daniels about honoring Sandburg, and Governor Luther Hodges agreed to issue the proclamation. Edwin Gill, the State Treasurer and a man of keen and wide-ranging interests in the arts as well as a talented writer, also became involved in the plans for the Carl Sandburg Day.

The date of March 27 had been agreed upon because that was the date when we could get the Sir Walter Hotel Ballroom in Raleigh, and also because that was the date for the opening of the Edward Steichen photographic exhibition of "The Family of Man" at the State Art Museum. Steichen was Sandburg's brother-in-law and the poet had great affection for the artist. He had written poems about him and had dedicated poems to Steichen.

Jonathan Daniels agreed to let Sandburg stay in his house while he was in Raleigh for the event. Jonathan and I went to the Raleigh-Airport at the appointed time but Sandburg wasn't there. We learned there was one more flight that night, so we waited for that, and I never breathed easier than when I saw the tall white-haired poet, a gray shawl over his shoulders, and carrying a small flight bag come down the steps of the plane.

Sandburg was in high humor, much pleased with the "Carl Sandburg Day" event, and after reaching the Daniels home promptly downed a glass of straight bourbon. This was followed by a beer, and then more bourbon, and he began telling tales, alternating the drinks as he talked. I left to go home at 3 o'clock in the morning and Sandburg was still talking.

Edwin Gill gave an address to talk about Sandburg. "His verse can be as mild as mist and as consoling as rain, but it can also be as hard as steel and as raw as a slaughter house. In Sandburg's voice you hear the plain talk of plain people, the gossip of farmers, laboring men, white collar workers. Through the wonderful poetry of Sandburg we experience sounds that we were never conscious of before. For instance, we may hear the stirring of the soil in springtime, the patter of the fog as it comes and goes, the movement of growing corn, the recoil of leaves grasses as they are smitten by the frost. We may hear the slow but inevitable turning of the seasons."

When Gill had finished speaking Sandburg leaned over to him and with a twinkle in his eye asked Gill for a copy of his remarks, saying, "On bad mornings I will read it to build up my ego." Sandburg's response was brief, eloquent and moving. It was obvious that he was moved by the tribute from his adopted state, and when he had finished with his words of deep appreciation the audience stood with sustained applause.

Sandburg later visited the Art Museum and the Steichen exhibit, and was enjoying himself so much he decided to stay over another day for the North Carolina Literary Forum which was held that night at Meredith College. Later at the Daniels home there were more stories, with several Tar Heel writers on hand to listen. Doris Betts sat at his feet, and Harry Golden, later to write a biography of Sandburg, was close by.

When Carl Sandburg died in 1967, Ragan attended a national memorial service for Sandburg at the Lincoln Memorial in Washington, D.C. It was during this time that he formed the outlines of a poem he would write.

Lincoln Memorial

The cars go around it
To get on to Constitution Avenue,
And you have to watch out
To keep from hitting
Children with boxes of popcorn,
Men with cameras,
And old ladies in print dresses
Who walk on flat feet.

They come from everywhere
And sometimes you can see their faces
In the reflecting pool,
Toward which he sits and stares
With eyes of bronze.

Jerry Erdahl, director of the N.C. State Student Union, visited Sam Ragan at his office at *The News and Observer* in 1959. The two men agreed to start the Friends of the College with the limited funds at their disposal. In the first year four concerts were held, and students attended free of charge. The mission was to present to the university and the general public "the best in music and dance to the largest possible audience at the lowest possible price." Over the next 35 years, Friends of the College would present 226 concerts to more than four million people in Reynolds Coliseum. The

New York Philharmonic with Leonard Bernstein, Van Cliburn, New York City Ballet, Leontyne Price, The Boston Pops with Arthur Fiedler, Vienna Boys Choir, Itzhak Perlman, and The London Symphony are just some of the examples of the artists and groups who performed on campus because of Friends of the College.

Marjorie Ragan remained very active, not only as a mother and wife, but in journalism as well. In 1960 she wrote an article in *The News and Observer* about the Parents-Teachers Association, and the article was reprinted in other newspapers and a couple of magazines. The PTA was a passion of Marjorie's, where she had served as state publicity director and editor of the North Carolina PTA Magazine. Along with being involved with the PTA, Marjorie edited a study that became the basis for public education reform in North Carolina.

Helen Bevington taught English, Creative Writing, and Literary Criticism at Duke University for many years, and wrote books of poetry and essays. Her book *Charley Smith's Girl* in 1965 was runner-up for the Pulitzer Prize. That book was banned by the library in Worcester, New York, where Bevington grew up, because the book tells of her minister father's having been divorced by her mother for affairs that he was having with female parishioners. Bevington won the North Carolina Award for Literature in 1973. Sam Ragan wrote a review of her book in 1961, *When Found, Make a Verse of*. Bevington wrote him a warm letter thanking him.

I hope you will let me say Sam, for by now I am thinking of you as benefactor and friend of long standing. The review is beautiful, perhaps the finest in my life, written with eloquence and grace, and choosing to say only the best. I am proud of it. It shows how generously you hold out your hand.

Whenever I think of that evening in Raleigh in the spring, I think of sitting beside you at dinner and having good talk. Since that time, I've been a follower of your column. Singlehanded, you do great good to poetry.

Since I can't send embraces through the mail, I send a very deeply meant thank you.

In 1960 the Ragan family went to Nags Head in July to celebrate Talmadge's 10th birthday. It was a beautiful day, the family was together, ev-

eryone was having a good time. Ragan looked out of a window, saw Talmadge, and from that came "The Girl in the Green Bathing Suit."

The Girl in the Green Bathing Suit

The girl in the green bathing suit
Swings in a swing near the sea.
I watch from my window.
There's a tree bent by the winds
That hangs over the roof of the house.
I can see through the tree's limbs,
Beyond the girl
In the green bathing suit,
Beyond the sea oats and sand,
Where the sea rolls,
Breaking white, as far out
As where the fishing boat
Sits motionless in the sun.

Sam's work at *The News and Observer* continued, where he had been
named executive editor. One year during his tenure, five *News and Observer* writers for the news staff won North Carolina Press Association honors,
this while Sam's job was running the news department. Ragan made good
hires and once people got there, they flourished under his guidance. Marjorie Hunter worked under Sam at *The News and Observer* before landing
a job with the *New York Times*. Simmons Fentress did an outstanding job
with *The News and Observer* while Sam was there before he took a job with
Time magazine.

Ragan's mailbox at *The News and Observer* office in Raleigh was always
full of mail from admirers of his, especially of *Southern Accent*. One such
letter came from Mona Cozart of nearby Knightdale, North Carolina, in
1961. Mona was a young girl at the time. The poem was written in 1960.

This is a poem I wrote. It has no title, only the date when it was written. If you think it's good enough, I'd like for you to put it in your
Sunday column. I have other poems, some worse, some better. They
all have rough edges, because I don't know very much about the rules
for writing poetry. I believe that expressing feeling is more important.

If you don't think it's good enough, I'd like to know if you think
it has any good points. If you'd like to see more of my writing, or talk
with me, please call me and I'll bring it to you. That would have to
be this week, because I'm going to Virginia this weekend for an in-
definite stay.

I would appreciate your criticisms and remarks.

November 7, 1960

> I am a smokestack
> > standing lonely,
> > > isolated,
> > > > ugly,

> an eyesore
> but lovely in the dark
> > > > and frightening

> > soaring tall
> > > alone...
> I have a fire down there in my guts
into which are poured flammable materials
> which I digest
> > then spurt into the clean air
> > befouling it
> > making myself ugly
> > > dirty
> > > > with soot particles
> which grind into the inside of me
> and around my big mouth like an infant's slobber.
> I can never be wholly cleaned
> never purged of the mess that has gone through me,
> has become a part of me.
> And others would perhaps not like to be as I am;
> But I have my consolation —
> I am myself — I am an individual.

In 1961 Ragan presented awards at the North Carolina High School
Football All-Star Awards Banquet in Rocky Mount. Ragan sat beside the
featured speaker that night, Bill Murray, the very successful head football
coach at Duke University. Ragan would later that year write about what

a fine man Bill Murray was. Ragan was a big UNC football fan, and even attended many games in Chapel Hill. But of course, Ragan got along with just about everyone, even the football coach of UNC's enemy, Duke.

In November of 1962 Ragan spoke to the University of North Carolina at Chapel Hill Journalism Club. Ragan was a good speaker, his many speaking engagements through the years made him very relaxed talking to groups of people, and his topics were usually about writing, poetry, and newspaper work, topics he knew thoroughly and topics he absolutely loved to share with others. He spoke as one would expect of such a Southern gentleman, in a smooth, melodic voice that got right to the point without using "polysyllabic words or phrases." The following is part of what he said to the UNC Journalism Club, and I think readers will agree that Ragan really gave them useful and good advice. Just as he believed poetry should not waste words, Ragan advised his reporters for *The News and Observer* and *The Pilot* in Southern Pines to get to the point, to use clarity and brevity when writing.

> Reporting, someone has said, is the second oldest profession. And in the eyes of some people, it is simply a natural outgrowth of the first.
>
> We should, perhaps, return to the clarity, brevity and strength of such early reporters as Matthew, Mark, Luke, and John. And who could improve on a lead such as "In the beginning God created the heaven and the earth"?
>
> A writer's duty is to report. Be he a newspaper writer or a novelist, he must deal with concrete things, facts which can be shaped into words and sentences that will inform, enlighten, or entertain. The first lesson a writer must learn is that you can't write something from nothing. Get the facts, and then tell them as simply and as clearly as you possibly can.
>
> It was Justice Brandeis who said that an opinion is worth no more than the facts behind it. And, as Thoreau pointed out, never ignore a fact, it may flower into a truth.
>
> I often suggest to our reporters to write their stories just as they would go home and tell it to their wives or husbands. This story-telling quality is one of the things that has made the quality that marks the work of such excellent writers as Sherwood Anderson and John Steinbeck.

There is, I feel, a certain compatibility in newspaper writing and creative writing. Some say that journalism is concerned with the head, and creative writing with the heart. But the best of each is a part of both.

There are two rules to guide the newspaper writer—accuracy and clarity. Do not let unnecessary words obscure the facts you have to present. [This statement is a great way to describe Sam Ragan's poetry.] And if you have a tendency toward the polysyllabic word or phrase, harken to the advice of that old prose master, Winston Churchill, who said, "Simple words are the best." Study the lean language of Churchill's best speeches.

As for accuracy, that, of course, is the first requirement.

What should a good newspaper story contain? It should contain the answers to all the reasonable questions a reader might raise.

What elements make a good story? A newspaper editor I know recently said that the ideal news story would include religion, royalty, sex and mystery. And this, he said, would be their lead: "My God. The Queen is pregnant. Who did it?"

The writing habits of writers always have intrigued me. A.E. Houseman wrote his poetry after downing two bottles of English beer at lunchtime and then going for a walk. It was this same stern English schoolmaster who said that, "Malt does more than Milton can to justify God's world to man." William Butler Yeats is said to have been content to write only 14 lines a day. When the 14 lines were completed, he stopped, and went walking, drinking, and wenching.

I hope that you will be haunted for the rest of your lives by blank sheets of paper crying out for the adornment of words. For it is words we live by. We take them and shape them into sentences and paragraphs, and if we are skillful enough our product will contribute something to man's enlightenment.

The late Oscar Coffin [longtime teacher of journalism at UNC] used to tell his Journalism students that the two books a newspaperman should read above all others were the dictionary and the Bible. It was good advice then; it is good advice now. There is no better place to learn the exact meaning of a word—and also how to spell it—than the dictionary. And there is no better place to give a writer a sense of the power and beauty of words than the Bible.

Freedom of the press exists in a democracy, not for the power or profit or pleasure of any individual, but for the common good. The right of the people to know cannot be denied or diminished without endangering democracy itself.

Every citizen deserves the stimulus of a strong editorial page, on which the editor voices his own well-informed opinion clearly and forcefully yet willingly provides space for contrary opinion. The good editor often takes sides, but without arrogance or intolerance. He has a special responsibility to defend the weak, to prod the public conscience, and to speak out against the injustices of which a majority can sometime be guilty.

The primary function of a newspaper is to report the news. The good reporter strives constantly to find and write the truth. This task, no matter how difficult, is his unescapable responsibility. To be true, a story, together with its headlines, must be honest. To be honest, it must be fair. To be fair, it must be accurate and complete. Honesty demands objectivity, the submergence of prejudice and personal conviction. Fairness demands regard for the rights of others. Accuracy demands courage, pain taking care, and perspective to assure a total picture as true as its individual facts. That is a good guideline, and a worthy goal for the press in North Carolina, or anywhere.

Along with many speaking dates, Ragan was involved with many other things besides being, by 1960, Executive Editor of the *News and Observer*. For example, there came a personal invitation in 1962 from North Carolina Governor Terry Sanford to come to the Governor's Mansion in Raleigh to have dinner with him and John Scott, the foreign correspondent for *Time* magazine. Sam accepted. Ragan and Terry Sanford would become close friends. Also during this time, Ragan did a regular show on WUNC Radio, talking about poetry and prose and what he was writing about in *Southern Accent*.

Ragan was also teaching a Contemporary Issues class and directing the Writer's Workshop in creative writing at North Carolina State University by this time. Many authors came out of these classes, and quite a few books were published by students who took Ragan's class from the years that he taught it. Ragan commented on teaching college classes. "I taught creative writing, journalism, and contemporary issues, which is a very fascinating subject. You have no textbook, but you just use the daily newspaper. I had a writer's workshop at North Carolina State University in creative writing. I taught that about 15 years. At last count, there have been over sixty books published by students from that class."

Ragan and his good friend, Thad Stem, both from Granville County, published a poem in 1963 called "In the Beginning." The poem depicted the development of North Carolina by the common man. The poem was judged the winner of the Poetry Division of the Literary Competition by the Carolina Charter Tercentenary Commission. This commission was formed to celebrate the 300th anniversary of the signing of the Carolina Charter in 1663. The Carolina Charter was by England's King Charles II granting the territory of Carolina to a number of his supporters who had helped him regain the throne.

"In the Beginning" was a poem written by Ragan and Stem describing what life was like in those very early days in North Carolina, and experiences common people would have gone through, and what they saw in this new land, such as Indians there before them, and the unspoiled land. The Tercentenary Commission awarded Ragan and Stem a cash prize of $500 at presentation ceremonies at the annual meeting of the North Carolina Literary and Historical Association. A short excerpt from "In the Beginning" is given.

Once, in the time of the long blue day,
When he plowed the green corn, the blades
Wet upon his knees, the Indian he had been told to fear
Stood in feathered silence in the tiny border where
Labor left off
And the wilderness began again.

And then the Indian was gone,
Melted silently into the grass and the stones
Beyond the river, leaving and carrying a trail
Of insoluble question marks to humor the wind.

And there was only the brutal cry of the hawk,
The spice of the wild orchard and the salt-water marsh
To join or separate the two.

Another big honor came to Ragan in 1963 when he was elected as President of the Associated Press Managing Editors at their national convention in Miami Beach, Florida. This was the largest newspaper organization in the United States, with over 1,700 members. Ragan had, in 1962, tallied the most votes of 12 editors from around the country to sit on the APME Board of Directors. By the early 1960s, he was among the most respected newspapermen in the nation. Being elected President of the APME was a prestigious position, one in which carried a lot of responsibility. But being able to lead, to get along, to get to the heart of a matter, and garner respect form peers was something that came natural to a man like Ragan. He tended to fill a room up with his presence, even though he was soft-spoken and devoid of a big ego. People noticed when Sam Ragan was among them, this despite the fact that he was someone who was content to listen and give other people the floor. But when he spoke meaningful words came from him, and those words would lead others to act in a purposeful way.

Ragan was overjoyed in 1963 when his daughter, Nancy, gave him his first grandchild, Robin, born on October 20. Nancy would also give birth to Eric on December 12, 1964. Ragan always loved Robin and Eric dearly, and they loved him back the same.

A poet Ragan had met and admired passed away in 1963, Robert Frost. Ragan had a chance to talk with Robert Frost on a visit Frost made to the University of North Carolina at Chapel Hill. On another time Ragan attended a reading that Frost made in Raleigh. It was on campus at North Carolina State University in 1957 on the very night that the University of North Carolina was playing the Wilt Chamberlain-led Kansas Jayhawks for the national title. Ragan wrote a poem of that night.

On Hearing Robert Frost Read His Poetry

The white hair and New England face
In querulous voice
Waving away a photographer —
That's enough, that's enough.
At first the fumbling words
And then the words catching hold,
The magic of words quieting the room.
They are standing along the walls.
The voice drones on

In those fixed faces.
A freight train rumbles by
But no one hears.
Did anyone ever call Robert Frost—Bobby?

In a 1974 *Southern Accent*, Ragan recalled meeting Frost.

> They used to say around Chapel Hill that "Spring is here when Frost comes."
>
> They were talking about Robert Frost, the white-haired New England poet who had a special affection for North Carolina, and for years along about this time he would come down to Chapel Hill to stay several days and read his poems at several campuses in the area.
>
> We thought about our first meeting with Frost when Nell Styron wrote about him in *The Pilot* last week and the issuance of a new postage stamp on the 100th anniversary of his birth. It was in the Carolina Inn and he was sitting alone in the lobby. He invited us to join him and we chatted informally for quite a while; he was talking about North Carolina and how wonderful the weather was in April.
>
> His poetry readings grew in popularity as his years mounted and there was the time he came to North Carolina State to read. It was the night of the finals for the national basketball championship and Carolina was playing Kansas. The game was on television and TV sets had been set up all over the campus, including the building where Frost was reading his poetry. The auditorium was full, and people stood along the walls and sat in the aisles while the game went on and the old poet read.
>
> In a state and in a town where basketball is an almost unsurpassed passion and can bring a populace to a fevered pitch that was quite a tribute to a poet and we doubt if anyone else could have done it but Robert Frost.
>
> Frost came year after year to Chapel Hill, but his visits to North Carolina started back in the 1890s. His first trip was to the Outer Banks and he wrote a poem about it. He came back on frequent visits.
>
> Years ago Huntington Cairns made us a member of the Society of Ontology, a small group which included Robert Frost as a member and its purpose was simply to sit on the Cairns porch at Kitty Hawk

and talk. We regret that we were never at a meeting of the Society with Frost, because he loved to talk and he especially liked that setting. He wrote several poems about his later trips to Kitty Hawk, humorous poems which caught the flavor of the place.

Frost was a complex man, as any reading in depth of his poetry will show. His poems were deceptively simple, but powerful, and almost daily some line of his poetry jumps into the mind. He could also be fierce as well as gentle, and he often poked fun at society and its institutions.

I am pleased that a stamp has been issued as a memorial to Robert Frost. He stands strong and sturdy on the American scene, and his poetry will be remembered and read long after lesser lights whose likenesses have adorned stamps are forgotten.

Ragan continued to write poetry. His poetry, for the most part, consisted of unadorned language with accessible imagery. The poems of Ragan, with their relative brevity, made them popular with a broad range of the public. A death that shocked the nation and the world in 1963 was when President John F. Kennedy was assassinated in Dallas. Sam Ragan was at work in *The News and Observer's* offices in Raleigh on a day that he and so many millions of Americans would never forget.

The Day Kennedy Was Shot

The shoeshine man at the hatter's
Came out of the door to say,
"The President's been shot."
There was a stricken look on his face.
There was the same look in the newsroom.
All the teletypes were going,
And he crowded up to read
The reports from Dallas.
He went to the telephone and said,
"Let's get out a special, an extra."
The thought kept running through his head,
"We've got to let the people know."
They would want to know everything,
And the next two hours,
Until the extra hit the street,

He was busy with that thought.
There would be time enough later
For lamentations.

John Fries Blair started his book publishing business in 1954, and it still is publishing books today in Winston-Salem. The first book published by Blair was *Whispering Pines*, a book of poetry by John Henry Boner, which had originally been published in 1883. An early success was *The Hatterasman*, written by Ben Dixon MacNeill, which won the Mayflower Cup, awarded for the best work of nonfiction by a North Carolina writer, in 1958.

Flannery O'Connor, the novelist, short story writer, and essayist, passed away in 1964 from the effects of lupus, at the age of 39. O'Connor had bought her first pair of peacocks when she learned she had lupus, and these birds brought her great joy roaming around her farm in Georgia. In an essay, "The King of Birds," O'Connor described the majesty of a peacock with its fan displayed. "When it suits him, the peacock will face you. Then you will see in a green-bronze arch around him a galaxy of gazing, haloed suns. This is the moment when most people are silent."

Ragan had a dinner with O'Connor once, and intended to talk with her about her writing life, but according to Ragan, O'Connor kept steering the conversation back to her beloved peacocks. So Ragan wrote a poem about her peacocks shortly after learning of O'Connor's death.

Flannery O'Connor

...the peacocks cry all night long: Help me, help me.
Four miles from Milledgeville on a farm
Of five hundred acres
She raised chickens (and peacocks).

She talked of grotesques,
Southern style—of freaks who felt
The call to preach,
Of praying violent men with something
In the blood driving them
Onward but inward.

Broiler prices had been falling,
And it had not rained for weeks.
The grass was almost gone in the pastures.

There had been a fire,
But the damage was slight.

She held their attention
With strong Georgia phrases
Drawing pictures of a people
In a land all their own, shifting
Suddenly from darkness to hard sunlight,
Caught in the giant hands of fate and the will of God.
      But the violent bear it away.
      And a good man is hard to find.

The crutches lean against the wall
Unnoticed and forgotten.
In the shade of the trees
The peacocks strut.

      But at night in the mellow darkness
      They cry...
      All night long...
      Help me.
      Help me.

There is much there in Ragan's poem of the conversation he had with O'Connor. It touches upon life on the farm in Milledgeville, her manner of speaking, and some of her books. "In the blood driving them" recalled her book, *Wise Blood*. And two lines, "the violent bear it away" and "a good man is hard to find," are direct quotes of two of her book titles. But the piece of the conversation Ragan remembered most, about the peacocks crying all night, begin and end the poem.

A very short poem Ragan wrote involved O'Connor also.

What She Said

O'Connor was talking
About William Faulkner.
"When the big train's coming," she said,
"You'd better get your mule and wagon
Off the track."

7

Poet, *The Tree in the Far Pasture,*
Professor, "In a perky bow tie"

I n 1964, Blair Publishing came out with Sam Ragan's first book of poetry, *The Tree in the Far Pasture*. Ragan had been writing poems since high school. And Marjorie Ragan once said that she had been in love with Sam Ragan since the day he read her some of his poems on "my vine-shaded porch at my home in the small town of Laurel Hill," back in 1937.

The first book of poetry that greatly influenced Ragan to fall in love with poetry was *Spoon River Anthology* by Edgar Lee Masters. In 1915, Masters published this book of poems written in free verse about a small fictional town called Spoon River. The poems in the book narrate the epitaphs of the people who lived in Spoon River. The poems resonated with a young Sam Ragan, who would go on to write free verse poems himself. *Spoon River Anthology* remains a staple of American literature today. Ragan wrote about the book of poems by Masters that so influenced him, and other writers and books that made strong impressions on him through the years.

The noted critic and literary scholar, Louis D. Rubin, wrote, "Just about every writer-to-be, I think, comes upon his or her Thomas Wolfe—which is to say happens upon an author who first shows the apprentice what is possible." For Dr. Rubin, it was the Asheville native.

As I look back on my life as a writer, I also claim Wolfe as a major influence. Baudelaire and his classic work, *Flowers of Evil*, remain strong in memory, as does the poetry of W.B. Yeats, and of course Shakespeare continues to stand tall as an unsurpassed observer of the human condition.

American writers, for the most part, have contributed to my consciousness—people such as Sherwood Anderson, William Faulkner, Erskine Caldwell, John Steinbeck, and the list goes on and on.

I still recall the pleasure and stimulation from the reading of Anderson's *Winesburg, Ohio*, Faulkner's *The Sound and the Fury*, Caldwell's *Tobacco Road*, Steinbeck's *Grapes of Wrath*, William Saroyan's *The Daring Young Man on the Flying Trapeze*, and Carson McCullers's *The Heart is a Lonely Hunter*.

Then there were the American poets—Carl Sandburg, Robert Frost, e.e cummings, T.S. Eliot, Ezra Pound, Wallace Stevens—and the galaxy of greatness grows even greater, even into today.

In North Carolina there are many people who have had an influence on both my prose and poetry—Paul Green, Jonathan Daniels, Thad Stem, Bernice Kelly Harris, O. Henry, Guy Owen and many more.

If I had to narrow it down to one writer and one book that had the most influence on me it would be *Spoon River Anthology*, by Edgar Lee Masters, first published in 1915.

This American classic was a liberating work of poetry for me. Masters wrote poetry about real people in real life situations. The people of Spoon River were like people I knew, and I read and re-read the Masters anthology, and I learn something new with each reading.

In *Spoon River Anthology* Masters portrays his characters with great insight and great sympathy. He delineates a life in a few short lines. For instance, his epitaph for a golden-voiced lawyer is that he became "a picker of rags in the rubbage of human wrongs."

I call Masters' *Spoon River* liberating because I realized that I did not have to write poetry like the stiffly mannered Englishmen and Americans who copied them. Of course, Whitman was an original, and I delighted in reading and appreciating his rolling rhetoric.

Everyday language began to appeal to me more and more, and I cannot deny how effective the prose of Ernest Hemingway, especially his short stories, and the splendid poetry of Carl Sandburg had upon my consciousness.

It's the simplicity of language, the insights into humanity, the feeling, the intellect, and knowing when to start and when to stop — it is all these qualities which, to me, make *Spoon River* the distinctly American classic which it is.

The *Spoon River Anthology* was not only a liberating influence on my writing, it also caused me to look closer to home for things to write about and to try to understand.

In *The Tree in the Far Pasture*, Ragan looks at everyday life and what ordinary people do. He does this with a simplicity of phrasing that is very direct. A few subjects in the poems are a deserted house, a handful of plums, an elderly woman knitting, a lonely man waving at a train, and a death in the country. The poems mostly deal with North Carolina, its history, its environment, and its people.

One of the poems in *The Tree in the Far Pasture* was "Portrait," which is where the title of the book came from. The "she" was his mother, Emma, and the "he" was his father, William, and the field, pasture, trellis, and pear tree came from his memory of the farm in Berea in Granville County where he grew up.

"This poem, 'Portrait,' was really special to me," said Ragan. "I was writing about my mother. This was in her last years. She would talk a little about her early life. It tells something of the relationship between my mother and my father. They were married for fifty-four years before he died. My mother was eighteen and my father was twenty-eight when they married. Though there was ten years difference in their ages, they had a very close relationship. In her last years she would go back and tell me about little things in her life."

Portrait

She spoke of things of long ago —
They were as yesterday.
She told of a dream:
It was a September
And it was not really warm until noon.
I had been sitting in the sun, she said.

I could hear a crow across the field.
On the trellis there were new roses.
I was sitting in the sun,
And he brought me three fresh pears
From the tree in the far pasture.

I think Ragan must have identified his poem "Neighbors" with the years he spent in Granville County growing up on the tobacco farm, miles from a town of any size, Oxford. Berea neighbors were mighty friendly, but few and far between. As he wrote "Neighbors" he surely thought about those days in rural Granville County, and even his days in Johnston County after his family moved there while he was still in high school.

Neighbors

I imagine he got rather lonely
Living that far from town
With no neighbors close enough
To drop by at night for a smoke and talk.
And living alone gives time for too much thought—
It's that way especially at night.

The time I saw him he was standing in front
Of his little house on the hill
Watching our train as it passed by.
He waved at us
And I fancy that meant something to him—
Waving at the train as it passed each day.
It was morning then and the man probably
Spent the rest of the day walking
Under the trees around his house.

But at night he doesn't have much
Except the wind to listen to
And a fire to nurse along
Until it's time to go to bed.
In the morning he can watch for the train
And wave at us as we go by.

"Final Edition" obviously was a poem included in *The Tree in the Far Pasture* that was an experience Ragan would go through many times in his life as a newspaperman, with all the papers he worked for before World War II, and with The *News and Observer* in Raleigh and *The Pilot* in Southern Pines. Long hours were common for Ragan, but after that final edition was ready, a sense of satisfaction on a job well done would be felt. After all, as Ragan often said, "I want each edition of the newspaper to be a work of art."

Final Edition

They have all gone from the city room.
Down the long hall the last footsteps have died away.
The teletypes are quiet,
But in the distance is the rumble
Of the fresh-inked last news.
The sweeper has come and gone.

A green eyeshade lies on the desk—
And there's no one to answer the telephone.

Richard Walser wrote a review of *The Tree in the Far Pasture*. Walser wrote many books about North Carolinians and their contributions to our literary heritage, such as *Literary North Carolina*, and became known as a leading scholar of Thomas Wolfe. Walser spent many years teaching at North Carolina State University. Walser wrote of Ragan's book, "Sam Ragan's style of writing poetry combines a freedom of line with a starkness made poetic by concrete images."

Guy Owen also praised Ragan's first book of poetry. "No one in North Carolina has done more to encourage young poets and to help the cause of poetry than Sam Ragan. *The Tree in the Far Pasture* is one of the most accomplished first volumes to come out of the South in some time. Mr. Ragan undertakes the greatest possible risk in his verse: the risk of simplicity. His poems move quietly. They do not churn for attention, there are no huge bow-wow effects, nor dazzling images nor fashionable subjects. Here are instead charming lyrics that talk and whisper, rather than sing and jingle."

Thad Stem reviewed this first volume of poetry. "These are the poems of a good man; and if aside from his family and newspapering, you wish to share his best thoughts, you will find these thoughts in this book, along with his sense of decency, the flowering of his experience, and the crystallizations of his profound observations. The style throughout the book is lean, pared lyricism. This is a book to own, to read, and to cherish. It isn't something to talk about. For Mr. Ragan isn't like this or that poet. He is like Sam Ragan."

A reviewer writing for the *Des Moines Register* in Iowa found much to like in the North Carolina poet. "There are two kinds of poetry. One only critics can understand; the other speaks to people and the heart. *The Tree in the Far Pasture* and the poems contained in it happily belong in the second category. Never labored or obscure, the images evoke the bright sunshine and shadow, the loneliness and poignancy of an Edward Hopper painting."

Another reviewer wrote this of the poet who favored free verse. "No observer of rhyme schemes that bind his imagination, Mr. Ragan ranges widely over the North Carolina landscape and the landscape of the human heart. He writes eloquently and movingly of nature and the seasons, of old deserted houses, of honeysuckle and kudzu vine, of birds and crickets and the beach, but mostly he writes about people, often lonely, and about what he calls 'the shining moment or the one small singing of every man.' What Poet Ragan does with remarkable skill is to give his readers an instant revelation of a mood, of a sight, of a sound, of an awareness which becomes a shared experience."

Perhaps the most moving tribute to *The Tree in the Far Pasture* came from a dear friend of Ragan's, Bernice Kelly Harris. Harris was born in Wake County, North Carolina, to a farming family. She graduated from Meredith College, and later attended The University of North Carolina at Chapel Hill where she studied playwriting under the well-known teacher Frederick Koch. In 1939 she published *Purslane*, which won the Mayflower Society Cup. Along with other novels, she wrote *Janey Jeems* in 1946, followed by *Hearthstones* and *Wild Cherry Tree Road*. Harris is now enshrined in the North Carolina Literary Hall of Fame. An excellent biography of Kelly, *Bernice Kelly Harris: A Good Life Was Writing*, was authored by Valerie Raleigh Yow. Kelly wrote to Ragan, from her home in Seaboard, shortly after publication of his new book of poetry. It is one of the most moving letters of tribute to a book this author has read.

Nelson Davis, a young friend of mine aged twelve, brought me *The Tree in the Far Pasture* from the post office. It was fitting that he should be the bearer of this beautiful book. He has collected wild flowers, transferred their colors to paper, observed a rainbow at Thanksgiving, and written a little Indian play for presentation in my back yard. We took a look at the book, then placed it in the fork of the apple tree to be relished later.

Nelson, little Jennifer, aged eight, and I continued to pick up pecans and burn leaves, to tend the sausages and apples roasting in the ashes. We had a sense of the chief nourisher in the day's feast waiting in the apple tree. So when we finished the roasted items I took *The Tree in the Far Pasture* down and said, "Now we're going to have some poetry." I was surprised at their reaction. After "Neighbors" little Jennifer said, "Read some more." Nelson looked at the contents and began to make selections. He chose everything about deserted houses and hunts and seasons. They kept asking for more. For myself I read "Country Saga" and "One Small Singing." Then we left the smoke and the ashes and went into the house—with a difference. It was a one-small-singing experience.

The title is beautiful, the physical book is. The poems are poetry as I want mine written. I love the sound of them read aloud. I nod my head in rapport as I turn the pages. I heard that crow across the field, saw the new roses on the trellis, received three fresh pears from the tree in the far pasture. I am moved by the "little living" in between birth and death. Thank you for recording the mood universal so beautifully.

All good wishes for this volume and the others you must write.

To be fair, not every reviewer praised Ragan's work. Robert Williams in the *Statesville Record and Landmark* took issue with some points. "At times the sustained mood is tiring, as is the repetition of language and tone. The symmetry of style and arrangement is unoriginal."

Ragan was awarded the Sidney Lanier Prize for the best collection of poetry by a North Carolinian for *The Tree in the Far Pasture*, which came with a cash prize and recognition at the annual meeting of the North Carolina Poetry Society. In remarks at the ceremony at the Battery Park Hotel in Asheville, Ragan commented about his poetry.

A poem is written long before it is put to paper. Any poem worth the name comes out of a lifetime of thinking and feeling. Poetry is the distilled essence of experience, emotion and thought, the use of the magic of words to pinpoint a moment in time and hold it. I write in free verse because I think I've gone beyond rhyme and meter which are really ornamental, structured things which to my mind, more often than not, create a false impression. When you seek to push an idea of feeling into a highly structured form, something has got to give, and so often its truth and beauty itself which will give to make it conform. Conformity, I think, is one of the things that all of us have to fight against all our lives. I'm not very ordered, I mean, I say a poem is more a compulsion than an act of will. I think a poem is written a long time before it's committed to paper. A word or phrase or something will lodge in your mind and then sink in and probably surface somewhere from the unconscious and start nagging at you until you have to write it down. In poetry both the poet and the reader bring something to a poem, and that something is imagination. There must be imagination on the part of the poet, and imagination on the part of the reader. I jot down things. I generally have a notebook in the car. Even when I'm riding, I jot down a word or two or a phrase or something I see that hits me.

Walt Whitman once added his thoughts about the reader bringing his own imagination to reading poetry. He seemed to agree with Ragan on this matter.

The reader will always have his or her part to do, just as much as I have had mine. I seek less to state or display any theme or thought, and more to bring you, reader, into the atmosphere of the theme or thought—there to pursue your own flight.

John Fries Blair, as Sam Ragan always referred to his good friend, passed away in 1986. Ragan wrote about the man and his publishing company quite a bit in *Southern Accent*, and they became good friends. After Blair's passing, Ragan remembered this man who did so much for North Carolina literature.

When John Fries Blair died on November 1 at the age of 83 he was seated at the large editorial desk in his publisher's office in Winston-Salem doing what he loved to do—reading the manuscripts and pondering the publication of new writers. John Fries Blair was my first publisher of a book of poems and it was a joy to work with him. He was an appreciative and discerning critic and when he expressed an opinion about a poem or passage he could cite the lines to support his view, and it was well to pay attention to him. His office in Winston-Salem was filled with boxes of books and manuscripts. His desk always was piled high with the work of writers, correspondence and his own notes. He approached the reading of every manuscript with a sense of excitement, and there was genuine regret when he felt he was not in a position to publish a work and had to return it to its author. He was one of North Carolina's most indispensable people.

The Tree in the Far Pasture was not the only book that Sam Ragan wrote in 1964. North Carolina Governor Terry Sanford and Ragan had become good friends. In 1964, as Governor Sanford was nearing the end of his term as Governor, Ragan, a lifelong Democrat, wrote a book about the Sanford Administration. The book was titled *The New Day*, and it covered Governor Sanford's accomplishments and some disappointments. But for the most part, it was a book in high praise of Sanford's term in office, 1961 to 1965. A controversial topic was the raising of taxes to invest in education.

The New Day included over 140 pages, and contained much written text, many pictures, and quite a few editorial cartoons. It was a handsomely crafted book published by Record Publishers in Zebulon, North Carolina. The book was released to coincide when thousands of Sanford supporters gathered at the Dorton Arena in Raleigh for the Terry Sanford Appreciation Dinner.

One accomplishment that Sam Ragan had a large role in helping Terry Sanford to attain was the establishment of the North Carolina School of the Arts in Winston-Salem. Ragan was an early supporter and consulted with Governor Sanford about establishing the school and sat on the original Board of Trustees and was appointed to the Founding Commission.

Author John Ehle is one of the founders of the school. Founded in 1963, and opened in 1965, it was the first public arts conservatory in the United States. Programs offered were dance, music, drama, and film, among others. This school is now known as the University of North Carolina School of the Arts, having become part of the University of North Carolina system in 1972.

In November of 1964, Ragan, the president of the Associated Press Managing Editors Association, spoke before the national delegation in Phoenix, Arizona. He talked about the healthy status of the newspaper industry as a whole but concentrated his remarks about how the newspapers had handled the assassination of President John F. Kennedy the previous year, 1963. "The crucible of the American press came on the bright afternoon of November 22, 1963, when President John F. Kennedy was assassinated on the streets of Dallas. In that hour, and the hours and days that followed, the newspapers of America were called upon to carry out their responsibility to the American people, to tell them not only what happened, but also how the country met the crisis. It was those facts provided by the American press that steadied a reeling and a shocked and startled world. Never before in history has any comparable news event been so quickly, accurately and comprehensively covered."

Ragan also talked about the newspaper profession. I feel this statement is a good summation of why Ragan loved being a newspaperman.

It is a good way to make a living, but more important, I think, it is a good way to live. For there is in newspaper work a daily sense of excitement of being present when history is made. It is also a career that gives one satisfaction in performing a service that is not only worthwhile but absolutely necessary.

Also in 1964, Ragan testified before the United States Senate in support of Senate Bill 1663, better known as the Administrative Procedure Act of 1964. This was a bill, championed by Ragan, that protected press freedom and citizens' rights to access criminal justice information. Ragan would be a staunch opponent of any type of censorship throughout his life, with many denunciations of it in *Southern Accent* and in speeches and papers. A debate raged in the 1960s that press coverage could undermine a defendant's fair trial rights. Ragan, as president of APME in a national leadership position, led the fight for press freedom as a way to protect citizens' rights to receive fair trials and to receive information about government activities. Press freedom, according to Ragan, would help to keep government from abusing its powers, and that freedom of the press would keep citizen's better informed. Ragan testified,

> The purpose of this bill is to make more accessible public information which the public has a right to know. Some time ago, for example, our newspaper, *The News and Observer*, published news stories regarding traffic violations on the Fort Bragg reservation. It wasn't too long before two counter-intelligence agents called on Editor Jonathan Daniels to question him about the source of the newspaper's information. When this bill was introduced, its author, Senator Edward V. Long, said so well what I feel about secrecy in government and the people's right to know. "A government by secrecy," he said, "benefits no one. It injures the people it seeks to serve." Speaking for myself and the 1700 members of APME, I commend Senator Long and his colleagues who are sponsoring this much-needed measure. Free and full information of what our government is doing is vital, fundamental, and absolutely necessary. The right of the public to know the public's business, which is government in all its aspects, has long been recognized, indeed, since the beginning of the Republic, as one of the first bulwarks of American democracy. An informed public is, in fact, a necessity if our form of government is to survive.

Out of the Administrative Procedure Act of 1964 and other legislation came the Freedom of Information Act, which allowed for the full or partial disclosure of previously unreleased information and documents controlled by the United States government. This went into effect in 1967, being signed into law by President Lyndon B. Johnson.

Sam Ragan played a major role leading to the enactment of a section of this new law, especially the part of the law that provided the public with more access to criminal justice information. The Spring 2017 issue of *Journalism History* magazine details this effort led by Ragan. The article is titled "Press Freedom and Citizens' Right to Know in the 1960s: Sam Ragan's Crusade to Provide the Public with Access to Criminal Justice Information."

Writing, along with running the news department of *The News and Observer* and the *Raleigh Times*, took up a big part of Sam Ragan's day. He wrote an article for *American Scholar* in 1965 titled "Dixie Looked Away." Ragan wrote about many southern states voting for Barry Goldwater in the 1964 presidential election, a Republican conservative. During this time of the push for civil rights by black citizens, Ragan wrote that this turn to Goldwater by white southerners was in part for the preservation of the white race.

Speaking invitations flowed in for this man who was by now recognized as one of the leading newspapermen in the United States. He went to Williamsburg, Virginia, to speak on "The Relationship of a Free Press and Fair Trials." Ragan debated Grant Cooper, an attorney and member of the American Bar Association's advisory committee. Ragan told the audience, "Censorship and secrecy need but little encouragement to flourish. Our historical experience of an open society could well go for naught if such restrictions on the public's right to know are not vigorously resisted." In San Diego, California, in 1965, Ragan addressed the Associated Press Managing Editors convention again, saying "There is no clear evidence that news of criminal matters published prior to a trial of a defendant has any detrimental effect on a fair trial." Many local organizations asked Ragan to come speak to their members; for example he spoke to the Goldsboro Rotary Club about poetry, for which he was given $25 and a free overnight stay in a hotel. As with many of his out-of-Raleigh visits, he took Marjorie with him, always wanting to be with the woman he loved so dearly whenever possible.

Add to all of these many responsibilities, Ragan continued to teach the Writer's Workshop at North Carolina State University. For the Spring 1965 class, he was paid $500 plus the course fees paid by students who were not North Carolina State students, which came to about an extra $300. In these classes, which produced many published authors, Ragan would assign papers to be written and he would take his red pen and make comments on the students' papers. Some of the comments were, "This is a very important subject but readers tend to read with more interest when you catch their attention in some arresting fashion, which you fail to do." "This would make a good lead to jump off with." "Good point made here, but try to tie these two subjects together."

Later in his life, Ragan also taught journalism and creative writing at St. Andrews College and Sandhills Community College.

Ragan wrote a poem he called "The Writer." It contains some of the techniques he used to teach writing, and some of the advice he used for his own writing.

The Writer

They call it writer's block,
And it is a terrible disease,
Which lasts for days, weeks, months, years,
I have had it several times.
There is nothing worse
Than a blank sheet of paper
Staring at you, and no words coming.
I've had it, but came out of it,
Some times with a word, a nod of a head,
The touch of a hand,
But most of the time God only knows
How or why.
I think I'm cured now.
The cure came when I decided
I didn't have to be perfect.

One of Sam Ragan's prize writing pupils was Sally Buckner. Buckner would go on to teach English at what is now William Peace University in Raleigh for 28 years. She got a job with the *Raleigh Times* when Ragan was Executive Editor, and that is when she decided to take his writing class at North Carolina State University. Buckner published two anthologies of North Carolina literature, *Our Words, Our Ways: Reading and Writing in North Carolina*, and *Word and Witness: 100 Years of North Carolina Poetry*. She also authored books of her own poetry, *Strawberry Harvest, Collateral Damage*, and *Nineteen Visions of Christmas*. Buckner passed away in 2018 as this book was being written.

When Buckner published her first book of poetry, in 1986, Ragan praised his former writing student in *Southern Accent*.

Sally Buckner of Raleigh is a very special poet of uncommon ability, and her first collection of poems, *Strawberry Harvest*, published by St. Andrews Press, is a delight. It has humor and irony and the language flows with remarkable precision. Ms. Buckner has an ear for human speech and an eye for the human condition, and her poems are filled with profound insights on our land and our people. There are 84 pages of poetry with an appeal which calls for reading and re-reading, and if we were to name our favorites, it would be a lengthy list. But "Cedar" is a good example. In this poem, written in the voice of Ms. Buckner's mother, she describes how her father, George, back in the Great Depression, made Christmas a happy time.

Cedar

Always cedar.
Fir trees didn't grow in Iredell County,
and George never considered pine or hemlock,
which suited me fine: I loved the scent of cedar
spicing the entire house from the very minute
those feathery branches ruffled through the door
until right after Christmas, when we flung
its carcass, picked as clean as chicken bones
outside where it could dry till fit for firewood.

In early years, he'd combine his search
For a tree with a hunting trip, return grinning,
Tree on one shoulder, rabbits on the other.
Later, when whatever disease the doctors
couldn't find a name for drew the muscles
in his legs so tight he could barely walk —
lurched like a drunken sailor — he would drive
far out in the country, scanning the winter roadside
till he found a likely candidate, straight and full,
which he could manage to clamber to, cane
clasped in one hand, ax in the other.

Never paid or asked permission. Lord, why would he?
We were all tree-poor those days, wouldn't miss a cedar
more than a dandelion. Nobody'd thought

of using tillable land for Christmas trees.
When Hoover was still making promises, who would have laid down
a cherished dollar
For something to toss away after just a week?

When George got home, he'd nail two boards in an X
for the tree's support. I'd swath them with a blanket.
The girls would help him string the lights, then wind
Cellophane garlands through the greenery.
Meanwhile I'd whip Lux Flakes to a frothy lather;
Dried on the branches, if you'd squint your eyes,
You'd swear that it was snow. Altogether,
It was some kind of pretty.

Eighteen years now, he's been gone. At first,
My boy still at home, I'd buy a tree—
Resenting every dollar—fix it up
The best I could all by myself. Then later,
Hoisting trees got to be beyond me.

I purchased one advertised as "everlasting,"
Needles, branches, trunk—all aluminum.
Don't use lights, just big red satin balls.
The children, when they come, never complain.
The grandchildren exclaim, "Red and silver!
Look at it shine!" And it lasts year after year—
Not half the trouble of a woodland tree.
But I still miss the scent of cedar.

Sally Buckner very well may have been a great poet without ever taking
Sam Ragan's writing class at North Carolina State University. But one can
see the influence of Ragan when reading a poem by Buckner; the free verse,
the love of country life, love of family, love of North Carolina, love of nature. Ragan often praised Buckner in his columns and felt awfully proud of
her, and surely knew of his influence on her. But never once did this most
humble of men ever mention this, although Buckner often wrote and told
about improving the craft of writing under her former teacher. Luckily to
those of us who love to read these two poets' works, we can turn again and
again to their magical and inspiring words.

Buckner wrote a poem saluting Ragan at a celebration of his life at the North Carolina Writers Conference in 1984 held at the Plantation Inn in Raleigh. The poem covers so much of what Ragan loved, did, wrote and stood for in his life.

Ode to Sam

Now to the business that's at hand:
Let there be no dissenter—
We've come to celebrate our Sam:
Poet, friend, and mentor.
Reared on a Granville County farm
On land which yet he praises,
He moved from turning earth by plow
To turning earthy phrases.
He used his dactyls and iambs
To record the life he knew.
With reporter's eye and poet's heart
Record it sharp and true.

He has taken us to the water's edge
And to the furthest tree,
On a journey into morning,
And there he lets us see
A squirrel and a butterfly,
The sunlight—how it lingers,
The bloom of plums, the slant of snow,
And a dying woman's fingers.
He has helped us hear the call of doves,
Mournful, strong, and sober.
He has helped us touch the spewing waves
And the ovens of October.

Yet though he wields the poet's tools
With panache and with power,
Not once has he retreated to
Garret or ivory tower.
Instead he trods the common road—
Let's make that point emphatic;

In fact, it's even known that he
Has voted Democratic.
His verses thus are peopled not
With king and financier;
But salesman, watchman, apple grower
Quietly appear
And breathe upon the living page
And breathe into our ear.

Now let us raise our glasses high,
Our steins, our jeroboams,
In tribute to our laureate,
In gratitude for his poems.
And let us add a hearty cheer
In clearest recognition
Of Marjorie, his partner in
His wide and worthy mission.
Let's dedicate this happy hour
And our best poetic lines
To the Prince of Weymouth Center,
The Bard of Southern Pines.

Buckner also wrote a poem to honor Ragan and Robert Frost, calling it "Stopping by Words on a Frosty Evening." The poem is excerpted here.

Whose words these are, I think I know,
His book is in my bookcase, so
He will not mind me stopping here
To watch his verses' gentle flow.

The words are never flip or fake,
But draw their point without mistake,
And help the heart to dance and leap
Beyond dark storms, beyond heartache.

The words are lovely, bright, and deep,
And offer visions I can keep,
And joy to know before I sleep,
And joy to know before I sleep.

Barbara Richie Pond, later in her life, wrote of taking Ragan's writing class at North Carolina State University.

I shall never forget the first time I saw him. I was in my late teens. With my insides literally rattling, I mounted those granite university steps. It was, I thought, one of the most profound moments of my short life. My palms were damp against the blue, rain-stained folder I clutched to my chest so tensely. It contained the outpourings of my soul. I hoped I would be accepted, even if I was only in high school. My dream was to become a great writer one day.

The thought of attending an N.C. State University creative writing class was terrifying, while awe-inspiring. As I entered the room like a frightened fawn, I was struck by a sea of too many elderly adult faces. I was overcome by the scent of success too, but it was the success of others, not my own. I looked across the room, and there, in the center of a roundtable was a man, smoke in hand, with a kind, calming, smile. He was the point upon which every eye in that room was fixed. When he talked, both fledging and experienced writers listened with reverence. I was mesmerized. He was most kind to me; he was not repulsed by my apparent youth, as were some others in the room. I sat down quietly, placing the blue folder in front of me.

My turn came to open the folder and share the well of my soul. Mentally, I made the decision not to read. My poems were too juvenile, too trite, too commonplace. Great tears welled up within me as I listened to the voice of Sam Ragan. "Have you something to offer?" he said. To my own surprise I said I did. I read my poem aloud, almost choking on my own words. Sam looked at me, smiled, and said in a grandfatherly way, "Writing is hard work. That has the potential to be a very good poem."

I thanked him. I listened for half an hour more. Then the class ended and the spell was broken. He walked over to me and asked me to come back. I did.

I remember so much about Sam—that straw hat, his snail-like driving, his cluttered office and his deliberate, Southern drawl. But what I remember most about Sam Ragan is not how he dressed. What I recall so well is the night Sam Ragan touched my life—me—a young, frightened girl, who had a great, big dream. I was not too small or insignificant to be taught or helped or encouraged by that great craftsman of words.

Sam Ragan showed me the magic of poetry, the intimate companionship of good literature, and that first blessed "ah-ha" moment every writer experiences.

Ragan's appearance, mentioned by Pond, was of a neatly dressed man, fedora atop his long, flowing hair combed straight back, bow tie tucked in his collar. He was a tall man, and with the fedora, seemed taller than his six feet. Even though he was soft spoken, and kind of spirit, he was a commanding presence, both from his success and respect he garnered, but because of his dress to a certain degree. But the bow tie was the item of dress that stood out. Linda Brinson of the *Winston-Salem Journal* once described Ragan as "the epitome of a Southern gentleman, with his patrician bearing, his Old South manners, and old-fashioned speech, his long, silvery hair spilling onto his collar and his hand-tied bowtie."

Lynn Sadler wrote about Ragan in a poem, and I excerpt here.

Trademark

The bow tie was his literal trademark.
But he had figurative trademarks, too:
his shyness, preference not to talk too much;
his quiet helpfulness and admiration for fledging effort,
as if we were all Paul Greens, just green in our trade;
his close observation of Nature, nature, and assorted leftovers;
his letting them speak for themselves in quietly shining poetry…
His biggest trademark? The mark he made on our poetry trade.
If ever required, he could provide the new face for Uncle Sam,
But in a perky bow tie.

Ragan explained his preference for bow ties.

I didn't always wear bow ties, you know. My wife gave me a dozen for Christmas in 1948. Of course that meant I had to wear them at least once each. After I started, I kept getting them as gifts. Pretty soon, if I didn't wear one, everyone would ask disappointedly, "Where's your bow tie?" So I haven't stopped in all these years. One thing, though,

I always tie my own, none of those pretend, snap-on things. My advice to the first-timer trying to put on a bow tie is don't look in the mirror. That might get you confused.

During the 1960s civil rights era, one day Ragan looked outside of *The News and Observer*'s offices and saw a group of people protesting against the newspaper. Ragan certainly had no problem with protests, making citizen's voices heard. Ragan was a supporter of equal rights for everyone. But he did find disappointment in that particular protest, because at the time *The News and Observer* had been experiencing a loss in subscriptions and advertising revenue from white readers and businesses who considered the newspaper too liberal and too much of a supporter of civil rights. This loss in part came because of positions of support the newspaper took on behalf of black people and civil rights. But even if he was disappointed at first when he saw the demonstrators, Ragan, being a very contemplative man, stood back and continued to look and listen, and to perhaps understand. Ragan wrote a poem about this day, "We Shall Overcome."

We Shall Overcome

They kept going round and round,
Clapping their hands and chanting,
"Unfair, unfair."
I was angry and hurt—
They had no right to say that
About me and my newspaper.
But later when they gathered
In the park across the street,
Linking arms, swaying, and singing,
"We shall overcome… some day."
I had to applaud.
And after it was over
I went upstairs and sat
Looking out of the window
For a long time.

Of course, Ragan continued to write *Southern Accent*, where his number one priority was to offer encouragement to North Carolina writers and publicize their works. In 1965 he wrote about Reynolds Price, who had found his name published for the very first time as a writer in *Southern Accent*, as mentioned earlier. He also wrote of other topics.

> Reynolds Price's new novel, *Clear Day*, is to be published by Atheneum in the fall. Word comes that Price has planted 60 rose bushes at his home in the country near Durham and will spend the summer tending the roses and working on a collection of short stories. Guy Owen has completed the writing of a sequel to *The Ballad of the Flim-Flam Man*, and is preparing a collection of poetry for publication next year. An English edition of *Paradise Preserved*, William Powell's story of the Roanoke Island Historical Association, was published last month by Oxford University Press.

In 1966, the annual North Carolina Literary Forum, which Sam Ragan had started, was held at North Carolina State University. Ragan moderated a discussion around the conversation of *The Writer and His World*. Other writers on the panel were Doris Betts, Peggy Hoffman, Fred Chappell and Charles Eaton.

Running a big newspaper with one of the largest circulations in North Carolina, Ragan expected, and received, criticism from time to time. In a letter he received, a Mrs. Bell told him she was offended reading about a couple of recent articles about "heinous crimes," and some of the words the reporter quoted in the article. Ragan replied as one would expect a Southern gentleman might. Ragan also mentioned a name that he always admired and knew Mrs. Bell would recognize, Josephus Daniels.

> It is the wish of *The News and Observer* to give to its readers a newspaper that meets their needs and desires, and for that reason any intelligent criticism such as yours is always welcome. I share your concern over the occurrence of news of crime and sordidness, but of paramount importance to us is the moral responsibility of presenting news as truthfully and as fully as possible.
>
> I do not feel that details about the two cases you mentioned were stressed any more than necessary to accurately present the news without unfair censorship to our readers. It is not our intention to ever use language that will offend any of our readers. However, we must report

the situations, be they good or evil. One of the journalistic canons of Josephus Daniels was "What the good Lord lets happen, I will print."

Thanking you for writing, and with all best wishes.

A letter by Ragan to a Miss Brown in February of 1968 tells a bit about his writing life. Miss Brown was doing a study of authors in North Carolina and she had written to Ragan as one of her subjects, and wanted to know more about him.

I am a newspaper editor, which is a full-time job in itself, but I also teach at North Carolina State University—a class in Contemporary Issues in the fall and a class in creative writing in the spring. The latter is more of a workshop than a class—in fact, it is called the Writer's Workshop—as I believe that the best way to learn how to write is to write, and that is what the students in the workshop do. I am not sure that writing can be taught, but I think it can be learned. All that a teacher can do is give encouragement, criticism, and guidance. Writing is really a personal thing, it is discovery, and quite often self-discovery. The teacher goes along, but the writer discovers.

I think of myself as a professional writer. I write for our newspaper, *The News and Observer*, each day and a Sunday column, *Southern Accent*, which is a collection of pieces of comment on the times, literary criticism, and poetry. In addition, I contribute fairly frequently to magazines, mostly articles on the press, or politics, or current topics, and some poetry. I have published one book of poetry, *The Tree in the Far Pasture*, which is now in its second edition, and I am also at work on another collection of poems.

This writing, of course, has to be done in free time away from the newspaper office and the classroom. I have found that it is best to set aside certain times for writing, and not to wait for inspiration. If one sits in front of a typewriter long enough something will come. Of course, it is better to have inspiration, and I think one must be alert and receptive to those moments of inspiration that come at odd moments during the day and night.

I often jot down fragments of thoughts and phrases, and they are very helpful later in jogging the memory or in recapturing the feeling so fleetingly experienced.

In the writing of poetry, I am inclined toward the belief of Theodore Roethke that writing a poem is more an act of compulsion than an act of will. It is difficult to will a good poem into being, as it is something that builds up inside you until it has to come out.

A good way to get into the writing mood, or to get the juices of creativity flowing, is to read from a writer one admires. A piece of writing that moves you, makes you feel, makes you think. I suppose, too, that is one of the best pieces of advice I could give a writer, read. Read anything, everything. To be sure, one who wants to write must also have eyes and ears for just about everything around him, so that they can absorb the sights and sounds of living. I think, too, that one needs to like people, and have a feeling for all living things.

Writing is one of the most satisfying things there is, if one can capture the meaningful moment, that experience, that feeling so that at some time in the future it will live again through a reader.

It is really amazing to consider what Ragan accomplished, say, in the period of 1960 to 1968. As he said in the letter to Miss Brown, he did his personal writing "in free time away from the newspaper office." How much free time did this busy man find? Just being a husband to Marjorie and a father to Nancy and Talmadge took up much time. He was a devoted family man, who made time each day to show his wife and daughters how much he loved them. He would patiently listen to them, hear their problems and concerns, revel in their joys and good news, and always talk to them in a calm voice that offered encouragement. His family knew how much he loved them, and nothing gave him more love in return, or more inspiration to work hard. Ragan would kiss Marjorie upon his return home each day and when the girls were young, sit with them and give them his full attention. Climbing in his lap, the girls would give him hugs and kisses, and he would ask them about their days. Today, those "girls," Nancy and Talmadge, still adore their father, and so do Robin and Eric, his grandchildren.

In 1967, this family had a new home to live in. Sam and Marjorie bought a 2,900 square foot house on Granville Drive in Raleigh, moving from their former residence at 2504 Kenmore Drive in Raleigh.

Along with being a husband, father, and grandfather, Sam Ragan also was the Executive Editor of one of the largest and most respected newspapers in the South. His days were long, and for most of his 25 years with

The News and Observer, he "ran the news department," according to an interview I had with Frank Daniels. But he found time for his many speaking engagements, his books, his magazine articles, his teaching, his many obligations to groups and organizations, his leadership positions, and his many requests for help and advice from others. Ragan established the "Tar Heel of the Week" feature in *The News and Observer.*

In a speech Ragan gave while he was still with *The News and Observer,* he talked about the function of a newspaper. "Your philosophy evolves, I think, through experience. An informed people can be depended upon to make the right decisions. It is the function of a newspaper to let them know what is going on so that they can make those decisions. There should be no censorship by anybody, including the publisher and the editor, of what is news and what is published in the newspaper."

He spoke at Meredith College in Raleigh in 1968 about a subject that he was by now considered a national authority on, free press and free trial. He went to South Bend, Indiana, to speak at the University of Notre Dame on the subject, and he also talked about the same at the University of California at Berkeley.

On another topic, the state of the short story, Ragan spoke at the Tar Heel Writer's Roundtable in Raleigh.

The short story, as practiced today, has reached its highest form. A short story should contain conflict, so that something should happen in the mind and the heart of the reader. The important thing is to make me as a reader see and feel something and to come to an understanding through his experience. Read such authors as Thurber, Hemingway, Faulkner, and E.B. White for those who write short stories. White may be the finest short story craftsman writing today. Frances Gray Patton is also a very good short story writer. My advice is to begin with a fact to establish a sense of plausibility, this is essential. Then let the story take its own course, but try to get inside the time and the place and the people of your story. Writing a short story is much like flying a kite. Get it off the ground and let the string out bit by bit, giving the reader what you want him to know a little at a time until the kite, or the story, is airborne.

Ragan received much mail, asking for his help or just letters of keeping in touch with an old friend. In one of the former, a young man, Robert

Lee Powell, from Oxford, had just graduated from high school, and wanted to attend Ragan's former college, Atlantic Christian. Powell explained the only way he could attend was if he could get a job at the college. Ragan, for sure remembering when he had worked also to get through college back in the 1930s, promptly wrote his good friend, Art Wenger, the president of Atlantic Christian at this time, 1968, and asked him to help Powell if possible. It didn't hurt that in his letter to Ragan, Powell told him that he had delivered *The News and Observer* in Oxford during his high school days.

Sometimes the letters Ragan received were from old friends just saying hello or trying to brighten a day. Paul Green wrote to him during this time.

Back in 1928–30 when women's dresses were getting shorter there was a doggerel poem going about entitled "The Flapper's Lament" one stanza of which ran as follows:

"If dresses get any shorter
    Said the flapper with a sob,
There'll be two more cheeks to powder
    And a lot more hair to bob."

I find this both amusing and innocent, considering the present hoisting of the miniskirts. No complaints from here, though.

The North Carolina Arts Council was formed in 1967. Philip Hanes Jr. was appointed by Governor Dan Moore as the first chairman, and Sam Ragan as vice-chairman. Ragan, even today, is inaccurately listed as the first chairman. Due to health reasons, Hanes resigned only months into his chairmanship, and Governor Moore then appointed Ragan as chairman. So by December of 1967, Ragan was chairman, and in this role he would play a huge part in promoting arts throughout the state. The North Carolina General Assembly made a two-year appropriation to the Council of $140,000, and the National Endowment for the Arts had given the Council a grant of $39,000. Along with these funds, the Mary Reynolds Babcock Foundation gave $5,000, the Mary Duke Biddle Foundation gave $2,500, and Hanes Dye and Finishing donated $1,000. Other corporate contributions came to over $7,500. So the Council started with about $200,000.

Ragan believed strongly in the literary magazines of North Carolina, and regularly wrote about them to give the magazines publicity in *South-*

ern Accent. But also, as chairman of the North Carolina Arts Council, he pushed funds their way, in many cases keeping some afloat financially. For example, in his first full year as chairman in 1968, the *Red Clay Reader* was given $1,500, *Greensboro Review* $600, *Southern Poetry Review* $600, *North Carolina Folklore* $1,000, *The Rebel* $1,200, *Crucible* $1,200, *Appalachian Harvest* $1,000, and the *Carolina Quarterly* $400. Other magazines got funds also. Ragan talked about funding of the literary magazines in North Carolina.

> I insisted that along with support of the other arts that we support the literary publications too. So we took a little money and made it go a long way. And a few other magazines started springing up around the state. And those magazines deserve recognition for giving writers a place to see their work and their talents which had been hidden away for years. When I talk about the early times — how in 1950 you could count the number of poets on the fingers of your hands — that's what I mean. Suddenly there was a burgeoning of literature in North Carolina and I think it was because of the Arts Council's small grants spread around. I remember one year we had applications from forty magazines in this state.
>
> As chairman, I called in Thad Stem and Guy Owen. We sat at a long table and we had samples of these magazines. We read through them and went over the applications. We didn't require forms. The applicants wrote letters, sometimes typed, sometimes just in longhand. And we spread the money out and I think that out of the forty magazines which applied we granted funds to thirty-six.

Of course, the Arts Council also donated funds to other arts organizations around the state in those first couple of years. The Rockingham County Arts Council got $3,200, the Vagabond School of Drama in Flat Rock got $4,000, the National Opera Company in Raleigh got $4,200, the Civic Arts Council in Asheville got $4,800, the Greensboro Little Theatre got $2,000, the Statesville Arts and Science Museum got $1,400, and the High Point Art Council got $5,000. The Surry County Arts Council got $2,000.

One program Ragan started as Arts Council Chairman was a program that had poets and writers travel to all parts of the state and read their works and poetry. This program proved to be very successful in promoting poetry in North Carolina. Ragan, in a *Southern Accent* column in later years, recalled that program. Of course, as usual, Ragan never mentions his role that he played.

In the late 1960s and early 70s a program of readings by Tar Heel writers was sponsored by the N.C. Arts Council and the impact was tremendous.

Poets in pairs scattered about the state and read their poems, sometimes to very large audiences and sometimes to very small groups. The readings took place in college auditoriums, classrooms, high schools, libraries, churches, theaters, hotel rooms, and once in a bar. Some of the writers and poets who took part in those early readings were Thad Stem, Tom Walters, Guy Owen, Heather Ross Miller, Betty Adcock, Ardis Kimzey, John Foster West, Reynolds Price, Doris Betts, Fred Chappell, Sylvia Wilkinson, Emily Wilson, Maria Ingram, Ann Deagon, James Applewhite, Sallie Nixon, Charles Edward Eaton, Ronald Bayes, and the list could go on and on, because these were heady times and these were talented and entertaining poets with something to say.

Heather Ross Miller said the highlight of her life was to arrive in Goldsboro for a poetry reading and to see her name in foot high letters in lights welcoming her to a Holiday Inn. In one city Guy Owen was challenged by a John Bircher who didn't like what he regarded as Guy's earthy poetry, and every place he went the inimitable Thad Stem could be counted upon to stir his audience into loud cheerings, and occasionally angry questions.

In Raleigh some of the poets were invited to read in a topless bar, and most of them went, although they admitted later they didn't compete too well with the twirling mammaries.

Evidently, from some correspondence between the two, Sam Ragan and Bernice Kelly Harris were in the initial stages of writing a book together. On August 21, 1968, Kelly wrote to Ragan, and he responded on two days later.

Dear Sam: I started to send two or three of the stories that are to demonstrate how creative writing can evolve from situations, incidents, pictures, characters. But I shall probably do further revisions. You'll see them later. I think we shall want to call it a how-to book, or words to that effect, unless textbook seems better. Mebane Burgwyn was here last week and was fascinated with the idea. When the weather is cooler and you have time, I hope you will come down to Seaboard for a fuller discussion of our book. I do have faith in it. If I should be disabled again (I am not cultivating that attitude) I want you to go on with it, using my stories if they seem to fit. I saved your essay on obscenity. This essay will be useful to me, and I am glad you wrote it.

Dear Bernice: My enthusiasm grows for our book, especially, when I hear about your story ideas. I am continuing to compile my notes which were rather hap-hazardly arranged and I hope to get started putting them in shape soon. We can call it a how-to, but I see no reason why it could not be used as a textbook for writing classes. As soon as I can unburden myself with work that has piled up, I want to come to Seaboard and see you.

What an absolute shame this book written by these two legendary North Carolina writers never got completed.

Louis Rubin was the subject of a *Southern Accent* in 1968. Rubin is credited with helping to establish Southern literature as a field of study within American literature. He was teacher and mentor to many writers at the University of North Carolina at Chapel Hill, and founded Algonquin Books, a nationally recognized publishing house.

One of the best of contemporary critics of American literature, especially the literature of the South, is Louis D. Rubin Jr., a Southerner himself and now Professor of English at the University in Chapel Hill. Rubin has not only written pointedly and with a fine style of clarity about Southern literature, as in *The Faraway Country*, but is also the author of a novel, many short stories and poems.

His latest book, *The Curious Death of the Novel*, is especially interesting. His conclusion in the first of the fifteen essays in the book is that there are "novels being written each year that I find greatly interesting and enjoyable, I suggest then, that we stop worrying so much over whether the novel is dead, and spend more time reading living novels."

A.R. Ammons was born on a tobacco farm near Whiteville, North Carolina. By 1964 he was hired to teach at Cornell University, where he would stay until he retired in 1998, eventually becoming Professor of English and Poet-in-Residence. He published many books, mostly poetry, in his lifetime. Two of them, *Garbage* and his *Collected Poems,* won National Book Awards. Ragan wrote about Ammons in 1968 in *Southern Accent*, and also about the death of Upton Sinclair.

A.R. Ammons of Whiteville has emerged as one of America's leading poets, and it is pleasing to have his recently published *Selected Poems* drawn from four previously published books. Ammons is a graduate of Wake Forest College. In his poems he has experimented with form, sometimes successfully and sometimes not, but it is the content which has made him a major poetic voice. A keen and appreciative eye and ear for nature give his poetry a freshness not often found today. Someone has written that his poetry delights the ear and challenges the mind. It does.

"I aimed at the public heart and by accident I hit it in the stomach." That's the way Upton Sinclair described the reaction to the most famous of his 89 books, *The Jungle*. Published in 1906, the book was intended to describe the human suffering in the Chicago stockyard area.

But in a few pages, more of an appendage than the main current of the story, he gave a description of meat production that horrified the public and brought reform in the industry. He gave details on the casual grinding of rats, refuse and even employees into beef products, and the generally horrible conditions under which the meat was prepared for the American consumer.

President Theodore Roosevelt was aroused by Sinclair's book and supported the reforms. It was also Roosevelt who gave a name to the whole school of writers of social protest by quoting from Bunyan's "Pilgrim's Progress" about "The Man with the Muckrake, who could look no way but downward." Along with Sinclair, others in the Muckraker class were Ida Tarbell and Lincoln Steffens.

Sinclair died a few days ago at the age of 90 in a New Jersey nursing home. He began writing at the age of 14 and beside the 89 full length books he wrote more than 20 plays and hundreds of magazine articles. His stated credo was: "My efforts are to find out what is righteous in the world, to live it, and to try to help others live it." Not bad for a muckraker.

At some point in 1968, Ragan wrote a report on the state of *The News and Observer* and *The Raleigh Times* to Frank Daniels Sr., son of Josephus Daniels. By 1968, Ragan had worked at *The News and Observer* for 27 years as State Editor, Managing Editor, and Executive Editor.

The News and Observer has a special character and flavor and distinction that sets it apart from other newspapers. The reader, of course, is the most important person involved, and I think that over the years our readers think of it as "my" newspaper rather than "the" newspaper. It is my hope that they will continue to think of it that way. I feel that long ago *The News and Observer* established and has maintained a rapport with its readers, that it is sensitive to and attuned to our readers needs and wishes. Any person charged with editorial responsibility needs to have a sort of built-in antenna to reader reaction. He must be aware of reader habit yet be sensitive to change and change the newspaper as reader requirements demand.

The real measure of a good newspaper, a great newspaper, in my opinion is how well it covers its own community, its own region or territory. I have given constant examination to this requirement and in recent days undertook a searching reappraisal of how we have met this measurement. In my opinion we have met it well. State news coverage, of course, has been our bread and butter, and I think it will remain so in the foreseeable future.

We have done well in coverage of state politics and government, a coverage which is well regarded and respected by our readers. This, too, could be made even better, however, with at least two good investigative type reporters. Efforts to strengthen the staff in this respect are now underway. I would like to expand the student trainee program, with a capable staff member in charge of such a program.

Our sports department ranks with the best. Our women's department could possibly be expanded to cover a wider range of news. Our farm news coverage is excellent.

All in all, I think the editorial department has done and is doing an excellent job and has demonstrated that it is so organized to cope with most any news situation. I cite the recent coverage of the racial disturbances and the prison riots as an example.

I am proud of what *The News and Observer* has done, and I am confident that it can continue to be a great newspaper.

In regards *to The Raleigh Times*, its development has been more difficult. Yet when I go through it carefully and compare it with other afternoon newspapers I think it is meeting well the standards of a good newspaper.

As you know, I have strong feelings about these newspapers. My involvement with *The News and Observer* has been a complete one for 27 years, and I want it to be the best newspaper in the country.

Claude Sitton was born in Atlanta, Georgia, in 1925. He joined *The New York Times* in 1957, and within a year was named Southern correspondent. Sitton covered the civil rights movement for the *Times* from 1958 to 1964. Some describe Sitton as the standard bearer for civil rights journalism. In 1964 he was named national news director of the *Times*. In 1968 *The News and Observer* in Raleigh made a big hire, getting Sitton to leave *The New York Times*. He was named editorial director and vice president of The News and Observer Publishing Company and was editor of the newspaper within two years. Sitton won the Pulitzer Prize while at *The News and Observer* in 1983 for distinguished commentary for his Sunday columns.

Having been hired to come to *The News and Observer* by June of 1968, Sitton wrote a short letter to Sam Ragan, then Executive Editor. He was looking forward to working with Ragan, although the two men knew each other already through their common work.

Having read *The News and Observer* for several weeks, I am even more impressed by the job you and others there are doing. Since the announcement was made that I was joining the paper, a number of newspapermen have spoken to me very highly of you and your efforts in the free press, free trial area and in the APME. You obviously have made a most substantial contribution over the years in maintaining and improving the national reputation of *The News and Observer*, one of which you can be justly proud. Further, Jonathan and others have told me of your fine work in cultural affairs and other undertakings in North Carolina and of the goodwill it has earned for the paper.

Needless to say, Sam, you are a valuable executive and I plan to rely upon you for help and advice in the years ahead. *The News and Observer*, to say nothing of Raleigh and North Carolina, has a most promising future. But while it may be promising, it's also going to be tough. Newspapers, generally, have a real scrap ahead of them. Only the good ones will survive. Only the best ones will grow. And to be the best means a star performance every day. That takes hard work and cooperation. You'll have mine. I'll need yours.

But Claude Sitton was not to work for very long with Sam Ragan.

William and Emma Long Ragan were the parents of Sam Ragan. William, born in Granville County in 1875, married Emma, born in Franklin County in 1886, in 1903. William was 28 years old and Emma was 18 years old when they got married. William and Emma had eight children, William, Sollie, Stephen, Lacy, Melvin, Sam, Margaret, and Dorothy. *Courtesy of Nancy Ragan*

Marjorie reads a newspaper on the porch of her family home in Laurel Hill, North Carolina, in 1919. Marjorie was born in 1917 to parents James Usher and Lula Frances McCall, who had married in 1915. Marjorie's father, James, died in 1918, when Marjorie was only one year old. James died from the terrible flu epidemic that came to America during this time period. From this scene, it is obvious Marjorie not only enjoyed reading newspapers at a young age, but she would spend much of her life working for newspapers and would marry a newspaperman, Sam Ragan. *Courtesy of Robin Smith*

Sam Ragan, third from the right, stands outside a Raleigh hospital with some of his siblings in 1960. Their mother, Emma, is in the hospital and would soon pass away. *Courtesy of Nancy Ragan and Robin Smith*

Shown is Sam Ragan as a young child while living in Berea in Granville County, North Carolina. *Courtesy of Talmadge Ragan*

PRESIDENT AND FIRST LADY—The North Carolina Press Association opens its Mid-Winter Institute here today, an annual meeting in Chapel Hill at which awards are presented for journalistic excellence. Breakfasts, luncheons, banquets, workshops and business sessions are held. Presiding during the weekend will be Sam Ragan, president of the Press Association. He is editor and publisher of the Southern Pines Pilot. Mrs. Ragan is associate editor of the newspaper. They are shown at their home in Southern Pines. (Newspaper color photo by Laura Richardson)

Sam Ragan holds his baby girl, Talmadge, in 1951. *Courtesy of Talmadge Ragan*

Sam and Marjorie Ragan walk the gardens of their home in Southern Pines on Hill Road in 1974. Sam and Marjorie were married in 1939 and had two daughters, Nancy, born in 1943, and Talmadge, born in 1950. *Courtesy of Talmadge Ragan*

Sam Ragan plays with his daughter, Talmadge, in 1954. *Courtesy of Talmadge Ragan*

Nancy Ragan, Sam Ragan's oldest daughter, plays with her Raggedy Ann doll in the 1940s. *Courtesy of Robin Smith*

Shown is the former home of James Boyd as it looks today. It is now the Weymouth Center for the Arts and Humanities. *Courtesy of Lewis Bowling*

This is the North Carolina Literary Hall of Fame Room at the Weymouth Center for the Arts and Humanities in Southern Pines. Ragan led the efforts to establish the North Carolina Literary Hall of Fame. *Courtesy of Lewis Bowling*

This is Ragan in the mid-1960s when he was still with *The News and Observer* in Raleigh. Ragan served as State Editor, Managing Editor, and Executive Editor with *The News and Observer* from 1941 to 1968. *Courtesy of Robin Smith*

Sam Ragan and Paul Green were good friends and collaborated often on projects. Green received the Pulitzer Prize for Drama in 1927 for his play *Abraham's Bosom*, but is best known for his outdoor drama, *The Lost Colony*, which Ragan attended dozens of times in Manteo. *Courtesy of Southern Historical Collection, University of North Carolina at Chapel Hill.*

The Sam and Marjorie Ragan Writing Center is located on the Barton College campus in Wilson, North Carolina. An annual "Walking into April" Poetry Day is held here to celebrate the written word in the spirit of Sam Ragan. Ragan was a 1936 graduate of Barton, then called Atlantic Christian College. *Courtesy of Lewis Bowling*

Sam Ragan sits at his desk in his office at *The Pilot* newspaper in Southern Pines. He has a cigarette in his right hand, is smiling, has his usual bow tie on, and as always, papers are scattered all over his desk and all over his office. Ragan's messy desk, his warm smile, his cigarette, and his bow tie were things people remember about him. *Courtesy of Glenn Sides*

Governor Robert W. Scott and Associate Justice Susie Sharp look on as Sam Ragan signs his commission as North Carolina's first secretary of art, culture and history on February 18, 1972. In the background is Dr. H. G. Jones who was appointed state historian and administrator of the Office of Archives and History.

Ragan signing Commission Papers for Secretary. *Courtesy of Robin Smith*

Courtesy of Glenn Sides

Sam Ragan speaks at the dedication of the Belk Dormitory at East Carolina University in 1966. Ragan worked for Henry Belk in 1938 at the *Goldsboro News-Argus*. Belk advised Ragan, who was 23 years old in 1938, to "Write with wonder. Write as if you are seeing something for the first time, and you want everyone else to see it the same way, with eyes of wonder." Ragan often recalled that advice from Henry Belk. *Courtesy of Southern Historical Collection, University of North Carolina at Chapel Hill*

Sam Ragan has copies of *The Pilot* hot off the press. *Courtesy of Ken Cooke*

Sam Ragan was chosen as the winner of the North Carolina Award in Fine Arts in 1979. *Courtesy of Talmadge Ragan*

Marjorie Ragan is shown in the office with Sam Ragan at *The Pilot*. As usual, papers are everywhere. *Courtesy of Joan Milligan*

Sam Ragan enjoys a moment of rest in his back yard at his home in Southern Pines. *Courtesy of Mae W. Bell.*

8

The Pilot, Arts Council, Word Man, "Desk is
always messy," "A forgotten flower has come
forth to receive the hummingbird's pause"

For a period of time, Katharine Boyd had been trying to persuade Ragan to buy *The Pilot* newspaper in Southern Pines from her. In late
1968, Ragan and Marjorie agreed to do just that, purchasing *The Pilot* for
$100,000. Ragan used his investments in *The News and Observer's* profit
sharing plan for much of this purchase. *The Pilot* investment would turn
out to be a good one. In 1996, several months before Ragan's death, he
sold the newspaper for $4.8 million. The buyers were Frank Daniels Jr.,
who was President and Publisher of *The News and Observer* from 1971 to
1996, Frank Daniels III, David Woronoff, Jack Andrews, and Lee Dirks, all
previously associated with *The News and Observer*. Woronoff is now the
publisher of *The Pilot*. Under Woronoff's leadership, *The Pilot* for three
consecutive years, 2015, 2016, and 2017 was named Best Community
Newspaper in the United States by the National Newspaper Association.

Sam Ragan's 27 years with *The News and Observer* ended officially on
December 31, 1968. Serving as State Editor, Managing Editor, and Executive Editor, Ragan had contributed greatly to the prestige and growth of
the newspaper. Frank Daniels Jr., in an interview with me, called him a
"good news man." Sam ran the news department for many years. He was
damn good at covering the state of North Carolina. We hated to lose him
at *The News and Observer*, but we understood that he wanted to run his

own newspaper. We lost a good man, but *The Pilot* and the town of Southern Pines got a good one."

Jonathan Daniels, who had worked with Ragan for most of Ragan's years at *The News and Observer*, and Ragan had become very close. "We are going to miss Sam Ragan. His contribution has meant much to the flavor of the paper and its growth. But along with all his other colleagues, I rejoice at his opportunity to have his own paper. *The Pilot* is something special in North Carolina, taking its tradition from the late great novelist James Boyd and from Katharine Boyd, who has made it an indigenous paper with a clear, strong voice for all that is best in town and state and country. Sam Ragan will bring to this tradition enthusiasm, talent and devotion to the highest ideals of a free press in a free and advancing land."

Stacy Brewer published the first issues of *The Pilot* in Vass, in 1920. Brewer sold the paper to Nelson Hyde of Southern Pines in 1928. In 1929 *The Pilot* was published in Aberdeen. By 1933 *The Pilot* had offices in both Southern Pines and Aberdeen. In 1941, Hyde sold to James Boyd. Boyd, as covered earlier in this book, passed away in 1944, and his wife, Katharine, takes over as publisher and editor.

In announcing the sale of *The Pilot* to Ragan, Katharine Boyd commented, "There could be no better person. To know only a few of the many important posts held by Mr. Ragan since he entered the newspaper field is to feel very proud. His choice of *The Pilot*, and Southern Pines as a place to live, is very lucky for us all. Clearly *The Pilot* is in extremely capable hands. And, more importantly, the spirit behind those hands is a spirit of justice, of integrity, of great kindness and a warm heart." Ragan said, "I am honored that Mrs. Boyd has chosen me to carry on *The Pilot* and the great tradition of this newspaper. I intend to see that this tradition of printing all the news and working for the advancement and betterment of the community, county and region is continued. Mrs. Boyd will continue to be associated with me in the newspaper which she has so long directed and which has earned a distinguished reputation."

Ragan recalled later in life moving to *The Pilot*.

I think every newspaperman at some time wants to own his own newspaper. The opportunity for me came in the fall of 1968. I had known Katharine Boyd who owned *The Pilot* all those years. She had been after me for four or five years, wanting to sell it to me. Finally,

I decided that it was the right time. Southern Pines is a very pleasant place to live, very enjoyable place. The pace is a little slower but it's a very cosmopolitan community, people here from all over the country, all over the world, very high level of education, tolerance is good. My editorial policies are probably anathema to the majority of the conservatives around here but still we get along. There was one man who used to come in here. He used to write me letters, giving me hell all the time. I printed them, of course. Then he just finally gave up on me. For a long time, the door to my office is always open, he'd come in about once a week and come to the door and look at me and shake his head and walk away.

Ragan must have had conservatives in mind, possibly the man who wrote all those letters to the editor, or perhaps he had Senator Jesse Helms in mind, when he wrote "Mr. Ibsen and His Trolls." Ibsen was a Norwegian playwright and poet who wrote *A Doll's House*, which became the world's most performed play at one time.

Mr. Ibsen and His Trolls

It was natural, I suppose,
For old Henrik Ibsen
To think in terms of trolls,
And he wrote: "to live is to fight with trolls"…
I have been thinking about that
For a long time—
I have never seen a troll.
But I know what Mr. Ibsen was talking about.

Congratulations poured in from around the country after Ragan bought *The Pilot*. Bernice Kelly Harris wrote, "Congratulations on owning your paper, and I am sincerely pleased at the possibilities that are ahead. It can mean much to the paper and to you. All the same I am less than happy at your leaving Raleigh. I found myself in the role of comforter at the creative writing group last night, as members lamented your leaving the *Observer*. You have become for several of them the *Observer*." Sallie Nixon, who once lived in Lincolnton, North Carolina, and an award-winning poet who was a past president of the North Carolina Poetry Society, wrote, "Although I know you will be greatly missed at the *Observer*, I am very enthusiastic about your new paper. It seems an appropriate time to tell you that I think you have done more to encourage good writing in our state than anyone I have known."

Doris Betts wrote, "You and Marjorie will be very happy in Southern Pines. *The Pilot* is an exceptional newspaper, with a literate history. And most of all the paper will be yours. There will be no one in journalism for miles on either side who embarks on a new enterprise with so much affection and loyalty from old friends as you will take with you to *The Pilot*. If you want a book reviewer for *The Pilot*, put me on your list."

At the time of the sale in 1968, there were four weekly papers in Moore County, where Southern Pines is located. *The Pilot* had the largest circulation at 3,700, followed by the *Sandhill Citizen* with 2,700, the *Moore County News* with about the same number, and the *Robbins Record*, with the lowest number of subscribers. *The Pilot* had the advantage of being located in and near a resort area, such as Pinehurst, and the people in the area were generally well off and well educated, a clientele that buys newspapers, at least in 1968. Moore County was growing in population at this time also.

In one of the very first issues of *The Pilot* under its new owner, Sam Ragan, Katharine Boyd was listed as a Contributing Editor, C. Benedict was Managing Editor, Julia Horner was Woman's Editor, Mary Evelyn de Nissoff was Pinehurst Editor, Michael Valen was Production Manager, and Glenn M. Sides was listed as working in the Composing Room. Fifty years later, in 2018, Glenn Sides retired from *The Pilot*. Sides was actually hired just before Ragan officially came on board. Sides did a little of everything when first hired in 1968. Ragan saw him laying out pages one day, liked what he saw, and assigned him to the darkroom. Sides has been taking pictures for the paper since then, and has won many photography awards, recognizing him as one of the outstanding newspaper photographers in the state.

Sides talked with me about his time spent with Ragan at *The Pilot*.

Mr. Ragan was always encouraging. He didn't just look at a person's education, but observed the person and put them where they would best serve the paper. He was the most generous person in the world. He got my wife a grant to go to nursing school. If you were in need of money or needed a loan, he helped to arrange it. He was a man of high integrity. The most important people to Mr. Ragan were the newspaper's readers. He was a chain smoker, when he first came to the paper, he smoked Camels, one after the other, and later switched to Salems. He drove a 65 Mustang for a number of years before he got an Oldsmobile. His desk was always a mess, stacked high with papers and letters and things. Whenever anyone would comment on his desk, he would say, "Oh, don't worry about such trivial stuff," in a joking manner. But if you walked in to his office and asked him for something, he would reach right for it in all that mess and pull it right out. He was organized in his own way. One day someone decided to go in Mr. Ragan's office when he wasn't there and organize things for him. When he got back, you would have thought she had set fire to his office. He didn't particularly like that. He would use that old typewriter of his and you could hear him down the halls, almost like a machine gun. I never saw him in anything but a bowtie, never in a necktie. He was always so well dressed and neat looking.

Also in that early issue of *The Pilot* under the new owner, January of 1969, there was a column by Betsy Lindau called *Some Looks at Books*, and a column from his good friend, Thad Stem. And in a sign of Ragan's progressive views, he put a picture and a story about Emry Little, who had just become the first black person on the Southern Pines Volunteer Fire Department. Little was a meat-cutter at the local A&P Store, and had made history earlier, in 1963, by becoming Southern Pine's first black policeman, which the article also pointed out.

"Sam Ragan Reports" started airing on WTVD television in Durham in 1969. It was a half hour program which aired at 1 p.m. each Sunday. The program, which ran for several years, dealt with most any issue in the news, but mostly featured guests being interviewed by Ragan about political, social, and literary issues. Television was not a new venture for Ragan, who along with the previously mentioned radio show he did for WUNC had also been on WUNC-TV many times. Some of the guests on the show in the first couple of years were future Governor Jim Hunt, Mayor Howard Lee of Chapel Hill, William Friday, Thad Stem, Dr. Charles Lyons, President of Fayetteville State University, Dr. Carlyle Sitterson, Chancellor of UNC-CH, Dr. A.C. Dawson, Executive Director of the North Carolina Association of Educators, Dr. Jacob Koomen, State

Health Director, Matthew Hogdson, Director of UNC Press, and many others. As you might expect, Ragan had authors from around the state on quite often, both to talk about their books, and to discuss the literary situation in the state.

Ragan received a letter from a lady quite upset with one of his guests, Thad Stem. The letter came from Oxford, where Stem was born and lived his entire life. Mrs. Watkins wrote, "I caught your show on Sunday in which you talked with the indomitable T.G. Stem. Several times I was sure he would swallow his cigarette, but somehow it always managed to get back in his fingers." But this was not the only lady Stem offended with his smoking while on television with Ragan. Another lady directed her anger at Stem through a letter to the offending smoker himself. "You spoiled the entire show for me yesterday by continually puffing away on a smoking cigarette. You made such a production of lighting then blowing the smoke in Mr. Ragan's face, making it appear that the studio was burning up, then mashing out the cigarette and drinking something! Doesn't your poise last even thirty minutes? No, not with nicotine clawing at you! You can tell by now I am against tobacco in all its forms. With all its dangers, how could you then puff the poisons at even your secretary? The odor of tobacco carries a hundred feet. You ought to be ashamed of yourself."

Regrettably, I never got to know Thad Stem. But I did visit with his wife on several occasions long after Stem passed away, Marguerite, whom every-one called Dety. She was a lady of many talents herself, among them writing and painting. And she was a tough, but good editor, working on one of my books. But I feel like I know Thad Stem through his papers, talking to many people who knew him, and visiting with Mrs. Stem. And my guess would be after reading the above letters, I'll bet Stem would have made a point of puffing away on his cigarette the next time he saw these ladies.

Ragan's inaugural *Southern Accent* column in *The Pilot* surely must have endeared him to readers of his new location, the Sandhills. As usual, he wrote with a folksy tone, sort of like having a casual conversation in his office. He touched on a number of subjects. The column appeared in the first week of January.

The making of New Year's Resolutions may have gone out of fashion. We were never for the making of resolves on December 31 or January 1, figuring that July is as good as January for such things.

Still, I suppose it does no harm to resolve to be better or to do better in a new year than one did in the year just past. Even if such resolutions fade as quickly as snow in a warm sunshine, the very making of them probably serves some good purpose.

Some people are very specific about New Year's Resolutions, mostly about things they will not do, things they feel guilty about, such as smoking or drinking or gambling. A few perhaps resolve to do certain things, positive things, such as clean out the attic, or visit someone they feel like they should visit and have not seen for a long time.

Perhaps most of us, however, hope to get through the year, and our lives for that matter, so that someone somewhere can say, as reported recorded on an old New England tombstone: "He did the best he could."

❋

We think it is a fine thing for the Post Office Department to issue a stamp in honor of Edgar Lee Masters, the poet. The likeness of the author of *Spoon River Anthology* will appear on a 6-cent stamp in 1970, the first in a series that will pay tribute to American poets.

Postmaster General Winton H. Blount, in announcing the series, said, "there is a place on our stamps for those quiet men and women of genius whose artistic endeavors have preserved our heritage and contributed to our cultural stimulation."

Who the other poets in the series will be, we do not know. Back in the 1940s, there was a Famous Americans series which did honor Longfellow, Whittier, Lowell, Whitman and Riley. There was also a stamp in 1949 for Edgar Allen Poe and one in 1967 for Thoreau. But not many poets and writers make it on stamps.

There was one writer who did serve as a postmaster at one time. William Faulkner did hold down that appointment at the University Station at the University of Mississippi in Oxford for a short while. But there were complaints that he spent his time reading in back of the post office and would not put up the mail or answer calls for service at the postal window. The complaints reached Washington and Faulkner received a letter demanding an explanation.

Faulkner replied to the Postmaster General and concluded his letter with this declaration: "I do not propose to be at the beck and call of every itinerant son-of-a-bitch with two cents to invest in a postage stamp. This, sir, is my resignation."

Of course, along with writing *Southern Accent*, Ragan got many letters and phone calls for help and advice from readers and writers from all over the state. In the years to come, *Southern Accent* would become the longest running column of its type in the United States, from 1948 to 1996, 48 years. It was syndicated in eventually 43 states and 24 foreign countries. Judy Griswold's letter from Chapel Hill to Ragan in June of 1969 is typical. "Recently, I completed a children's book of free verse which I am interested in having published. Ed Hamlin of *The Orange County News* suggested that I ask you to look over the poetry and evaluate its potential. I would appreciate you taking the time to look over my work and criticizing it in light of its applicability to publishing."

Chairman of the North Carolina Arts Council since December of 1967, Ragan continued to work hard for all of the arts in the state. In May of 1969, Charleen Swansea, who founded the *Red Clay Reader* in 1964, wrote Ragan thanking him for funds received from the Arts Council. There were times when the money received from the Arts Council kept literary magazines in the state afloat financially, especially in the early years when many of these magazines and journals got their start. "I was so very relieved and pleased to receive another grant from the North Carolina Arts Council. I am sure that no one knows better than you the mushrooming costs of printing, and I was getting rather desperate about the next issue. The $1,500 will make it possible for us to pay contributors, and as you know, I think this is important. Thank you for all the work and concern you have invested in the Red Clay Reader. I hope that I can deserve your faith."

Another gracious letter came from Mildred Hartsock of *Crucible* produced by Atlantic Christian College in Wilson, Ragan's alma mater. "I have just received a letter and a check for $1,000 from the North Carolina Arts Council. I want to tell you how much the editors and staff of Crucible appreciate this grant for 1969–70. The encouragement and the interest mean as much to me as the money itself; and I just can't begin to tell you how grateful we are for both. Thank you again for all you have done to help us."

Elizabeth "Buffie" Stevenson Ives was the sister of Adlai Stevenson, who was the Democratic Governor of Illinois and the Democratic nominee for President of the United States in 1952 and 1956. Elizabeth Stevenson lived in Southern Pines and was very active in the community. Elizabeth and Adlai had a North Carolina heritage. Most of their link to North Carolina was from ancestors in Rowan County. Adlai visited the state many times, to see his sister, of course, but he also had many friends in the Tar Heel state. Sam Ragan got to know Elizabeth rather well, and they decided to collaborate on a book about Elizabeth's famous brother. The book was published in 1969, four years after Adlai had passed away in 1965, by Heritage Printers in Charlotte, and was titled *Back to Beginnings: Adlai E. Stevenson and North Carolina*.

Elizabeth and her husband, Ernest Ives, were winter inhabitants of Southern Pines, for the most part. Adlai particularly enjoyed visiting Elizabeth's home at Paint Hill Farm in Southern Pines. He enjoyed the quiet life and serene setting of Paint Hill Farm and found getting work done there to his liking.

One of the most celebrated writers in all of America, Carl Sandburg, also was a staunch Adlai Stevenson supporter, like Sam Ragan. Sandburg was at this time living at Connemara, his home in Flat Rock, North Carolina, where he wrote and his wife, Paula, raised goats. Sandburg said about Stevenson, "Adlai Stevenson sees America not in the setting sun of a black night of despair ahead of us. He sees America in the crimson light of a rising sun."

Ragan became friends with Elizabeth after he bought *The Pilot* and moved to Southern Pines. They would later both be very instrumental in saving Weymouth, James and Katharine Boyd's home in Southern Pines. Ragan, being a staunch Democrat, certainly saw a kindred spirit in the politics of Adlai Stevenson, and personally liked and respected him. So the collaboration with Elizabeth on the book was a welcome and enjoyable one.

Back to Beginnings was a successful book and sold well around the state. Bernice Kelly Harris, the well-known author who was a good friend of Ragan's, and is now In the North Carolina Literary Hall of Fame, wrote to Ragan about the book from her home in Seaboard, North Carolina.

> Congratulations most hearty and sincere on the new book you and Mrs. Ives have written. My interest of course is on your authorship and on the subject. I still call Adlai "President Stevenson" because he will always represent for me the qualities I want most in the President of the United States.

Sam, you don't know how proud I am of you and of your place among outstanding North Carolinians. I like the introduction to your Sunday TV program. It isn't often that I can get your program, as my TV set picks up the Virginia stations. But yesterday you came through clearly and distinctly. I was so glad to see and hear you.

My revisions are taking place slowly. But the zest to get out another book is present. I have written one new story which I personally like. The idea of making fiction out of unvarnished fact does have validity, doesn't it? I still hope for the resultant book we have talked about.

Santford Martin wrote to Ragan also about *Back to Beginnings*.

Attached is a $4.62 check for payment and shipment of your book on Adlai Stevenson. It arrived yesterday. I have already read it, last night, and I must admit to a proud tear when I ran into some of his eloquence once again.

I hope the book is going well. And although you were very kind in sending it with your good wishes, which I value, I do want to pay for it because I do not believe people buy enough books. They squat in front of TV tubes and gape, slack-jawed, but read too few thoughts and think too few thoughts for themselves. So please accept this check for a fine book which I will keep in memory of a great man, but far more important, a good man.

Ragan wrote some wonderful columns in his *Southern Accent* in 1969. Reading his newspaper column is a way to get to know this man. He wrote like he talked to someone, easy and amiable, conversational, and informative.

John Steinbeck won fame as a protest novelist, and the powerful story of the plight of the dispossessed of the depression-ridden 30s placed him in the lead of the proletarian writers of that era. But his fame should not rest solely on *The Grapes of Wrath*. He should be remembered too for his other works of robust, often ribald, humor, and for the many gentle, tender tales of people in the everyday world. Steinbeck, who died a few days ago at the age of 66, was a great writer who will be long remembered by the American public.

In musing upon the career of this California-born writer, I think about *The Grapes of Wrath*, of the Joads and their struggle to survive. But I also think of the tender and moving vignettes in that novel — the turtle crossing the road, the two-for-a-penny candy which a hard-boiled waitress sold to a poverty-stricken farmer for his two children. I think of the simple and moving stories of *The Pastures of Heaven* and *Tortilla Flat*, of the lively humor of *Cannery Row* and *The Wayward Bus*, of the strong and compassionate *Of Mice and Men*, of the patriotism and love of freedom in *The Moon Is Down*, and of dozens of other stories which are his legacy to us.

John Steinbeck wrote 24 books of fiction. Most of them can be brought forth again today and read with pleasure.

❊

The newest literary publication in the state is also one of the most unusual of the three dozen or more "little" literary magazines now being printed in North Carolina. *The Long View Journal* came out just before the Christmas holidays and offers a good variety in its 119 pages of fiction, articles, poems, reviews and graphics.

Most of the contributors were students in the Writers Workshop at N.C. State University. But when the classes came to an end in the spring on the campus they were still too fired up over writing to stop. So they continued meeting once a week in an office on the grounds of Longview, the home of Mr. and Mrs. Calvin Criner and former home of the late Dr. Clarence Poe in Raleigh.

[What Ragan fails to mention here is the teacher of the Writers Workshop was himself. In all of his hundreds and hundreds of *Southern Accent* columns, you will never find where he ever mentions his role in what he is writing about, even though in many instances he played the largest role in what he was referring to.]

No one seems to know how the *Saturday Evening Post* got its name. It never was published on a Saturday. And after the February 8 issue it will never be published at all.

Nearly everyone says it was inevitable that the *Post* would fold. It was losing $3 million a year, and was reported as responsible for the

$60 million loss of the Curtis Publishing Company since 1961. It had a good circulation, but was not getting sufficient advertising to meet operating costs.

In recent years the *Post*, which had its beginning with Benjamin Franklin, had not looked like the *Post* of old. Its new editors had jazzed up the content and format, concentrating on the sensational and expose type feature stories.

That was not enough, and somehow the suspicion exists that it was too much. It may well be that the *Post* could have survived if it had stayed with the good, solid editing which characterized it during the days of George Horace Lorimer, who was editor from 1899 to 1936. Those were the days when there were such contributors as William Faulkner, Rudyard Kipling, Sinclair Lewis, Carl Sandburg, Edna St. Vincent Millay, Dorothy Parker, Stephen Vincent Benet, Scott Fitzgerald, Ring Lardner, James Branch Cabell, Joseph Conrad, Theodore Dreiser, H.G. Wells, and many other luminaries of literature.

The *Post* was conservative in look and often in viewpoint. But its content was unsurpassed, and we are still of the opinion that substance counts more than form.

It may be that the *Post* had lived beyond its time. But we are sorry to see it go.

※

Jonathan Williams writes some of the most outrageous and delightful poetry published today. He is 40 years old and says he is "afflicted with the same Buncombe County Virus" as another Asheville native, Thomas Wolfe. "It's something in the water, demanding that one go everywhere, eat everything, read everything, drink everything."

It's all there in *An Ear in Bartram's Tree*, selected poems from 1957–1967 — poems playful, profound, and perhaps put-on. There is wit and wonder, sensitive observations, and a lot of good lusty humor in Jonathan William's poetry. It's a delight to read.

※

A visit to Bandon Plantation was always a treat. There in that old house and on grounds that looked out over the broad sweep of the river was a charm not often found in our times. Adding to that charm were a gracious host and hostess, John and Inglis Fletcher.

When word came the other day that Inglis Fletcher had died we thought back to our last visit to Bandon near Edenton, only a few months before the old house burned. Inglis Fletcher had shown us her writing room where she turned out a dozen novels about early North Carolina, a state she loved and a state to which she had come from her native Illinois because the Chowan country was the home of her ancestors.

"I believe," she once said, "that North Carolina comes nearer to the original idea of democracy than any other state."

Inglis Fletcher and James Boyd are among the only ones who have tapped the rich lode of material on North Carolina's development in those early years. Her *Raleigh's Eden* was published in 1940, and there followed many more in that vein. She had hoped to solve the mystery of Sir Walter Raleigh's Lost Colony, but she did not live to finish her painstaking research.

Mrs. Fletcher helped found the North Carolina Writers Conference, and was always on hand at the annual summer meetings until her health failed. She was the first North Carolina writer to receive the North Carolina Award in Literature, and she won many prizes for her work. But she would be most pleased, I think, if people continued to read her books and find in them the history and romance of a land and a people she loved.

Inglis Fletcher called me one day from Edenton. She lived outside the town at a plantation she called Bandon. Inglis was interested in *The Lost Colony*, as I was. She said, "We've got to get more people to come see it." Her idea was to get some writers to write some pieces about *The Lost Colony*. She asked me if we could get them published in *The News and Observer*. This was around 1948 to 1950. I said, "Sure, be glad to." She asked me when I would be down there. And I told her that my wife and daughter planned to come down to see *The Lost Colony* and that we'd be staying over in Nags Head for a few days. She said she'd see me then. I went down and we saw the play and I got to my room and there was a note waiting—"Come to my room." Signed "Inglis." So I went by and she told me she wanted to invite some people to come down to see *The Lost Colony*. And that's how the North Carolina Writers Conference got its start—out of that desire to promote Paul Green's most popular symphonic drama.

※

We were present a few nights ago for the 1500th performance of *The Lost Colony*, Paul Green's first symphonic drama and today the longest running play in America.

It was a beautiful setting in Waterside Theater, the very site on which the first English colonists settled in the New World. Beside the milestone in performances, which began in 1937, it was also a special night for two distinguished North Carolinians.

They were Paul Green, the Pulitzer Prize-winning playwright, and Dr. Benjamin Swain, who is now in his 31st season as director of the North Carolina Symphony. Both were being presented the Morrison Award, a beautiful medallion, for having achieved the "highest standard of excellence" in the performing arts in North Carolina.

Rain had been falling in the afternoon and early evening, but miraculously it stopped just before show time, and we were witness to one of the finest performances of *The Lost Colony* we have seen.

I don't know how many times I have seen the drama—at least two dozen times, I'm sure—but each time I am moved by the great poetry and the story of love and courage and sacrifice that unfolds. The play has wonderful movement and music, and a vibrant quality that seems to be forever fresh.

We think every Tar Heel should see it, at least once. It is good to get back to our beginnings and to live again an experience both pertinent to history and to our times.

※

We like to drive through the Carolina country-side, especially on those Scott roads that take you out where the corn rows run down to the edge of the road and one has the feeling of green and growing things. It's the best way to get the feel of the country.

On a recent such jaunt we got to thinking about what makes August a month so different from all the others. Around us the cornfields already were turning brown, and fields were less green than autumnal tan. There was a haze over everything, and not much stirred in the summer heat.

August is a hot month and often dry. Everything seems to slow down in an almost imperceptible walk, even though it remains a harvest time.

The browned fields tell us that this is the dried husk of summer. And we round a curve and see an old man in a cane-bottomed chair leaning against a tree and dozing in the filtered sun.

Then it comes to us. Somnolent is the word for August.

I pause here from *Southern Accent* to include a poem about August that Ragan wrote. It describes the somnolent August he mentions in his newspaper column. Reading *Southern Accent* is like reading poetry.

One Moment on an August Afternoon

The green vine hangs on the hidden wall.
A forgotten flower has come forth
To receive the hummingbird's pause.
The sun's gone past
The hickory tree.
The shadows fall across the yard.
A white cat yawns,
And a bird
Resumes its singing.

❋

It is a fitting thing, I think, for Connemara to be a national historic site. The old house, built in 1838 by Charleston's Christopher G. Memminger, was Carl Sandburg's home the last quarter of his life.

A few days ago the federal government paid Mrs. Sandburg $200,000 for the home and farm. Representative Roy Taylor presented her the check in special ceremonies at the home outside Flat Rock. Mrs. Sandburg is now living in Asheville and the Blue Ridge Parkway people are taking over the administration of the place.

Next year it will be opened as "The Carl Sandburg Historic Site," and more than 100,000 visitors are expected the first year. There will be guided tours and many of Sandburg's works and possessions will remain. There will be some changes in the upstairs room where the poet worked. But last week the cluttered desk remained as it was when he died in 1967, and the old typewriter still stood on an apple crate as he had left it.

The farm was the special province of Mrs. Sandburg and the Parkway people said they plan to maintain a herd of the same prize-winning goats she had kept on the 240-acre farm.

Connemara was a special place. It is good that it is being preserved.

Carl Sandburg came to fame as the poet of the prairies and as the biographer of another prairie man, Abraham Lincoln. Chicago was his town in those early years as newspaper reporter and new-style poet. But it was North Carolina he chose as his home a quarter century ago, and it was here that he continued to work, as a poet, as a novelist and singer of songs.

*

Sherwood Anderson has always been one of our favorite writers. He was clumsy, sometimes shallow, but in his early years his style and story was something to hold the reader. The reader, in fact, became involved. He also became the story-teller, as he groped with Anderson for the words, the meaning.

Anderson set the pace and gave the vision to a whole generation of American writers — such as Ernest Hemingway, William Faulkner and a host of others.

Before he died in 1941 after swallowing a toothpick at a cocktail party aboard ship during a Caribbean cruise, Anderson had spent nine years on his autobiography. His *Memoirs* were published soon thereafter and provided a fascinating look at a man and his times.

We are pleased that the University of North Carolina Press has brought out a new edition of Sherwood Anderson's *Memoirs*. Edited from the original manuscript by Ray Lewis White, former teacher of English at N.C. State University, the book is wonderful reading as well as an invaluable work for the study of the American literary renaissance of 1910–30, and of America itself in the time of its coming of age.

✳

They called him the father of the beat generation, and Jack Kerouac's *On the Road* has been called the Bible of the hippies.

But Jack Kerouac, who died in Florida a few days ago, had long and heatedly repudiated any link with the hippies. He had defined beat as "beatific," and had said, "I'm only a jolly story teller and have nothing to do with politics or schemes, and my only plan is the old Chinese way of the Tao, 'Avoid the authorities.'"

Kerouac wrote *On the Road* while staying with a sister at Whitakers Crossroads in Nash County in 1956. He once promised the manuscript to the University of North Carolina at Chapel Hill, but I don't think he ever showed up to deliver it.

The Massachusetts native thought of himself as the father of "modern spontaneous prose," a sort of stream of consciousness style which appeared in *On the Road*. He had other books. *The Dharma Bums* preached Zen Buddhism, and his last book, *The Vanity of Duluoz*, was more of his autobiography. Published last year, it received mixed reviews.

Kerouac was 47 when he died — older than many people thought him to be — and he was not being discussed as much as he was a few years ago. His generation had gone over the hill, over the 30 mark, and so perhaps had his appeal waned.

He did not write great literature. He was not as good a story-teller as he wanted to be, and he never achieved the status of poet he so long desired. But he was the leader, the father, of a movement that has gone into the language, and he did contribute something fresh and appealing in his books. And for that he will be at least a significant footnote in literary history. And he will be remembered.

✳

Thus far we have failed to make contact with the young generation in at least one area. That is the area of music. We simply have different drummers.

There does seem to be one criterion, however, for judging the new music of the young. The louder it is the better it is.

The amplification of sound by assorted means has made the new music a pollutant of major proportions.

Noise pollution is no laughing matter. Studies show that urban noises contribute to tensions, and it may well be that one of the biggest problems of our urban society is noise.

And though the new music may be a jungle sound, it is probably just a reflection of our tension-ridden urban society.

Manly Wade Wellman wrote to Ragan in 1970. Wellman was born in 1903 and passed away in 1986. By 1951 he came to live in Chapel Hill. By his 80th birthday he had written 80 books. Wellman wrote about most everything, demonstrating his versatility. He wrote adventure novels for young adults, folklore, biographies, history, and developed a genre in writing called speculative fiction. Wellman taught creative writing classes at UNC-Chapel Hill and won the North Carolina Literature Award in 1978. His *Silver John* series of books featured a young hero who battles supernatural forces in the North Carolina mountains. Wellman's best known biographical book, *Giant in Gray*, was about Confederate General Wade Hampton, Wellman's namesake.

Wellman and Ragan were good friends and corresponded often. Wellman thanked Ragan, still Director of the North Carolina Arts Council, for money granted to *Colonnades* magazine. *Colonnades* was and is the literary and art journal of Elon University. *Colonnades* has been published since 1937, and contains poetry, fiction, non-fiction, and art. From Wellman's letter, one can tell *Colonnades* was struggling financially, as many of the literary magazines in North Carolina would, and money sent from the North Carolina Arts Council, which Ragan as Director signed off on, saved many in these times of lack of operational funds. Wellman also mentions Ragan's defense of the song "Dixie" in one of his *Southern Accent* columns.

I feel compelled to write with heartfelt thanks in the name of *Colonnades* at Elon College. Help to the extent you gave will make a huge difference. Just now, the unsinkable Marion Brown, the cookbook lady, you know her, is impelled to do something about raising the rest of what the operation may take. I'm past praying about most things, but if the Bible's right and the prayers of the wicked avail, then I'll say one for the success of this publication and the eager, fumbling kids whose hearts are in it.

Let me say also, cheers for the honesty and courage of your remarks on beautiful Dixie. To be Southern is not to fail to be American. Many sane and fair-minded people are going to realize the value and validity of looking away, looking away, to Dixie.

Ragan's defense of the song "Dixie" was very strong. All his life, he was against almost any kind of censorship. He believed that adults should have the right to decide what they wanted to read, see, and participate in, within reason. This song, of course, was opposed by many people, especially black people, for obvious reasons. Ragan defended the song in *Southern Accent* in October of 1970.

Count us down as a dedicated devotee of "Dixie." We like the song as a song and not for chauvinistic reasons. For many black people the song represents repression and a hated past. White racists have misused the song as well as the Confederate flag, and have used both to flaunt views rather than as exhibits of pride. Hopefully we can continue to hear "Dixie," "Yankee Doodle Dandy," "The Battle Hymn of the Republic," "We Shall Overcome," and all the other songs that have become part of the warf and woof of America, the happy songs as well as those that saw the downcast, the dispirited, the dispossessed through hard times.

This is what America is all about. Let every man have his say, as well as his song.

The North Carolina Arts Council met in March of 1970 at the Quail Roost Conference Center in Rougemont, not far from Durham. In an opening statement, Chairman Sam Ragan said, "We have been very active in supporting the arts, the good things in North Carolina, and yet so much remains to be done. I want to stress the importance of getting closer to the people throughout North Carolina by awakening interests in local communities and by working closer with the public schools."

Staying exceptionally busy, as always, Ragan also continued his Ragan Reports television show for WTVD. One of his guests in 1970 was the head of the University of North Carolina system from 1956 to 1986.

William Friday and Ragan often corresponded and became good friends. In short, Friday wrote, "After seeing our television program yesterday, I felt it was the best appearance I ever made on any TV program and that is directly attributable to your good questions and your easy manner in working with someone. You, more than any other friend in the media, have given the University more opportunities to put its best foot forward; and this program, Sam, was the best yet. Please give Marjorie our warmest regards."

Jonathan Daniels and Ragan, after working together at *The News and Observer* for so many years, stayed in touch. These two men had much respect for each other. Daniels was writing from Hilton Head Island in South Carolina, where he had moved. Daniels had served as Press Secretary to President Harry Truman, and also founded *The Island Packet*, a newspaper in Hilton Head. He wrote many books, such as *The Times Between the Wars: Armistice to Pearl Harbor, A Southerner Discovers the South,* and he did write about the Randolph's of Virginia, which he mentions in the letter to Ragan.

My favorite biographical statement of myself was written by Vermont Royster in a column he wrote on *The Time Between the Wars*. He said, "Mr. Daniels is a journalist by trade, a novelist by dream, an iconoclast by habit and a philosopher in spite of himself."

The new book to be published in September is called *Ordeal of Ambition: Jefferson, Hamilton, and Burr*. My editor at Doubleday thinks it is the best book I've ever done. I think it is pretty good myself. It's about their tragic triangle of enmity. I've been amazed at the amount of new material I have been able to dig up which has been glossed over by historians. The next book is still unsettled. Doubleday wants me to do one on the Randolphs of Virginia.

One thing I hope you will make clear is that while I have been spending much time at my writing hide-away down here my true locus is Raleigh.

Jim Boyd was James Boyd's son, and in 1970 living and working in New York City. But Boyd kept in touch with Ragan, and didn't mind offering his advice on *The Pilot*, his parent's former newspaper that Ragan was now running.

I think your decision to go offset is wise and timely. It will give you much more flexibility. You might even consider going bi-weekly if there is demand and enough advertising to do this. I was impressed with the special 50th anniversary issue. As you know for many years, *The Pilot* got the top award in the state for makeup of the front page. I would like to see, therefore, a little more effort of design of headlines, placing of stories, pictures on the front page. You are handling many more stories but at the present, it is a jumble on the front page.

Sam Ragan loved the newspaper business; he was always proud to be called a newspaperman. He accepted that title proudly. But as with any business, there were always problems popping up. Evidently from the following letter, *The Sanford Daily Herald* was printing *The Pilot*'s paper for a time in 1970. And Ragan thought the number of papers delivered to him one day was short of the number he expected. W.E. Horner, Publisher of the *Daily Herald*, saw it differently. Also, a reader of *The Pilot* was not pleased with the way the newspaper covered a story, as seen in the second letter below.

We are going to plead not guilty to your apparent shortage of papers last week. 4,715 good issues of *The Pilot* left our building. There is no doubt of that. I counted the spoils personally; exactly 234. I set up the press run, personally; 4,715 for you plus 234 spoils, total press run of 4,949. When the press actually stopped the counter showed 4,949. And our counter works properly; we use it on our own runs so it can't be off.

✳

Your lead story on Congressman Earl Ruth's visit to Moore County last week was such a distortion of the original news article that I gave to you and other county papers that I would like to request that you give your readers the benefit of the original article, verbatim, and a copy of your version, in adjacent columns for comparison. Such front page editorializing does neither you nor the newspaper profession much credit.

Richard Walser wrote *Literary North Carolina* in 1970. Ragan commented on Walser and his new book in *Southern Accent*. After reading Ragan's comments, Walser wrote a letter to him.

Over the period of many years, while serving as professor of English at North Carolina State University, Richard Walser has written about and edited the poetry and prose of writers in his native state. He has resurrected many of them from oblivion, made many discoveries of talent, and in his criticism given new meaning to the works of the well-known.

His new work, *Literary North Carolina*, pays tribute to James Boyd and his novels and short stories. "It was James Boyd's *Drums*," writes Walser, "one of the classic works of North Carolina literature, which established new rules for the genre and lifted the historical novel out of its mediocrity. Boyd was a scholar no less than a writer. Before penning even the first sentence of his great story of Eastern North Carolina just prior to and during the Revolution, he read deeply and thoroughly into all the documents and histories of the period." Not only that, but the Southern Pines writer visited the places, walked the old fields and plantations, the cemeteries, to get the feel of the places about which he was to write.

A whole chapter is devoted to Thomas Wolfe, "the greatest writer North Carolina has ever produced," Walser writes.

As far as we can tell, there are no omissions of individuals, the large and the small talents, who contributed to North Carolina literature. All North Carolinians can read *Literary North Carolina* with pride and pleasure, and no student of the state's history and literature can be without it.

※

The most consoling thing in your pleasant words about my *Literary North Carolina* was when you wrote: "As far as we can see, there are no omissions of individuals, the large and the small talents, who contributed to North Carolina literature." In the kind of stuff I do, what I dread most is being accused of leaving out somebody who, by general consensus, should have been included; and I think your opinion expressed above will give me ammunition when the accusations come, as come they will. You relieved my soul with that statement. After all, you're an authority on such a matter.

Thomas Walters was born in Tarboro. He taught in the English Department at North Carolina State University from 1964 to 1983, and also wrote books and poetry. In 1973 Walters was awarded a creative writing fellowship from the National Endowment for the Arts, which he used to write one of his novels, *Always Next August*. He wrote to Ragan in early 1970. Another frequent correspondent was Paul Green, who wrote to Ragan later in 1970, thanking him for publicizing one of Green's books, *Home to My Valley*. The book was about the folklore of the people of the Cape Fear River Valley in North Carolina, which was published in 1970.

I want to thank you for all your help this year. I won't even try to mention all the ways in which you encouraged me, but I appreciate your asking me to read and participate in your creative writing class; I appreciate very much your mentioning me in your annual Christmas season poem; and I have gotten some wonderful response to your television show which you were thoughtful enough to have me in.

Probably you are discomfited by such gratitude, and I would not be so fulsome with it in conversation, but in writing, I can tell you fully what a true, grand gentleman you are. It's downright inspiring, Sam, and I mean that. *Tom*

I've just seen the issue of *The Pilot* with the reprint of the introduction piece to the little book *Home to my Valley*. Man, it's nice. I too along with thousands of North Carolinians keep falling deeper in your debt. Repayment can only come in increased effort. Love to you and Marjorie. *Paul*

Southern Accent continued to pick up readers from all over America, and it was being read in many countries around the world. Following are some topics Ragan wrote about in 1970.

The other day during the course of a talk, the Rev. Martin Caldwell of Southern Pines said the outstanding book of the Sixties, in his opinion, was Dag Hammarskjolds's *Markings*. He said he had read it three times and still finds pleasure and profit in its re-reading. We agree that *Markings* is a monumental book, and it may well stand the test of time more than any other one of the quarter-million volumes published in the Sixties.

My wife Marjorie said that Carl Jung's *Reflections, Memories, and Dreams* stands out for her as the best of the decade. And she added that her candidate for the worst book was John Updike's *Couples*.

I suppose Joseph Heller's *Catch-22* will have to stand as the best novel with the most impact. There were a lot of novels that entertained and impressed—Walker Percy's *The Last Gentleman* for example, but few stand out as truly great.

Some new poets emerged—William Stafford, Heather Ross Miller, William Dickey among them—who will be heard from in the Seventies.

⁕

Scattered Lights is the first book of poems by Christopher Brookhouse, who taught English at the University of North Carolina in Chapel Hill. Brookhouse's poems have a good lean quality about them. He has a good eye for the world around him, and his poetry comes forth free of fog or pettifoggery. The most distinguishing characteristic, I think, is its fine irony.

⁕

We were in Wilson to take part in the latest of the series of Poetry Fairs sponsored by the North Carolina Arts Council across the state. This one was held at Atlantic Christian College and it was a good feeling to return to the old campus, which also has taken on a new look with several handsome new buildings. The poetry readings took place in one of the new buildings, the music building with an auditorium seating over 150. The auditorium was more than filled, with students, faculty members, townspeople and some from other towns, as far away as Fayetteville and Raleigh. Thad Stem took part in the program, as did Juanita Tobin of Pine Level.

From Mae Woods Bell of Rocky Mount we pass along this observation.

> When a censor is mentioned
> My temper is sorely tried—
> I've always resented a character who thinks
> His conscience should be my guide.

⁕

Another book published this past week which also deserves wide reading is Guy Owen's third novel, *Journey for Joedel*. Owen's mythical Cape Fear County bears a strong resemblance to his own Bladen County, but it could also be Columbus, or Robeson, Scotland, Hoke or Moore. His county is mythical but his people and his time and his place are real.

The action in this novel takes place on one day—opening day of the tobacco auction market—and the story is concerned with what takes place within and around Joedel, a 13-year-old half white, half Indian boy, who accompanies his strong-willed, prideful sharecropper, Clint Shaw, to the market to sell their first wagon-load of tobacco. Owens captures well the scene—the very heady smell of it— the excitement, the philosophy, the speech, everything.

The time is the Depression-ridden 30s when the Eastern Carolina tobacco farmers are seeing hope in FDR's New Deal after the hard times of Hoover. In this book, we live with those farmers and we share their hope and despair, their fears, tears and laughter. For there is humor here, too, good lusty humor— and they are people not easily forgotten. They are not stereotypes, not Southern grotesques, they are people, real people.

A strong theme in this excellent book is the love of the land, a dominating early American trait which seems to be disappearing from the scene. At one place in the book, Mr. Jim Eller, the finely drawn landlord, speaks about the transition then beginning in North Carolina.

"It's what's ruining us farmers, to say nothing of the land itself," he says. "Merchants that buy up the land and never live on it, never hold a plow handle in their hands, not even drive a tractor across it once. What do they know about the land, how to treat the earth right so it'll go on treating us right, us that have always lived on it and off it? They buy it and the land suffers, maybe dies. Folks move off it to town, and the land goes back to sedge and briars."

There is a great deal to this book. Guy Owens writes out of his own knowledge, his own heart, and he writes with affection and love. With *Journey for Joedel*, Guy Owen moves into the front rank of novelists.

When Ragan started working at *The News and Observer* in 1941, he used a 1940 Royal typewriter. When he left to take over *The Pilot* in 1969, he paid $5 for it and took the typewriter with him and installed it in his office. He used that old Royal typewriter until he passed away in 1996. It was a manual typewriter. Ragan would never want to use a computer. With that old typewriter, he wrote stories that comforted the afflicted and afflicted the comfortable.

It is a feeling that there is only one typewriter in the world—only one typewriter that understands the writer and the writer understands. I'm reminded of an editor who was a one-typewriter man and who was so devoted to his ancient old L.C. Smith that he wouldn't work without it. The man was Neil Hester, who was Telegraph Editor of *The News and Observer* for nearly 50 years. In all those years, the L.C. Smith (of undetermined but undoubtedly early 20th century date) was his machine. He could make it perform, and with it he could turn out as much work as it takes six or seven people to do today.

One day, however, someone in the front office decided that Neil was entitled to a new typewriter. They felt sorry for him having to contend with that old beat-up machine he had used for so long. So they traded in the old one for a new typewriter. Neil didn't come to work until after 5 in the afternoon and when he did he quickly noticed the change. It was a case of shock. He walked around and muttered and refused to work. Finally he found out where his old machine had gone and he called the typewriter man at his home and made him come down and open up his shop so Neil could get his old machine back. From that time on there was no more talk of getting Neil a new typewriter. When he retired he took it with him—a gift from the newspaper.

We feel the same about our old black beat-up Royal.

Our first typewriter was a Remington portable, which was purchased for $5 from a graduating senior when we were a junior at Atlantic Christian College. It was well worn when we became its owner, and typing on it was difficult, but we did learn our hunt-and-peck system on it. The various newspapers on which we worked the typewriters were always old and difficult.

It was only when we joined the staff of *The News and Observer* in Raleigh in 1941 that we were assigned to a brand new Royal typewriter—a 1940 model—and it's a machine on which we have recorded a lot of North Carolina history. When we left the N&O in 1969 we paid them $5 to take this old Royal with us. It's still on the job with me and I face it with both love and awe almost every day.

When we entered the Army in 1943 we were taught touch typing and we became fairly good at it. However, when we returned to this old Royal we also returned to the old hunt-and-peck system—mostly two fingers and occasionally four.

Sometimes we fling an "o" or an "e" across the room, and other repairs are needed, and those repairs are becoming more and more difficult to find. Sanford is the nearest place now for repairs, and when our old Royal is in the shop we use another Royal substitute. It's not the same, however, and the relationship is not the same.

We often have been asked why we do not use today's darling, the computer, and we tell those who ask that the computer is not for us, and that we are in a long-standing relationship we do not want to abandon. We tell them that our Royal understands us and we understand it—and that's the truth.

Before the year is out it will be back in the shop and we will fall back on the substitute—but we know that this old Royal will be with us at *The Pilot* for many more years to come.

Other writers got attached to their typewriters. Betty Smith, author of *A Tree Grows in Brooklyn*, lost a typewriter she had used for years. In 1952 a portable Smith-Corona of hers was lost while being shipped from Nevada. Smith bought a new typewriter but said that no other typewriter could replace the one she had. She even started writing in longhand for a period of time after this.

April and October were Ragan's two favorite months. He wrote about them often.

April is the awakening, the pulsing of new life, and the flowering of first fruits. October is the time of their dying. But it is not a somber dying but a colorful panorama and wild excitement of a last fling, in which the last fruits are sweeter and the last blooms are more fragrant and of deeper hue.

There is also something about October which calls for contemplation. It is a time of lonely walks in old fields, of measurements of months past, a time of stock-taking, questions which bring forth only muddled answers.

North Carolina's Thomas Wolfe, who would have been 70 years old on October 3, often wrote of the month in his native land. Long ago he wrote of its special quality, saying:

> "Now October has come again which in our land is different from October in other lands. The ripe, the golden month has come again…The chinquapins are falling. Frost sharps the middle music of the season, and all things living on the earth turn home again."

Thomas Wolfe knew that feeling. He had written "You can't go home again," but he knew that at sometime in someplace we all turn home again. And it is in October when that call comes strongest.

❊

In the past we have commented upon the strong feel for the sea which is found in the poetry of Paul Baker Newman, a teacher at Queen's College in Charlotte. Now again in his third volume of poetry *The Ladders of Love* we see his widening range as a poet. There is a good lean economy in his language and many strikingly good lines of perception.

❊

John Moses Pipkin is a professor of religion at Guilford College and president of the North Carolina Poetry Society. He is a poet of considerable accomplishment and we have been reading his first collection of poems, *Half-A-Love*, with delight and appreciation.

Mr. Pipkin has the facility to get to what I consider the heart of poetry, the distilled essence of an emotion, a feeling, an experience. His language, though sparse, is filled with warmth and humanity, and his statement is clear and concise. He makes use of rhyme as well as free verse, letting each poem, as it should be, call for its own telling.

The above critique of Pipkin's poetry is a good example of Ragan's ability to read and be a critic of poetry written by others. He once gave an explanation of what he thought were some good guidelines to use when writing poetry.

A poem comes from the imagination, is a feeling that keeps nagging you, forms an idea and becomes something more. It's taking the old truths and putting them in a new light. Be honest, be able to say "this is what I really see, this is what I really feel, not someone else." Read everything; it's all there somewhere. Rewrite, go back and tighten it up, ask if there is a better way to say it, and try to use active verbs. I like active verbs. Be honest in the expression of yourself, which means you must know yourself. Poems are written a long time before it's committed to paper. All writing, whether a newspaper article, a short story or a lawyer's brief, is essentially reporting. A poem is a report on a feeling of an emotion. When it comes down to it, all writers are just tellers of tales. There is nothing mystical about poetry. I don't know why people are scared of it. The writer and the reader only have to bring their imaginations to it in order to appreciate it. It doesn't matter what it meant to the poet, it's how the reader interprets it that counts.

Regarding his use of words in a spare way, he once remarked, "I respect words too much to waste them."

Ragan could be very critical if he thought it was warranted. Of a Norman Mailer book he wrote this. "One has to work at reading Mailer on Mailer. His over-blown ego keeps rising as a wall between the reader and the book, and we become convinced that this giant superiority complex is simply a cover for a tremendous sense of insecurity and inadequacy."

Ragan also wrote a few poems about writing poetry.

A Poet Is Somebody Who Feels

A poet, said e.e. cummings, is somebody who feels,
And expresses his feelings through words.
Something that cannot be taught like thinking can,
Something that makes you nobody but yourself.
Feeling and finding words.
For April mornings and winter nights,

Birds against the sky on October afternoons,
Old fields and lonely streets,
Or sunlit days
When a girl walks by,
And the heart is crying
For things that have no names.
Feeling…

Nobody…
Nobody but yourself.

On Writing a Poem

I am caught in this spilling of words,
In this gathering of words
Spun out like fog in the valley,
And the driving of nails,
Hammered in and pounded down,
Nails driven through fog,
Hammering down the fog.

Go ahead and put it down,
Put down the words,
Shape them into evenings, nights, mornings,
Catch the calls that come out of darkness,
Out of sunlights, out of memorized things
That were not to be remembered,
Out of vastness, out of smallness,
The small things we clutch and hold,
Out of questions which become rhetorical answers.
We begin with the word,
We hold, we see, we hear, we feel.
These are the fragments,
We put them together and fasten them down
With the strong glue of words.

Poems are not to be dissected
Like frogs or earthworms
Or the way people are
When they are dead.

Put the scalpel to it
And it comes apart like the fog
In the mid-morning sun.

In "On Writing A Poem," Ragan states that "poetry comes from fragments of living," as he once said, that our experiences in life form our
poetry. "We hold, we see, we hear, we feel. These are the fragments." Zoe
Kincaid Brockman, who was born in Gastonia and wrote poetry, including
two books, *Heart on My Sleeve* and *Unguarded Moments,* agreed with Ragan
about living shaping poetry. "I suppose you might call it inspiration which
the poet waits for, but beauty, and sorrow, and life itself are always about
us. This I know: you can't decide you're going to write a poem and then sit
down and do it. The poem has to take you by the hand—you don't take it."

"Poems are not to be dissected like frogs or earthworms or the way
people are when they are dead. Put the scalpel to it and it comes apart like
the fog in the mid-morning sun," Ragan writes in "On Writing A Poem."
He was not one to constantly go back to his words of poetry and "take
a scalpel to it," or revise endlessly. He let the idea of a poem stay with
him for some time, adding lines and words as he lived life, working at the
newspaper, being with his family, lying in bed at night. He might jot down
lines and phrases and stick them in a drawer of his messy desk at *The Pilot,*
or in a drawer in his bedside table. By the time he decided to write a new
poem, his life experiences and having turned the poem over in his mind
many times enabled him to write much of the poem. He certainly would
read and re-read, make additions and subtractions, but usually not on a
mass scale. Zoe Kincaid Brockman, once again, agreed with Ragan. She
once said, "A poem simply can't be labored; it can't be manhandled, else it
shows; it's easy to know when the thing has been worked over until all the
lilt and the shine are gone."

Ruth Moose, a novelist and poet, and a winner of the Sam Ragan Fine
Arts Award, which is presented annually for outstanding contributions to
the Fine Arts of North Carolina over an extended period. Moose once said
this about Ragan's poem, "On Writing A Poem": "I keep his poem Scotch-
taped next to my computer. I read it whenever I get stuck."

Another poem by Ragan, "The Writer," covered earlier in this book,
gives good advice about writing, especially when a writer is struggling for
words, such as Moose mentions.

Like "On Writing a Poem," another Ragan poem, "Where Does a Poem Come From?" gives similar advice. Ragan would sometimes use these poems when teaching his writing classes.

Where Does a Poem Come From?

Where does a poem come from?
No one knows.
Bits and pieces are lodged within
From days, months, years, lifetimes,
And then something nudges them
Into the sunlight.
You suggest and imply,
Something happens.
A poem is written a long time
Before it goes down on paper.

Sally Hall, a teacher at Broughton High School in Raleigh, wrote a letter to Ragan in March of 1971. She sent a poem by one of her students for hopeful inclusion in *Southern Accent* and told him that she quoted him regularly in her classes. Sally had taken Ragan's Writer's Workshop at North Carolina State University and told him that she had enjoyed it so much, and found it very helpful, that she planned to take it again the next year.

Ragan received poems by hundreds of aspiring poets from around North Carolina each year, hoping that perhaps he would choose one of their poems for publication in *Southern Accent*. Or if not publication, they relished words of critique from him. Worded in a different way, these readers and fans of *Southern Accent* must have felt a little like Emily Dickinson in a note to Thomas Wentworth Higginson, when she wrote, "Are you too deeply occupied to say if my Verse is alive?"

The Pilot won first place in the state for Ragan's *Southern Accent* for newspaper columns from the North Carolina Press Association. *The Pilot* also was awarded third place for news coverage and third place for editorials, which also were written by Ragan. Subscriptions to *The Pilot* were increasing. Ragan believed in readers having their say, evidenced by some issues devoting an entire page to letter to the editor. When Christmas came, Ragan included a page of Christmas messages, such as his annual Christmas poem, Bible verses and stories, excerpts from books about the Christmas season, Santa Claus stories, and anything else related to Christmas. One entire page, and sometimes two or three, were devoted to literature, and you can bet it was mostly North Carolina literature, just as most of his *Southern Accent* columns were. *The Pilot* was a well-respected newspaper, had been since the days of Jim and Katharine Boyd, and that continued under Sam Ragan. That fine tradition went on after the Daniels family bought it in 1996, and it is the same today under the leadership of David Woronoff.

Speaking engagements kept Ragan on the road quite a bit around North Carolina. Ragan, along with Ron Bayes, Lew Barton, and Charles Joiner led a panel discussion on "North Carolina Literature: Then and Now" at Pembroke State University.

Continuing as Chairman of the North Carolina Arts Council, Ragan made decisions that aided and even sustained arts and literature organizations all over the state. It certainly is no exaggeration to write that without grants from the Arts Council while Ragan was Chairman, many of these organizations would not have survived, and very well might not be with us today. The letter that follows from John Haber and J.E. Dietz of Carolina Repertory Company in May of 1971 is just one of many examples.

> We just wanted to write you a brief note to thank you for your support. The $5000 will be a real boost, and will help us cover some of our expenses. We feel very deeply that professional theatre, if it lives up to all the standards that the word "professional" implies, is needed and can be sustained in North Carolina. You trusted that instinct enough to give us a good start. We hope we live up to your trust.

The North Carolina Arts Council, under Ragan's leadership, partnered with the Department of Public Instruction in 1971 to start Poetry in the Schools. Under the program, a well-known North Carolina poet would go into a school as a poet-in-resident for one week. The poet would talk to the students about poetry and encourage them to write poetry themselves. It started with 30 schools and expanded to 68 by 1972. This program proved to be a big success.

With all of his immense responsibilities, Ragan cared for nothing more than to be with his family, his dear wife, Marjorie, and his beloved daughters, Nancy and Talmadge. They were the reason he worked so hard. But by 1971, Nancy and Talmadge were out of the house in Southern Pines, making a living for themselves, going to school, and becoming women that made their parents proud. Talmadge wrote her father a letter from New York City, giving an update on her recent activities and plans.

> Just a short note before my rehearsal. Joe Layton came Sunday and we're doing a run-through for him tonight. I tried out and got a good understudy part—one of the principals. It's Joyce Archard, who is a friend of Eleanor Dare's.
>
> Terry came Monday, and those six months finished our relationship. I'm pretty upset about it, although I kind of expected it. I just didn't want to admit it. I hope time will either bring us together, or wear out my hurt.
>
> I've decided what to do next Fall. I think I'll go to school first semester, then see if I can teach modern dance at Chatham during their winter quarter.
>
> Will you get new pads on my flute please? Troutwein wants me to accompany the choir with some number. Must go. Got back lesson 4, got an A-. I'm trying to keep busy, so I won't cry. Love.

The "Terry" mentioned above is Terry Mann, who has had prominent roles on the Broadway stage for the past three decades, in such plays as *Cats, Les Miserables,* and *Beauty and the Beast.* He was nominated for a Tony Award for Best Actor in a Leading Role in 1987 in *Les Miserables* and received a second Tony nomination for Actor in a Musical in 1994 in *Beauty and the Beast.* Mann also starred in the television soap opera *All My Children.* Talmadge and Terry met while both were acting in *The Lost Colony* in North Carolina.

It is hard to imagine much leisure time Ragan would have, considering his many responsibilities. But there were activities he participated in that led to real enjoyment and relaxation. He enjoyed listening to music and would sing songs with his family. He once talked about that. "I like all kinds of music. I am very fond of jazz, and I like the old blues. I know them way back. I like classical music."

Sitting on his back porch at his home on Hill Road in Southern Pines, perhaps chatting with Marjorie, Nancy, Talmadge, or his grandkids, Robin and Eric, always gave him joy. Or just sitting alone, listening to bird song, watching the wind blow the branches of trees was a way to relax and think. He also enjoyed strolling around the yard. On Saturday afternoons he enjoyed sitting in his rocking chair and watching college football. According to Robin, his granddaughter, this was "his time. He would stare at the television like it was transporting him to another place. It was during these games that his ability to hear became very selective. I remember the dramatics displayed by both my grandparents when Marjorie decided this was the time that her question was of the utmost importance." This is similar to something else Marjorie observed about her husband. She often commented that she knew Sam was working when he was sitting for hours up in his study looking out the window.

"Rockford Files" was also a favorite television show of Ragan's. And along with college football, Washington Redskins football on Sunday afternoons was a regular habit, and Ragan also enjoyed some ACC basketball games.

Another thing that Ragan enjoyed, in fact, really enjoyed, was watching the Miss America Pageant. He had been a judge for the Miss North Carolina Pageant a couple of times. Ragan earned the title of "Southern gentleman" on merit, as he was always very respectful to women, and treated them with utmost deference. And women found this tall, handsome man, always dressed well, attractive also. Betty Hodges, who wrote a column called "Book Nook" for the *Durham Morning Herald*, once described his dress this way, "resplendent in a striped suit, cut with the new wide lapels, textured shirt, and a flamboyant new bow tie." Robin said of this mutual admiration of women by Ragan and women's admiration of him, "My grandfather always appreciated women, and they most definitely appreciated him appreciating them. Always the consummate Southern gentleman, Sam's admiration was never overt and always respectful."

One characteristic Ragan possessed in abundance was optimism. He wanted to see the goodness in every person, knew they had it in them. He could, and did, deal with tough issues forcefully and promptly, but he liked to dwell on the positive.

Sally Buckner, a former student of Ragan's writing class at North Carolina State University, wrote about Ragan's optimism in a poem.

Word Man

Straight back, straight talk:
The language of the people,
A red carnation in its lapel,
     wresting truth from packaged lies,
     sculpting remarkable form
     from unremarkable moments.

You listen to a plan,
     a heartening bit of news,
     an evocative phrase from a new poem—
and your spoken Splendid! Swings in the air
like cherry blossoms at Weymouth,
casting rosy glow upon the morning.

And no matter
How bleak the releases quivering through the wires,
     how tangled the connivings,
     how thunderous the horizons,
you turn to the plum blossoms,
     the ovens of October,
     the apple man,
     the hands that ask questions, then give answers—
and you say, with a smile as wide as the brim of your hat,
as generous as your snappy tie,
what we have seen through knowing you:
the News is basically good.

Reading was always a favorite way for Ragan to relax. Books were everywhere, at home and in his office at *The Pilot*. He read several newspapers a day, and up to a dozen or more different papers weekly. This was enjoyable to him, but it also was necessary, he reasoned, to keep up with his competitors. Exercise was never a priority for Ragan, but of course, he worked long hours and he must have felt hard work was his exercise.

He also was fond of driving through the countryside of North Carolina, passing through small towns. Many of these drives ended up in *Southern Accent,* commenting on what he saw, such as a field ready for harvest, a farmer plowing tobacco, children at play, a vegetable stand along a remote country road, wildflowers close to a pond, neighbors sitting on an old bench in front of a rural store, or an older couple rocking on their front porch and waving a friendly hand. Not only did some of these scenes end up in *Southern Accent,* but they were the seeds of new poems.

"Feeling is what prompts a poem," Ragan once said. "I keep a notepad in my car and at home. Sometimes I'll jot down just a word or phrase to preserve the feeling. It may be years before I'll try to write the poem."

Ragan loved to take Talmadge to the local Kentucky Fried Chicken, whether it was for his taste buds or to make his daughter happy is debatable. One food that left no debate was his love of Southern barbecue. His favorite family dinner out was in Aberdeen at Jimmy's Barbecue. Usually Ragan's main course of barbecue would be served with green beans, cole slaw, and hushpuppies. Another favorite was the Howard Johnson Restaurant, and for special occasions, the Ragan family would go to Mid Pines Country Club in Southern Pines. Another food that Ragan really liked was pinto beans. To supplement this diet, he constantly smoked his beloved Camel cigarettes.

During the Christmas season, the Ragans would fill the car and drive around the neighborhood and look at the beautifully decorated homes. And before they went home, a stop would be made at the drive thru Dairy Queen for some ice cream. Ragan loved ice cream, and his favorites were rum raisin and butter pecan.

Talmadge Ragan remembers how much her father loved ice cream. "When we were living in Raleigh, every night about 11 o'clock, Mama, Daddy, and I would get in the car and drive downtown to get the first edition of the next day's *News and Observer.* We'd get the paper usually from a man on the street, or at the bus station, and then we'd stop at a local drive-in: Finches or Krispy Kreme, the Dairy Queen or Shoney's, get some ice cream, and head home. My father then would look over the paper and call in corrections every night."

Ragan loved ice cream so much he wrote a poem called "Ice Cream." He remembered what his father, William Ragan, obviously an ice cream lover too, had once said.

Eating ice cream, my father said,
Is like lying down
And letting the moon
Shine in your mouth.

One thing that did not take much of Ragan's time was attending church. He always called himself a Presbyterian, and I do think he was religious in his own way. But regular church attendance just was not part of his routine. More so than church attendance, Ragan's relationships with people and nature was a huge part of his religion, or spirituality might be a better way to put it. Ragan, I feel, found in nature not only great beauty and peace but felt it was a way to find meanings in life. One could certainly find religious aspects in his poetry, as many of his subjects were searching for purposes of life. Much more so than attending church, Ragan lived his life helping others, being kind to people, loving and cherishing his family, appreciating the wonders of nature, and devoting long hours to his work.

Work occupied a big part of Ragan's life, as in the past and as it would for many years to come. He enjoyed being a newspaperman, and writing his *Southern Accent* column, now in its 23rd year. He touched on many subjects in *Southern Accent* in 1971.

It was during the 1956 Democratic National Convention and Jonathan Daniels called to give me his daily report and observations on what was going on. "Everybody is talking about David Brinkley out here," he said.

I wasn't surprised. The Brinkley wit I had first observed in Wilmington in 1939 had simply found a national audience. David Brinkley has remained himself. He showed while still a high school student that he was a "natural" newsman, and he has remained a newsman. After 27 years as a reporter for NBC, years in which he has reached the peak of his profession, Brinkley retains the natural curiosity and keen observation that marked his beginnings in the profession. Over the years he has become knowledgeable and an erudite commentator on national and world affairs, but he insists on remaining the reporter.

They're still talking about Brinkley in Wilmington, and everywhere else in the United States. And well they may, for he continues to show that wit and grace both as a person and as a reporter.

✳

We have been reading Norman Mailer's *Of a Fire on the Moon* and find it irritating in the extreme but in some spots exciting and provocative.

Still, we know that Mailer can write, and he could possibly become a good reporter if he did not continually intrude in the telling of his story.

Someone does need to write about America's adventure into space, and Mailer does raise some interesting questions about the trip to the moon. Some of the questions get to the hard core of why, and of values, and whether those values are misplaced. But we come away without answers, and the feeling that Mailer, once questions have been asked, did not care to stay for an answer.

The story of the Apollo moon shot was an assigned story, but near the end of the book Mailer himself wonders if "he might have blundered in accepting the hardest story of them all."

We think he did.

✳

A social critic or satirist treads on delicate ground. To be successful his arrows must hit true and his barbs must be sharp. But if he is malicious in what he says he is doomed.

This, I think, is why Ogden Nash was successful. He hit the mark and his acute observations were stinging but not fatal. There was no malice in his genius for satire.

The master of light verse died the other day after a long illness. Since 1931 he had devoted all of his time to writing and he had nearly two dozen books to his credit, and there are few Americans who do not have at least one of them around for occasional reading. Nearly everybody has a favorite line or two.

The delightful verses of Ogden Nash over the years have often dealt with the ludicrous aspects of human frailty, but he always wished his subjects well.

We recall a long conversation with the poet on a visit to the State a few years ago. He was very proud of his Tar Heel ancestry, of beginnings in Edgecombe County, and he called the names of many kinsman about the state. And we remember the story of a visit with some of them, Mr. and Mrs. Kenneth Sprunt, at Orton Plantation near Wilmington. On leaving, Mr. Nash was asked to write something in the guest book, and this is what he wrote:

> Ogden Nash.
> Social failure.
> Says ca-mee-lia.
> Not ca-may-lia.

Ogden Nash had many imitators, but none could match his unique talent, and even though he is gone his books will be around a long time, helping a lot of people around the rough edges by pointing up some of the ludicrous aspects of human frailty.

✻

Diane Wakoski has a way with words, and once wrote a poem that speaks to why poets write poems.

> Forgive me then,
> if the poems I write
> are about the fragments,
> the broken bridges,
> and unlit fences
> in my life.
> For the poet
> the poem
> is not
> the measure
> of all he's lost, or
> never seen,
> or what has no life,
> unless he gives it life
> with words.

John Ehle passed away in 2018 at the age of 92. Ehle was born in Asheville, and married the British actress Rosemary Harris, who has won Tony, Emmy and Golden Globe Awards. They lived in Winston-Salem. Ehle is best known for his Appalachian novels, such as *The Land Breakers* and *Last One Home*. Those novels were partly inspired by stories he heard from his mother's family, whose roots in the mountains went back several generations. Ehle is also one of the founders of what is now the University of North Carolina School of the Arts. Ragan wrote about Ehle in *Southern Accent* many times, but this one is from 1971.

Most writers will have at least one favorite writer, one who influenced them to some degree. Ernest Hemingway liked Rudyard Kipling, John O'Hara admired F. Scott Fitzgerald and Thomas Wolfe liked to read Ecclesiastes from the Bible to get the writing juices flowing.

John Ehle says that there is no one writer who has influenced him or that he admires more than another. But Paul Green, as a man, has influenced him more than any other. He admires the work of Green. He does talk over his own writing with Green, and has received a great deal of encouragement from him.

Ehle also says when he is writing he sets himself the task of turning out twenty pages a day. He rewrites his novels five or six times, and figures it takes him from nine months to three years to complete a book.

Ehle and his wife Rosemary live in a huge castle-like house surrounded by six acres of land in the heart of Winston-Salem. There are a lot of fine antique furnishings in the house, as well as some beautiful paintings, but the first thing that catches the eye when entering the front door is a gleaming copper liquor still. Ehle says he knows about liquor making, but all he plans to do is keep the still for ornamental purposes. "It's a work of art," he says.

To The Water's Edge, Ragan's second book of poetry, was published in 1971. Good reviews flowed in. Zoe Brockman wrote, "A shining web of words, each one is perfect, each one is complete, all are executed without a single superfluous word or phrase." Franklin Cooley of the *Richmond*

Times-Dispatch wrote, "Lyrics, personal and topical, they evoke scenes and fragile moods with a great deal of charm." Ronald Bayes wrote, "Ragan creates great beauty for the ear and eye in the lines of his verses. He is as earthy as Sandburg when it suits his purpose, and as insightful as Frost with a Southern Accent." Heather Ross Miller wrote, "In this age of strident hysteria, his poems are quiet. He asks us to pay attention to stones and gulls, violets, dogs, the eyes of owls. He asks us to slow down. And he makes us see those real things, precious and unpredictable, that slip through our fingers every day." Thad Stem added his praise, "While this book is a living record of the outer and inner passions, chills, and fevers of a sensitive man's total existence, the reader makes the same journey the poet makes." Betty Hodges had this to say, "A collection marked by emotion, by feeling, however, that emotion is always under control. Sam Ragan is a poet to make people who don't read poetry read poetry." Jonathan Yardley wrote, "He captures, accurately and affectingly, the particular mood of this state and its people."

One of the poems in *To the Water's Edge* was "Markings," with a nod to Robert Frost.

Markings

These are the markings that I make
The trees now gold that will be green again,
The stone that brings the horse to halt when
Plowing furrows which must be begun again,
The slope of land to where the willows grow
Along a stream that flows to woods
Where birds now fly.
I make the markings with my eye.
For I have not traveled this road before,
And the markings I make are to remember it by.

"A Walk on the Beach," a poem in *To the Water's Edge,* gives the book its title, but also gives the reader vivid images to ponder. The speaker of the poem walks with the birds along with the movement of the waves.

A Walk on the Beach

On the beach
The birds go walking—
Ahead of me in my walking.
With each wave a feeding,
A movement to the water's edge,
And then away,
Always away, always returning,
Even as I return
To the water's edge.
But I reach the point of turning back
　　The birds go on.

To the Water's Edge was named the winner of the Oscar Arnold Young Memorial for the best book of poetry published in the state. The award was presented to Ragan at the North Carolina Poetry Day program in Asheville. In his acceptance speech, Ragan likened his philosophy of poetry to Camus. "The aim of poetry and the arts is to provide a privileged image of our common joys and woes. Poetry is the distilled essence of a feeling, an experience, and a poet, if successful, can say in twenty lines what it takes a novelist 100,000 words to say.

To the Water's Edge was published by Moore Publishing Company. Moore Publishing printed 2,000 books and they sold out, and another 2,000 were printed. Ragan was very pleased with the reception to *To the Water's Edge.*

In an address to the 1972 graduating class at North Carolina Wesleyan College, Ragan encouraged the students to take advantage of opportunities in a changing society and to make decisions based on their conscience. And as always, he urged the students to enjoy arts to improve their lives.

The arts are not just for an exclusive elite, any more than economic opportunity is for an exclusive few. We must make better economic opportunity available for the disadvantaged and dispossessed. But we also must add to the quality of their lives by bringing to them that extra dimension which the arts provide. In this way our people will be able to not only make a living, but their living will be made more worthwhile. In speaking of transition, of change, we should be grateful that in a free society we do have a choice. But if that choice is not open to all, then it is diminished for all. The individual needs the freedom to choose, to choose alternatives, to take a different road. I hope that you graduates will not hesitate to take the road less traveled by, that in the making of choices you will follow the dictates of conscience and principles rather than always follow the dictates of the popular.

9

Secretary, "My Old Mule Is Dead," Weymouth, Jonathan, Thad, Paul, Bernice, Guy, "I watch this field of yellow daisies"

A great honor was bestowed on Sam Ragan in 1972, as Governor Bob Scott appointed him as the very first Secretary of the Department of Art, Culture, and History, what is now the Department of Natural and Cultural Resources. Even though Ragan had been appointed Chairman of the North Carolina Arts Council in 1967 by Governor Dan Moore, Bob Scott had been governor since 1969, so Ragan had worked with Governor Scott since then as Arts Council Chairman. The two men were very close in their politics and in their visions for the state, along with developing a close personal relationship. Ragan outlined his goals in his new position in his acceptance speech.

> The measure of man and his civilization is by his arts and his view of history, and the culture that goes to make up a people, and indeed I think that the measure of a people and its state is in how it treats its arts, its culture and history. So I would like to see a renaissance burgeoning forth in the arts in North Carolina, to see us open new vistas for our people, to bring new horizons into their lives. I have been told that North Carolina is the only state that has such a department as this now. And that does give me a sense of pride and also a little feeling of ominous fear of what we have to live up to.

Arts and culture are measured by the light of wonder that comes into the face of children hearing the North Carolina Symphony for the first time, in the quiet glow of satisfaction which comes to the man or woman feeling a piece of pottery they have made or seeing a picture they have painted.

There are tangible things we can point to, the powerful and moving drama of *The Lost Colony,* for instance, the exciting summer drama program at East Carolina University, the magnificent historic restoration of Tryon Palace. But I'd like to find a permanent home for the North Carolina Symphony. It needs an adequate office and rehearsal space. Now its office is in a trailer in Chapel Hill, and it rehearses in an auditorium in Durham. I'd like to expand the symphony's programs so each year it appears within 25 or 30 miles of every citizen, so everyone will have a chance to see it. As a long-range plan, I'd like to see and work for a number of counties going together to form regional arts councils, to promote arts and history within the region. I would like to expand the archives and history department's work with local historical societies in the state to write about and emphasize the local points of historical interest.

It is my firm belief that what the state is, what it hopes to become, the measure of its strength, its character, is shown in its arts and how it regards its history. The meaning of life is how well we cultivate those things which are the essence of our hopes and aspirations. And no matter how we thrill to the achievements in outer space, it is still the inner space, the soul of man, which is more important.

There were many branches of government under Ragan's Department of Art, Culture, and History, and he did an outstanding job of coordinating these agencies. There was the N.C. Arts Council, the N.C. Art Society, the N.C. Museum of Art, the N.C. Symphony, the Office of Archives and History, and the Office of the State Library, among others.

Bob Scott, later in life, remembered the job that Ragan had done as Secretary of Art, Culture, and History.

Sam came to Raleigh to become a member of the cabinet. It was his job to preside over the shotgun marriage of many departments, boards, and commissions that were brought into the newly created

Department of Art, Culture, and History. It was, I honestly believe, the only major appointment I made during my eight years in state government that met with universal approval. At cabinet meetings, sitting at the huge, oblong table, and surrounded by his colleagues, Sam was like a rose in a briar patch. Sam has that remarkable quality of exhibiting grace under pressure, and he needed every bit of it to mold and build the new department. And a fine job he did, as the record shows. Sam was not new to state government, having served previously as chairman of the North Carolina Arts Council, and, of course, for years having scrutinized the comings and goings of assorted governors and legislators from the hallowed halls of *The News and Observer*.

Another great honor was awarded Ragan in 1972 when his alma mater, Atlantic Christian College, conferred upon him the Honorary Degree, Doctor of Literature, during commencement exercises on May 26. Ragan had graduated from Atlantic Christian in 1936, 36 years before. Since that time, he had done as much, if not more, than any single person in the North Carolina to promote literature and the arts. This was one of the most satisfying awards Ragan once said that ever came his way, from his beloved former college that had meant so much to him, and that had played such a huge role in shaping him into the good man he had become.

Many events kept Ragan busy throughout 1972, such as moderating a discussion on the topic of "Sexual Freedom and the Novel" by Reynolds Price at the University of North Carolina at Charlotte. As usual, many people wrote to Ragan asking for his help with their writings and poetry, and as always, he patiently tried to help them as best he could. To Joan Warlick of Raleigh, he wrote, "These are very good poems and I particularly like 'The Mad Dogs' and 'The Birds Know First.' I am keeping the latter for use in my column at some early date. I think you are right to submit these to some of the North Carolina magazines and, in addition, the *St. Andrews Review*. You should keep in mind entering the contest sponsored by *Crucible* at Atlantic Christian College." To Ellen Johnston of Mooresville, he replied, "I enjoyed reading your poems very much. I think you have something new and fresh to say, and I see no reason why you could not get a good book out of this collection. It is very difficult to get poetry collections published by the regular royalty-paying houses, but I suggest that you send this manuscript to John P. Blair, Winston-Salem, for his consideration. Of course, you could publish it yourself and take on the task of distribution, and I think that the NCAE would be of help to you. At any rate, I would be very interested in how things develop."

Many topics were covered in *Southern Accent* during 1972. One technique Ragan used to get readers to keep reading was the way he grabbed a person with his first sentence. Who would not want to read further after reading the opening sentence in the following column about the famed writer, Betty Smith, author of *A Tree Grows in Brooklyn*?

We walked home with Betty Smith from a football game one afternoon and sat talking until late that night about books and the writing of books. She had to show us clippings of reviews of her novels, the good reviews and the bad ones, and she talked about the novel she wanted to write about Chapel Hill.

She never did get around to finishing that novel, but Chapel Hill was in all of those things she wrote after *A Tree Grows in Brooklyn*, that marvelous book about her early life, a book both tender and tough, with many poignant moments. It is easy to understand why it became one of America's all-time best sellers.

We appeared on programs together on several occasions, and once we had a long visit in the hospital at Louisburg where she was recuperating from a broken leg suffered in an automobile accident near there.

Betty Smith was a more complex person than most people realized. She was well aware of her weaknesses as well as her strengths, and she could talk quite candidly of both.

Her first husband had been a young law student from Brooklyn and they had lived in Ann Arbor where he was in school. *Joy in the Morning* came out of that experience. Her second husband was Joe Jones of Chapel Hill and they met after she was moved by his stories in *The Chapel Hill Weekly*, stories he wrote from Camp Lee, Va., where he was stationed during World War II. Those stories became a book, *Class B Soldier*. Betty went up to see him at Camp Lee and not long afterwards they were married. Because she was divorced her church excommunicated her, and she saw some irony in the fact that she was back again in the church's good graces after her third husband, Bob Finch, died suddenly of a heart attack.

Betty had come to Chapel Hill in the late 1930s. She had been traveling with a WPA theater group, which folded in Raleigh. She had heard of Paul Green and spent her last money on a bus ticket to go see him in Chapel Hill. Out of that visit came her long stay there. Once, she said, things were going so badly she decided to leave and go back to New York. In fact, she was already on the bus and it was getting ready to leave. But she couldn't go. She got off and stayed, and finished work on her novel, and when *A Tree in Brooklyn* became such an instant success she never had to worry about money again.

She had a special feeling for Chapel Hill and the "Old Mangum Place" which she bought and restored. Even in her last years she loved to work with her flowers in the yard of that handsome old house.

We read about Betty Smith's death in a Connecticut rest home last week, and we thought about some of these things and other times when we had talked and of letters she had written. And we went back and read some passages from that first book and were moved again by them.

We will long remember those things she had written — and Betty Smith too.

＊

Yevgeny Yevtushenko knows how to milk a cow. With a little grin, he demonstrated his two-handed technique at the Governor's Mansion one night last week. He grew up on a farm in Siberia.

The world's most famous living poet was visiting and had a delightful dinner and the Russian poet enjoyed it immensely. Yevtushenko had read to more than 6,000 persons in Carmichael Gym at Chapel Hill the night before, and he had been delighted with the response.

He told me he had once read to 60,000 people in Moscow Stadium. I told him, "Well you got me beat. The largest crowd I've had was 600 in an outdoor theatre in Chapel Hill, counting the dogs and the dogs kept running back and forth across the stage in front of me and one of them was in heat. What they were doing was far more interesting than what I was reading."

At the Governor's mansion, the poet who is known for his explosive expressions at times, sat relaxed and talked about American poets.

He likes Whitman, but sometimes his poetry is a "monotone."

He admires the poetry of Robert Frost very much, and he wanted to know more about William Stafford. He likes some of the things by Allen Ginsburg, but he finds Ferlinghetti "a bit coarse."

Yevtushenko told us that he wrote his first poem when he was seven. There have been thousands since, and when the dinner was over he presented an autographed copy of his latest book, *Stolen Apples*, to Mrs. Bob Scott.

Yevtushenko knows a great deal about America, and despite his occasional Russian sloganeering, it is obvious in his poetry and his talk that he feels a rapport with this country. There is something of Whitman in his poetry, he celebrates himself, his country, the world. In one of his poems, he says:

"I love immeasurably this whole earth."

We thoroughly enjoyed the dinner and talk with Yevtushenko, and found him responsive on just about every subject. When he left he said, "I would like to come back."

✳

Ovid Pierce likes to lean back against a pecan tree in the back yard of his Halifax County farm house with a ruled pad of paper in his lap and write his novels.

It's a good place for writing and it's a good place for a special view of what's going on around him.

It is the things he had seen from that vantage point, the things he had heard, the things he has felt that are going into his new novel.

Pierce says this about being on his farm. "The country means a lot to me. I'm happy to refresh contact with the world. It enables me to increase my own sense of awareness. The exposure to the open world is important to me as a writer."

He is about half-way through it now, but expects to finish it up this summer and send it on off to Doubleday for publication. It could be his best novel to date, and that's saying a great deal, because those books by Ovid Pierce — *The Plantation, On a Lonesome Porch, The Devil's Half* — rank with the best of Southern fiction.

This new novel by Ovid Pierce, who spends most of his time as writer-in-residence and teacher at East Carolina University, deals with a very important contemporary theme, the movement of farm families from the rural South to the big cities of the North.

Ovid Pierce is attempting to tell that story, and we are confident that this fine craftsman will tell it well.

☀

The other day tobacco prices hit a high of more than 88 cents a pound as an average on North Carolina markets and we suppose there was some excitement about it. We doubt, however, if the excitement of farmers will ever reach that of 1919 when tobacco sold for a dollar a pound.

That wasn't the average, of course. The 1919 average for the season wound up at 53.6 cents per pound, and that was a record that wasn't reached for a long time. The next season the average tumbled to 25.3 cents.

It was that dollar a pound which many farmers received for some grades that brought on the excitement and for years afterward they talked about it with something of awe in their voices. In the Depression days when tobacco prices were five cents or eight cents a farmer standing in a hot August sun would get that far-away look in his eyes and whisper reverently the words "a dollar a pound."

They also talked about that time back in 1919 as the "silk shirt days."

It was the silk shirt that also set that year apart from all others. It wasn't the fact that the war was over and the Roaring Twenties were about to begin. Those farmers in Granville County never heard of Scott Fitzgerald and they wouldn't have understood, or even cared much, for the whole world apart he wrote about. But they did understand dollar a pound tobacco and that they could buy silk shirts for the first time in their lives, and wear them.

Some of them, of course, bought T-Model Fords, or an Overland or a Durant, and one bought a Buick which he was still driving in

1940. But it was the silk shirt that gave them the status that only dollar a pound tobacco could give them.

It didn't last long, but for Tar Heel tobacco farmers it was a year long to remember, and something to talk about as they sat around the curing barns on those long nights many years after 1919.

✳

It was a little too early for the full flavor of the mountain's color show and *The Asheville Citizen* was somewhat apologetic about it, explaining in a special front page story that an extended rainy season in the Great Smokies had given the leaves enough life to hang on awhile longer.

Still, the North Carolina mountains were lovely enough for a mid-October weekend, the red and gold of maple, dogwoods and sourwoods blazing forth in forests of green.

It was a pleasant journey and a fine occasion — the celebration of Poetry Day in North Carolina, a day proclaimed in special ceremonies recently by Governor Scott, who took the time to talk on the need for more poetry in our lives.

This was a special occasion but poetry is an everyday thing. We saw it on the journey home in a mountain farmer who stood by the road with his baskets of apples. They had been polished bright red and the sun caught their colors and gave them back to us.

From his meeting with the famous Russian poet, Yevgeny Yevtushenko, Ragan wrote the following poem, "Poetry Reading."

Poetry Reading

Yevgeny Yevtushenko was pleased with himself.
He told me he had read his poems
To sixty thousand people
In a Moscow stadium.
I told him I couldn't match that —
The largest audience I had
Was six hundred at the Outdoor
Theater in Chapel Hill,
And that didn't count the dogs.

There were ten or twelve dogs
(At least one of whom was in heat)
Who kept chasing each other
Across the open stage
As I read my poems.
It wasn't long before the audience
Was much more interested
In what was going on
Right in front of me
Than what I was reading.

Norris Hodgkins, President of the North Carolina Symphony Society, sent a letter to Ragan in 1973 thanking him for his help with the symphony's financial problems. It shows how Ragan, time and again, went to bat for arts organizations. "I am delighted that the Council of State approved the request of the North Carolina Symphony Society to cover our current deficit of $62,000. That was possible only because of the efforts that you personally made on behalf of our request. I want to thank you and express my sincere appreciation."

Ragan spoke, with Guy Owen, at a program called "The Individual's Right to Entertainment and Use of Leisure Time" later that year. As always, Ragan was adamantly opposed to most forms of censorship, even including pornography. He often spoke out against censorship, in speeches and in his writings. "No man is wise enough to be a censor for another man. Even now, no one has been able to define obscenity adequately. We have to recognize the rights of individuals to write, publish, and distribute and even show pornography. Is censorship the duty of law, or is it up to the individual? I'm afraid that in the case of censorship, the cure would be worse than the disease."

Ragan was elected as President of the North Carolina Press Association in 1973, so this added to his many responsibilities, but yet was an honor for him to receive. Journalism and being a newspaperman were professions that Ragan would always love. It could justly be said he was born with printer's ink in his blood and bones.

While serving as Secretary of the North Carolina Department of Art, Culture, and History, Ragan managed the mergers of many departments of state into his. The State Library, the Department of Archives and History, the North Carolina Historical Commission, the North Carolina Museum of Art, and the North Carolina Symphony all came under the auspices of Ragan's Department of Art, Culture, and History. Ragan's department's name was changed in 1973 to Department of Cultural Resources, and today it is called the Department of Natural and Cultural Resources.

While Ragan served as Secretary of Art, Culture, and History, the budget request for the first ten million dollars for the new State Art Museum was granted.

When Republican James Holshouser was elected Governor and started his term of office in January 1973, he decided to appoint a new Secretary of Cultural Resources, so Ragan's time in that office lasted less than two years. But he had set the precedent of the office, had established it as an important office of state government, and had promoted the arts as a vital part of North Carolinian's lives.

Writing editorials, poems, books, and columns kept Ragan busy, along with speaking, running *The Pilot*, and serving as Secretary of the North Carolina Department of Art, Culture, and History. Neil Morgan, his good friend and also a newspaperman, wrote this about Ragan.

> His long gray hair awry and his outsized bow tie askew, Sam Ragan looks like a Southern country editor on deadline. Behind barricades of books and papers in his newspaper office in Southern Pines he attacks his old Royal Standard typewriter as though it was the enemy closing in. It is, instead, his lifelong ally, and with it he has helped to prod his state into cultural leadership in the Sun Belt bonanza.

Ragan, in the period of 1973 to 1976, continued expounding on various topics in *Southern Accent*. And *Southern Accent* continued to grow in popularity.

> We prefer the watermelon red but any of the profusely blooming crepe myrtle trees we see nowadays are pleasing to the eye. The Chinese call it "flower of a hundred days," for that is its blooming period.
>
> It is classified as an Oriental shrub, whose botanical name is "lagerstroemia indica," and it is a warm climate flower. It came out of the Orient and in so many small towns of the South there are long

avenues of crepe myrtle to delight the eye of the traveler through these towns.

Years ago in *The Progressive Farmer* Dr. Clarence Poe would urge the people of North Carolina to plant crepe myrtle in the yards and along the roadways, and he practiced what he preached by planting the shrub all over Longview gardens east of Raleigh.

Even though it is labeled a shrub, the crepe myrtle grows to tree size proportions in these parts. Across the street from *The Pilot* is a crepe myrtle that is 40 feet high.

Another beautiful tree of Oriental origins which we see much of these days is the mimosa. It grows wild in many parts of the State, especially in the Sandhills area. There are several varieties of mimosa, which is also known as the "sensitivity plant." In fact, its botanical name comes from the Latin "Mimus," or mime, meaning an imitation of animal sensitivity.

Anyway, both are trees which gives much pleasure to those who plant them, and to the traveler who comes upon them in his journeys.

⁕

Conrad Aiken died the other day at the age of 84 in his birthplace of Savannah, Ga. Early this year he had been named the Poet Laureate of Georgia by Governor Jimmy Carter and there were signs of a rediscovery of his marvelous poetry, as well as his beautifully written short stories.

His constant theme was creation and his own place in it. Poetry to him was also music and there is music in his verse. Aiken is best known for his poetry, but we remember many of his stories—"Secret Snow, Silent Snow," is one which we frequently recall.

When he graduated from Harvard, Aiken settled in Cambridge to pursue a career as a writer, and he published his first major work, *Earth Triumphant*, in 1914. He continued writing poetry, and when World War I came along he refused to serve in the armed forces on the grounds that he was engaged in "essential industry." Oddly enough, his draft board granted him a deferment so he could continue to write poetry. As far as we know, he is the only poet who ever received such treatment.

Aiken won many honors for his poetry, the Pulitzer Prize in 1930 and the National Medal for Literature in 1969 among them. He also held the chair of poetry in the Library of Congress.

＊

A little more than a month ago a lengthy letter came to us from Bernice Kelly Harris. It was written from the Durham Medical Complex where she had been a patient for several months and where she died a few days ago.

It was a letter of grace and charm, sprinkled with that special wit so characteristic of this lady who was one of North Carolina's, and indeed the nation's, finest writers. She was North Carolina's First Lady of letters, and the State had conferred upon her such honors—the Mayflower Cup and the North Carolina Award for Literature.

Even in those years following her heart attack, the months after her stroke and in her last illness, she continued to write and to plan her next book.

Mrs. Harris had gone to Durham for therapy and she was looking forward to returning to Seaboard. "I am supposed to use a cane when walking," she wrote, "but I put it aside when the therapist is not looking."

The indomitable spirit, the wit, and charm were there to the last—and she did go home to Seaboard for those last rites and burial, leaving heavy hearts with all her friends, but also a remembrance of the wonderful woman who was so long with them.

When I think of Bernice Kelly the word "gentle" always comes to mind. She was a gentle person, with a tolerance for human frailties and an admiration for the fullness of the human spirit. She wrote with a gentleness, but there was also a tough-mindedness in the keen eye and ear she had for the realities of the human condition.

Her books are treasures—*Purslane, Portulaca, Sweet Beulah Land, Wild Cherry Tree Road, Janey Jeems*—and in them she captures the heart of Eastern Carolina. As one critic wrote, she "portrayed the drama of the everyday, the mystery of commonplace people, and the triumph of the human spirit."

She was, without question, North Carolina's best loved writer. And she loved writers. For many years she had taught creative writing in her Writer's Workshop at Chowan College. Her students, young and old, came from many miles to sit with her and learn the wonders of the craft of writing.

Among our most pleasant memories are visits to her "commencements," held each year in the form of an outdoor picnic in one of the towns of the Roanoke-Chowan region. On one of our last "commencements" we drove down with Thad and Dety Stem and sat in the backyard of a Weldon home and listened to that gracious lady encourage her students to talk about themselves and their writing.

When we left after a very pleasurable evening she walked with us to the gate.

"Thank you for coming," she said. "Hurry back."

We promise that we will. We will be hurrying back to the memory of this great and good woman—Bernice Kelly Harris.

"Soliloquy" is by Katherine Bright Gurkin of Clinton:

Sweet Jesus, that a man can come to this!
Eyes failing, and the curse of Cain
Laid on him with a trowel.
I never asked for nor expected
So much time, nor this
Too public tremor of the hands.
The thews and sinews that I boasted
Melt like mist.
I swam the river, once, six miles—upstream—
Without a cramp or breathing hard.
Now this; the short breath knifing
On the stair, the lassitude,
The days like millstones dragging into dark—
And doubt (sweet Jesus, will I make it?
Will she even care?)
And I could use a smattering of splendor
In a woman's smile.
I'd settle for the hand-to-shoulder of a friend.
One who remembers how it was with me
When we were strong…

Gurkin would go on to write *Terra Amata*, a collection of poetry which won the Zoe Kincaid Brockman Book Award from the North Carolina Poetry Society in 1980.

We remember a few years ago we got a postcard from Phillips Russell inviting us over to his home in Chapel Hill for "an evening of Heine." We were not aware that this famed writer and teacher had an interest in the German poet but we accepted the invitation. There followed a second postcard asking us to bring along a bottle of rye whiskey.

We did and a very pleasant evening followed. Heine wasn't mentioned, but Phillips had invited several writers—Doris Betts was among them—and after dinner he asked her to read a short story on which she was then working. Others were asked to read from their work or to talk about writing. It was very enjoyable.

It was the type of get-together which Phillips Russell enjoyed. He loved to be with writers and to talk about writing. He had taught it for more than a quarter of a century and practiced it for nearly three times as long.

There were several other such sessions in which we participated, and although we were never one of his students in his famous writing classes at the University of North Carolina we felt we were learning from a master teacher. He was certainly that, and in the days which have followed his death at the age of 90 we have read dozens of editorials and columns of reminiscences in North Carolina newspapers from former students who wrote about this quality.

Phillips and James Forrestal, later to become Secretary of Defense, were once partners in publishing a small newspaper in New York State. He had been a publicity man for Jack Dempsey, the prize fighter, and had met such notables as Mark Twain.

But he had a special love for North Carolina, and when Frank Porter Graham persuaded him to return to Chapel Hill and teach he readily accepted. In newsrooms all over America there are scores of editors and reporters who recall the lessons he taught. Among them is Marjorie Ragan, associate editor of *The Pilot*, who says he was the most inspiring teacher she ever had.

Up to the last Phillips Russell had a keen interest in people and both state and national affairs. He had written many books—fine biographies of Benjamin Franklin, Thomas Jefferson, Ralph Waldo Emerson among them—and he had a special insight into this state and this nation's character. He had lived through so much of our history himself.

The last time we saw him was a few weeks before he was found dead in his Chapel Hill home. He was at Merritt's Filling Station just down the hill from his house and when we walked in he was talking about Adlai Stevenson, whom he greatly admired, and Stevenson's grandfather, who had served as Vice President with Grover Cleveland. He stayed alive and interested in everything until the end.

✳

We don't know what the mule population in the South is today but the number has greatly declined as machines have taken the place of this endurable animal. In the South of yesteryear a man and his mule were inseparable, sharing good times and bad.

After the Civil War there was a slogan which ran throughout the land—"forty acres and a mule." With that acreage and that animal a freed slave could make a livelihood. Not many got that gift, but in the sharecropper years which followed the pattern did follow that line.

The portrait of a lone man and a mule with a plow marching across the landscape became indelibly implanted in the minds of Southerners and non-Southerners alike. In that lonely march it was inevitable that a strong kinship and affection would develop between the two.

Not much is heard about man and mule today, but some weeks ago the story of such a pair hit the national news wires and stirred a storm of protest centered on Hartsville, S.C.

An elderly black man named Early Wilds owned a 16-year old mule named Red. They lived within the town limits and someone discovered that it was against an eight-year old zoning law to keep a mule in town. The town council said Red had to go and they stuck to that decision despite impassioned appeals from Early Wilds that both were old and needed each other. The case went to court, and the court ruled that Red could stay. He had been a resident of the town before the zoning law was passed and therefore was exempt from the law under a "grandfather clause."

Now Early Wilds and his mule can live out their lives together, the town council of Hartsville accepting the court's decision and recognizing Red as the only legal mule in town.

This report of the attachment of a man to his mule reminded us of another poignant and tragic story of a few years ago. It happened in Sampson County. The body of an old man was pulled from a farm pond. His clothing was found on a path near the pond and on the clothing was a note scrawled on lined tablet paper. The note read: "My old mule is dead."

Ragan recalled the sad event of the mule and his owner.

When I first went to *The News and Observer* as state editor there, I had correspondents in every little town all over eastern North Carolina, in some forty-five or fifty counties. Some correspondent in this little town sent me a story. At that time stories were sent by telephone or Western Union by press rate and sometimes by letter. Well, this was a very brief story, sent by Western Union in a telegram. It was about a man being found drowned in a small farm pond. It said there was a note left. The man had taken off his jacket and he'd left a note, written on tablet paper with a pencil and he'd put a rock on the note so it wouldn't blow away. And the note told a story. And it stayed lodged in the back of my mind for years and years. One night I woke up in the middle of the night and I remembered it. And I had to get up and write this poem. I didn't change anything. It stayed the way I wrote it that night. I knew people I grew up with. This man and his mule, they are off in the fields plowing. They are the only two beings in this landscape. And sometimes the man talks to his mule, tells it his joys, his woes. Sometimes he even sings to his mule. They become very close in that relationship. When this man's mule died, he'd lost his closest friend, his closest family member.

Sam Ragan never forgot where he came from. His Granville County, North Carolina, roots greatly influenced his life. Growing up in Berea, Ragan was not too far away from the town of Creedmoor, a little further south in Granville County. Creedmoor was known as the "Mule Capital of the South," because of the huge mule auctions that took place right there on Main Street. Those were hard times growing up poor in the small community of Berea on a farm where his parents struggled to put food on the table and clothes on their eight children. Ragan once said that he knew the front end from the back end of a mule. And he said he knew what end of a mule to put the halter on. What he was saying was he had experiences with mules. From that sad event in Sampson County, described above, Ragan wrote a poem.

My Old Mule Is Dead

They found his body in the pond,
And on the banks there was his jacket
With a note under a rock.
The penciled note told it all:
"My old mule is dead."

…only a country man
Can understand that.
The relationship between a man and his mule
Is something special.

When he was *writing Journey for Joedel* Guy Owen needed to know the exact feeling, the sights and sounds, for a scene so he drove from Raleigh to Bladen County and slept under a tobacco barn shed all night in order to capture it for the opening of that marvelous book.

Later he went back to a tobacco warehouse in Clarkton in order to relive the same feeling of an auction sale, and he has taken other trips to see what flowers are blooming along the field's edge, what trees have leaves on the creek bank.

This is an essential part of writing, essential for such writers as Guy Owen, certainly, which most people do not know about or realize has to be done.

Owen talked about this kind of personal research as well as other approaches to writing at St. Andrews College in Laurinburg the other night. The occasion was the first annual awards night of the *St. Andrews Review*, the excellent literary magazine published at the college and edited by Ron Bayes and Malcolm Doubles.

Owen held his listeners as he lead them through the interesting paths of his Cape Fear County, his fictional territory which he has staked out as his own much like William Faulkner created and staked out as his own his Yoknapatawpha County in Mississippi.

"I write under many shadows," Owen said, "and Faulkner's is one of the long ones."

Cape Fear County, is, of course, Owen's own Bladen County, the place where he was born and grew up and he writes out of the things he has absorbed by some form of osmosis. "I don't want to read something that sounds like it was written by a tourist," he said. "I want to read something that is rooted in something real, the earth, the land."

It was an enjoyable evening made even more so by Owen's entertaining talk.

᠅

For much more than a quarter of a century I have been reading Thad Stem's prose and poetry and with each reading and re-reading finding new delight therein.

It's that way with his newest book — his 15th in all — and each of the 326 pages of *Thad Stem's First Reader* contains something special. This book is a remarkable blend of fiction, prose, and poetry.

Jonathan Daniels, who has written the Foreword, touches upon the unique qualities of the writer when he says: "the only phrase for Thad Stem, sui generis. There is nothing or nobody like him. So he is as precious as he is rare. Yet, in a world which rejoices in labels, he is catalogued in the coterie of the poets. And, of course, he is one — and one who in rhythmical turn and whirl is cathedral singer and carnival barker, a nightingale on a rose bush or Chanticleer on a Granville County dung hill. This salty selection is certainly among the best he has written. They prove that at Stem's hand poetry never lapses in his prose. Wise man and smirking boy by turns, and always the maker of the secretly sophisticated country music he brings. Stem clings to his small town residence as tenaciously as Diogenes did to his barrel. No great Alexanders owe him. But the light of his lantern, held high in broad daylight, will help honest men to find the true America and hold it closer to their hearts."

*

Butterflies have no other purpose but to be beautiful, and that is reason enough to want them around.

For a while there during recent years we had thought that the urbanization of our countryside, the draining of swamps, and the clearing away of the wildflowers on which they feed had sent them away.

But then suddenly last spring we noticed the butterflies were back, and that was cause for rejoicing. All the butterflies want is a little nectar from the flowers to keep them flashing beautifully about the grounds. They are around to give pleasure by their beauty.

"The Butterflies Are Back" is by Ragan.

You came in excitedly to say
The butterflies are back,
And I looked out that morning's window
To see the fragile fluttering
Of bright wings over bright flowers.
It had been a long time—
Someone had said there would be no more butterflies
Because they had drained the swamps,
Filling in the low, cool places where they lived
For a highway clover-leaf,
And rows and rows of houses.
But this morning in the early slant of sun
There are butterflies in the garden.
…It was cause enough for celebration.

Jonathan Daniels wrote to Ragan from Hilton Head Island, South Carolina, in 1977, where he had started the newspaper *The Island Packet*.

You must be getting rich, as well as famous. We are pleased when an issue of the *Packet* goes to forty pages but it seems cadaverous beside your *Pilot*. I wish I could be at the Writers Conference. I would particularly like to participate in the applause for Paul [Paul Green]. I've just written a piece about him for the *Pembroke Magazine*, which is embalming him along with you. Also am enclosing a little piece. If at any time it seems appropriate at the Writers Conference use it as you will or feed it to the animals in the Asheboro Zoo. I hope it is funny but Lucy [his wife] thinks it is a little morbid. Lucy sends her best with mine to you and Marjorie.

Anne Russell is a playwright, poet, and writer whose novels include *Tropical Depression* and *The Wayward Girls of Samarcand*. She has also written a children's book, *Seabiscuit, Wild Pony of the Outer Banks*. Russell was the recipient of the 2015 North Carolina Sorosis Award for Creative Writing. *Waystations* is her latest book of poetry, released in 2017. Russell also wrote *The Porch*, an award-winning play. Russell has been a Professor of Journalism and Communications at Atlantic Christian College, now Barton College, UNC Pembroke, and UNC Wilmington. This is only a partial list of this very talented woman's achievements.

In an interview, Russell talked about Sam Ragan.

I was 20 when I got to know Sam. He was a father figure to me and a lot of other women. I had been at UNC and I went to *The News and Observer* in Raleigh and Sam hired me as entertainment editor. He served as a mentor to me. That was in the 1960s. Sam was good at spotting talent. I took a writing class of his at N.C. State. He got me a writer-in-residence at Weymouth. I later became a professor at UNC-Pembroke and Eric Smith, Sam's grandson, was a student of mine. I also taught at Atlantic Christian. Sam helped me get that job. I remember when Sam died, there was an event for him at Weymouth. Lots of people were there. All the women wore big hats, because Sam liked women with big hats.

Ragan wrote a poem called "Butterflies" about Anne Russell. At the age of 4, Russell was at an outdoor party in Decatur, Georgia. She saw what she thought was a butterfly and reached out to touch it. But it was a bee and stung her on the hand. Shortly after getting hired by Ragan to be entertainment editor at *The News and Observer*, Russell told him this story. She told him that she "had always had difficulty distinguishing good people from people who might hurt me, harmless butterflies from harmful bees."

Butterflies

She had run after it
Down the steep lawn
Toward the river, her eyes
Upon the flying thing
Bright upon the sun,
And then the sharp pain,
The sting, and she ran back
Crying.
Her fingers moved as she talked,
She was trying to explain things.
I thought it was a butterfly,
She said, but I could never
Tell butterflies from bees.

Butterflies were a favorite topic of Ragan to write about, especially in his poetry. Ragan, an avid reader of poetry, would surely have enjoyed an excerpt from one of Emily Dickinson's poems about hummingbirds.

Within my Garden, rides a Bird
Upon a single Wheel—
Whose spokes a dizzy Music make
As 'twere a traveling Mill—

He never stops, but slackens
Above the Ripest Rose—
Partakes without alighting
And praises as he goes

Southern Accent continued to pick up new readers.

One of the many quality literary publications in North Carolina is the *Carolina Quarterly*, which has been around for a long time—its latest revival dating back to 1948. The 1976 Spring-Summer issue is at hand. The quality of some of the stories is good, but this issue devoted to stories and poems is not as balanced as some of the others which have offered critical essays and other non-fiction pieces.

What bothers us about this issue of the *Carolina Quarterly* and so many others of this magazine in recent years is the absence of North Carolina writers and poets. In the current issue out of 18 contributors there is only one from North Carolina—a woman from Greensboro. Surely, with the fine writing program at Chapel Hill, there are some writers from that town worthy of being included in the magazine.

The new editor is Michael Carter and we hope that some future issues can discover some North Carolina writers.

※

Paul Green stopped by the other day on his way home from his annual visit to his plays on the eve of their openings for the 1976 summer season. There was one more to go and he was headed that weekend for the opening of the granddaddy of all of his symphonic dramas, *The Lost Colony*, on Roanoke Island.

If we count them correctly, there are ten Paul Green dramas showing this summer, including two new ones, *Louisiana Cavalier*, in Natchitoches, La., and *We, the People*, at Columbia, Md.

What a remarkable accomplishment that is, and Green, who was 82 last March 17, shows no slackening in the zeal and the fervor. His symphonic dramas on historical events are written to entertain and to inspire, and in each there's a message which he seeks to apply to today's world.

Green is excited about his new plays, and he's also excited at the showing again of his old dramas. "It's the people's theater," he says, and he feels that people feel a kinship with America's historical past.

These symphonic dramas go back a long time—to *The Lost Colony*, which had its beginning in 1937. In them he blends all the elements of the theater—the drama itself, the music, the dance—and America has been receptive to this great art form. Green's plays range from Manteo to west Texas.

On the way back to Chapel Hill he did stop over for a visit with old friend and Carolina classmate, Jonathan Daniels, at Hilton Head Island, S.C. "Jonathan and I have a pact that one of us will serve as a pallbearer for the other," Green said, "and Jonathan looked at me real hard this time."

There's also an understanding that a bottle of whiskey which was given to Jonathan by Thomas Wolfe some 40 years ago will be broken out for the wake of the first to go.

But neither one is thinking very much about such an event. Jonathan Daniels is at work on a new book, and Paul Green has plans for more plays, and for rallying America to march forward toward the "American dream."

I never knew anyone who could write a better editorial than Jonathan Daniels. He had a style which was a delight to read and he had the ability to cut through the fog and hit the point of an issue in a few words. He rarely missed the mark, and he was always out front.

We still read him. He has a front page column in the *Island Packet* at Hilton Head and the old style and flair of this gifted writer is still evident.

The Pilot continued to grow under Ragan's leadership. Operating under Ragan's maxim of "I want every issue to be a work of art," the newspaper garnered many statewide awards in editorials, news coverage, photography, and advertising. In 1976, seven years after Ragan took over the paper, *The Pilot* had a subscription of 8,500. Southern Pines at this time had a population of just over 7,000. By 1981 *The Pilot*'s circulation had reached over 12,000, and by the early 1990s had gone over 14,000, remarkable figures for a bi-weekly newspaper in a town the size of Southern Pines. *The Pilot* averaged 16 pages an issue when Ragan became publisher in 1969. By 1976 it averaged 44 pages. In the 1980s most issues contained 80 pages.

Ragan talked about the growth of *The Pilot*. "We have the newspaper with its circulation that is probably the only newspaper in the country with twice the circulation of the population of the area where it is published. Southern Pines is a resort town. It is a retirement community. The readership is generally quite sophisticated, and they also, most of the people around there, appreciate the arts."

Many items of interest were in *The Pilot*, as Ragan knew the readers liked variety. One issue during this time included the Sandhills Scene, Pinebluff News and Personals, Literary Lantern, Some Looks at Books, Dear Abby, Teeing Off with de Nissoff, and Stamps and Coins. Horses and golf were and are today popular in the Southern Pines and Pinehurst area, so many articles were devoted to them. For example, there were 20 pages covering a PGA event in Pinehurst and the new Golf Hall of Fame inductees that year.

Speaking engagements kept Ragan busy also. He spoke at the Hoke County Library in Raeford on "Life Enrichment Through the Arts," and at the dedication of the Pittsboro Memorial Library, just to name a couple.

Katharine Boyd, from whom Ragan had bought *The Pilot*, passed away in 1974. Katharine had taken over *The Pilot* in 1944 at the sudden death of husband James Boyd and ran the newspaper with much success for 25 years. She jumped right into the daily grind of running a newspaper. Mary Evelyn de Nissoff, a longtime staffer for the paper, wrote, "It was a familiar sight to find Katharine seated on a high stool or standing hunched over the proof-reading desk, her nose pressed against the galleys she held in hands badly crippled by arthritis, proofs of editorials she had written or stories someone else had written. She wanted to know, even though she had another editor or two or three, what was going into her paper."

Ragan once said of his good friend, Katharine Boyd, "Katharine Boyd was both tender and tough-minded in her views and outlook. She was gentle, generous, and gracious, but she could be equally strong against sham and hypocrisy."

Katharine Boyd's acts of philanthropy enriched the lives of many in Southern Pines, Moore County, and the Sandhills area. She deeded 400 acres of wooded land to the State of North Carolina in 1963 for the establishment of Weymouth Woods-Sandhills Nature Preserve. She left Weymouth, her Georgian-style house, and the surrounding land, to Sandhills Community College.

But soon Sandhills Community College decided to sell Weymouth, and afraid it would be sold to developers, residents in Southern Pines and the area asked Ragan to help. Ragan was a leading force in forming "Friends of Weymouth," a group that went about raising the purchase price of $700,000. By 1979, Friends of Weymouth had purchased the home and land. In return for a $412,000 grant, which went toward the purchase of Weymouth, 168 acres of surrounding wooded land of long leaf pine trees were transferred to the State of North Carolina as a nature preserve. The Friends of Weymouth owned the stately home and outbuildings and 24 acres of land. The first President of Friends of Weymouth was Pete Galantin.

Ragan, as President of Friends of Weymouth in 1979, wrote a letter to members.

One of our first goals has been achieved.

On April 24, 1979, the Boyd Estate (Weymouth) was purchased for the amount of $700,000 from the Sandhills Community College Foundation. In return for a $412,000 grant, 168 acres of woodlands were transferred to the State of North Carolina which will be added to the adjoining Weymouth Woods Sandhills Nature Preserve, which was established several years ago through a gift to the State by the Boyd family. Thus we are assured that the stand of longleaf pines and woodland will be preserved.

The Boyd house and the surrounding 24 acres, which also includes a formal garden, a gate house, a stable, a garage and a pool house, will become the Weymouth Center for the Arts and Humanities.

We are now embarked on the second phase of our goal, the development of the cultural center to serve North Carolinians. Several programs, including a writer-in-residence program, are now under way.

With your help the Weymouth Center for the Arts and Humanities can become a shining reality to stimulate the mind and lift the spirits of the people of our state.

Shelby Stephenson and Sam Ragan were close friends. They admired each other's work. Stephenson would be appointed Poet Laureate of North Carolina in 2014. He wrote to Ragan in 1978. The poem Stephenson refers to of Ragan's is "Notes on the Margins of our Times."

I want to thank you for asking me to read with you in Southern Pines. As you know, I love your poems. I love them for the feeling and the images I understand. That final poem you read from *To the Water's Edge* absolutely works. The bits and pieces of history and song give structure to the lyrical moments. As I told you once, the poem reminds me of Dos Passos' *U.S.A.,* particularly *Big Money,* and Faulkner and so many more "modern" writers have used the contrapuntal devices effectively.

Ragan, in a *Southern Accent* column in 1990, praised the work of Shelby Stephenson.

Shelby Stephenson is that special kind of writer, teacher and editor—a real literary scholar whose thoughts and talk have stayed and keep going back to his roots in Eastern North Carolina.

Not long ago, in an interview for another publication, Shelby said that everybody has to be from somewhere. It was his way of saying that place is important in the lives of everyone and it is something always with us.

Shelby's place is McGee's Crossroads in Johnston County, and even though he has traveled far from there, he never really left that place where he was born and brought up.

It's the same with William Faulkner, about whom Dr. Stephenson wrote his doctoral dissertation at the University of Wisconsin, and of another great literary figure whom Shelby admires and of whom he also is an authority, Paul Green of neighboring Harnett County. Faulkner created his own Yoknapatawpha County, which is as real as any place in his native Mississippi and for which there always was a deep and abiding love and affection.

Paul Green, also the subject of a lengthy and scholarly work by Shelby Stephenson, wrote with love and honesty of his beloved Cape Fear Country.

There's something about the land where you start from that gets inside you and stays with you for the rest of your life.

That's the way it is with the beat of Shelby Stephenson's poetry and poetic drama, in the tales he tells, and the wit, poignancy and haunting melody of the songs he sings. That farm in Johnston County hovers in our thoughts and feelings which his words and music evokes.

We have been reading Shelby Stephenson's latest collection of poetry, *The Persimmon Tree Carol.*

It is really one long poem, which is about and dedicated to the memory of his father, William Paul Stephenson (1901–1981). Robert Morgan calls it "a wonderful celebration of the mystery of kinship," and Fred Chappell says the book is "warm, funny and deeply touching."

These are apt descriptions, but the book is even more—a deeply felt, honestly told story of growing up and looking back with clear eyes on a time, a place and a family relationship that in many ways was something special.

In a *Southern Accent* column in 1978, Ragan wrote about his beloved South, the mystiques of the region, and how to understand the unique characteristics of the South through books about the South. Not many men ever epitomized the South more than Sam Ragan, known as a true Southern gentleman.

The South is not monolithic, despite the characterizations and caricatures which used to flourish. Indeed there are many Souths, in fact as well as accents, with noticeable shades of differences.

Still, there is a Southern mystique, even though it is hard to define and even harder to capture on paper.

Some writers, however, have come close, even though their writing might range all the way from the Gothic and grotesque to the simplicity found in an Ovid Pierce or Bernice Kelly Harris novel.

Anyone writing to understand the South as a region, with all of its simplicities and complexions, its flavor and mystique can go a long way toward understanding by the reading of some three or four dozen books by Southern writers.

In the understanding of any region, of course, one must know the past to know the present, and many of these books may not seem at first glance to be relevant to what some call the "New South." But, in fact, they are — and if one wanted to start off seeking to know, here are some of the books I would recommend.

One of my favorites is *Red Hills and Cotton*, by the late Ben Robertson. It was also a favorite of William T. Polk, whose *Southern Accent* I would also include on the list. (Bill Polk had called me about use of that title for his book before publication.) Then there would be *Lanterns on the Levee*, by William Alexander Percy, and, of course, Jonathan Daniels' *A Southerner Discovers the South* and *Tar Heels*.

Some scholars of the Southern realm start off with W.A. Cash's *The Mind of the South*, but I would save that until I had savored several others. Cash's book is monumental, and is at the top of the list for several "Southern Studies" programs in universities in other regions, but it is not an introduction to the South.

Entries From Oxford and *Thad Stem's First Reader* are two necessary books for the journey, and add to them Stem's poetry for further pleasure as well as insight.

Several works of fiction can add to informative pleasures, including Guy Owen's *The Ballad of the Flim-Flam Man* and *Journey for Joedel*, Ovid Pierce's *The Plantation* and his other three novels, Walker Percy's *The Last Gentleman*, Robert Penn Warren's *All the King's Men*, and other novels, the short stories of Frances Gray Patton and Doris Betts, the novels and stories of Flannery O'Connor, Carson McCullers and Eudora Welty, *A Long and Happy Life* and *A Generous Man* by Reynolds Price. Novels by William Faulkner and Erskine Caldwell will provide another dimension.

Dozens of plays by Paul Green, as well as his essays, can give a poignant understanding of the region, both in reading and viewing, which no other work can do as well.

One of Bernice Kelly Harris' last books, *Southern Savory*, is high on my list, and so is John Foster West's *Time Was*.

James Dickey's flamboyant long poem, "Jericho: The South Beheld," belongs in a special category, as well as Stephen Vincent Benet's classic "John Brown's Body."

There are dozens more, but these provide a good start. Each presents a different facet of the South, so that one discovers many Souths, but taken all together the portrait emerges of a land with distinctive characteristics, yet with basic universality.

Jim Boyd was James and Katharine Boyd's son and living in New York in 1978. He seemed rather happy about the new owner of *The Pilot* and what he had done with his parents' former newspaper in this letter.

I've taken the month of August off as usual. Wanted to thank you for the check. This would have pleased Mrs. Boyd very much. One of her dreams, never realized, was for *The Pilot*, one day, to be able to produce income for the stockholders.

The size and contents of the paper would indicate Southern Pines is now almost as active in the summer as during the rest of the year. Very impressive! Mother would have enjoyed the general tone and observations of your editorials, often, in my opinion, better than the *New York Times*.

Demonstrating his firm desire to establish James Boyd's former home, Weymouth, into a center for the arts and humanities, a goal which he led the fight for, Ragan donated $5,000 to the Friends of Weymouth, in September of 1978.

Ragan received quite a coveted invitation in 1978. On August 24, 1978, a letter arrived at *The Pilot* from the White House. The letter was from Patricia Bario, Deputy Press Secretary to the President. Ragan had been a supporter of President Carter since he was elected in 1976, and this visit to the White House only enhanced that support.

On September 7 we will hold a day-long, on-the-record briefing session for 30 editors from across the country. We would like you to be one of them. The 8:30 a.m. to 4 p.m. session will give you a chance to question senior White House, Cabinet or agency staff—and the President for a half-hour. Charles Godwin of our office will be calling on Friday, August 31, for Secret Service clearance. I look forward to seeing you September 7. We'll have coffee at 8:30 a.m. in Room 160 of the Old Executive Office Building.

Ragan's good friend, Thad Stem, was experiencing some major health problems in 1978. Stem was born in Oxford, North Carolina, and lived there his entire life. From his home on Front Street, he would walk a couple of blocks through downtown Oxford to his office above Hall's Drug Store on Main Street. Most of his writings came from his small, cluttered office in Oxford, a town incorporated in 1816 which is now over 200 years old. Stem tried to inject some humor, in his own way, into a bleak outlook when he wrote to Ragan in 1978.

I will not know until January 17 whether or not I am to go on dialysis. I fear my condition is serious, and perhaps, inexorable. In the meantime I take six medications a day and I am on an austere diet. Never again can I eat sugar, salt, or potassium, and all the fruits I love contain potassium.

I eat lots of raw radishes and carrots, and I have eaten so many goddam radishes and carrots that twice I have jumped into briar patches trying to fuck rabbits.

Ragan was named the winner of the North Carolina Award in the Fine Arts in 1979. This was the highest award given by the state of North Carolina. The awards ceremony was held in the Raleigh Civic Center. Governor Jim Hunt presented the award to Ragan. A reception was held after a dinner at the Governor's Mansion.

In 1979, Grace Gibson wrote to Ragan thanking him for coming to Pembroke State University to speak with her students.

My students and many faculty members have told me how much they appreciated this opportunity to know you. They especially admired the clarity and wisdom of your comments on such a wide-ranging list of concerns, not only to journalists and other writers, but also to every thoughtful citizen. With you as an advocate, the press can face down its critics.

I have just been talking with Jim McDuffie, fine young writer and student, who was telling me how much your help has meant to him, as it has to so many others. Certainly through the years Alton and I were always grateful for your support, especially for your interest in my poetry.

Again, many thanks for a visit that enlivened my classroom and provided the high point for the semester for my students.

Ragan also spoke at St. Andrews College, now St. Andrews University, in 1979, at the invitation of his good friend, Ron Bayes.

Would you be willing to come down to St. Andrews and give a little talk to my senior core curriculum class? These are all graduating seniors and the topic which we would like you to explore would be: "What Jobs Are There for a Writer in North Carolina Professions?" We would be able to come up with $50 which might pay for your gasoline.

Thad Stem passed away in 1980. Stem had been one of Ragan's closest friends for many years, and their wives, Dety Stem and Marjorie Ragan, had also been close. Ragan wrote about his fellow writer and good friend.

Thad Stem often pointed out that he lived on the same street in Oxford in which he was born. He grew up in the same county of Granville as I did, but I didn't know Thad (except as the son of Major Stem) until after he had published his first book of poetry. I was charmed, in fact, excited, with it and we soon came to know each other. In the years since we collaborated on books and dozens of other projects, compared notes on hundreds of persons, places and events, and shared a deep and abiding friendship.

In his work there is a strong sense of place, which marks the best of American literature. His poetry was written in a style all his own, and his prose bears the mark of the poet and are delightful excursions into the realm of ideas, sights and sounds, indeed, the entire human condition.

One of his books, *Entries from Oxford*, is what he called "autobiographical fiction," and it tells the story of his town and time.

I can speak appreciation for his many contributions, I can speak for the pleasure he has given in his poetry and prose, but I can speak more and treasure more deeply his friendship over these many years.

Ragan wrote a poem about his very good friend and fellow writer from Granville County.

Thad Stem and Words

He was in love with language,
And being in love is different
From the loving of words,
Of making them dance and sing.
Thad Stem could make words
Stand up and cheer, turn somersaults,
Walk a tight wire,
Or wander through the woods and fields
Like a creek.
When writing a poem he would create
Images different from anyone else,

But even the words had to walk the line.
He would declare, I want people to say
That's the way it is, or maybe,
If you are lucky, they will say:
I never saw it that way before.

One of North Carolina's greatest men of letters, and one of Sam Ragan's dearest friends, Paul Green, passed away in 1981. Also, Guy Owen, another friend and writer, died in the same year. And Ragan's close friend with whom they spent many hours together at *The News and Observer*, Jonathan Daniels, passed away in 1981 too. Ragan wrote about Green, Owen, and Daniels in *Southern Accent*.

A few weeks ago Paul Green sat in the great room at Weymouth and listened to his granddaughter, Nancy Green, in a splendid performance on the cello, and later he remarked, "Jim Boyd and Katharine would have liked it."

Later that evening Paul Green recalled incidents from the times he spent in Hollywood as a writer for many movies. There were recollections from the times of his growing up in Harnett County.

It was a wonderful evening, as always, spent in the company of this great man, and we thought about it, and others, a few nights ago when we heard Paul Green had died.

He was the evangelist of the good life for all the people of North Carolina. His was a life of affirmation. We thought about the dozens of plays Paul Green had written, their impact on America, and the fervency with which he espoused such causes as world peace, the abolition of the death penalty, and upholding the dignity of man.

One of the causes he was greatly devoted was the preservation of Weymouth, the home of James and Katharine Boyd, where he had visited as far back as the 1920s. In that same room where he heard his granddaughter play the cello he had joined to talk about writing and the arts with Boyd and other writers such as Thomas Wolfe, Struthers Burt, Scott Fitzgerald, Lawrence Stallings, Sherwood Anderson, and others, including Boyd's and Wolfe's editor at Scribner's, Maxwell Perkins. Green and Boyd had once collaborated on writing a play, and Paul once described how they worked together in the upstairs study, one pacing back and forth and talking while the other wrote down what was said and then exchanging places.

I remember the first meeting of a group of people here a few years ago when the Friends of Weymouth was formed to preserve the Boyd estate. Paul Green was there and he was the first Friend of Weymouth with a gift of $1,000 after Robert Drummond had offered to contribute $20,000 to the cause.

He continued his interest and contributions, helping to interest others in the establishment of a center for the arts and humanities, talking about what it would mean to the people of the Sandhills and to all of North Carolina. He saw it as a place for creativity, where people could explore their highest aspirations, and he agreed when we spoke of Weymouth as a concept as well as a place.

At one of the meetings when the center was being discussed Paul Green looked across the meadow and envisioned an outdoor theater there. He talked about writing a play for Weymouth and some months ago he said he was still thinking about it. "I have some ideas and I've been making some notes," he said.

Paul Green was pleased that one of his dreams—the Weymouth Center—was realized.

He had many dreams, and in his talks, his exhortations, he often talked of "the dream," man's dream for a better life, a full life of joy and celebration, and his own life was dedicated to fulfilling that dream for everyone.

Even when he wrote of the ugliness and the meanness of spirit and body of people who abused other people there always was a hope that "the dream" would become a reality.

Paul Green was a man who had won many honors, had achieved great acclaim, had walked and talked with great men and women, and yet he had time to listen and talk with young writers and artists to offer them encouragement. He never failed to applaud the achievements of others.

I treasure what was perhaps his last letter, written on the evening of May 1, three days before he died, when he wrote, "Sorry I am incapacitated and cannot be present to honor ourselves in honoring you. Great and blessed going be yours for good time to come. And I know it will—as long as you are you. Love to you and Marjorie."

My friendship with Paul Green and his wonderful, strong and gentle wife Elizabeth, goes back nearly 40 years, and I treasure every minute of it.

The News and Observer in an editorial recalled that Green once said, "I lean on some sort of philosophy that declares for an optimism and growth among men. Bring on the jubilation even if mixed with tears," and the newspaper quoted a statement by Katherine Anne Porter about Green in Hollywood. "The honest, tender and gifted soul stood out like a stalk of good sugar cane in a thicket of poison ivy."

We think of Paul Green as one of the greatest of North Carolinians, and we think of him as the author of *The Lost Colony*, the greatest of his 16 symphonic dramas. And when we think of that drama we think of those stirring words he wrote, words which will always remind us of Paul Green himself:

Now down the trackless hollow years
That swallowed them but not their song
We send response—
"Lusty singer, dreamer, pioneer.
Lord of the wilderness, the unafraid.
Tamer of darkness, fire and flood.
Of the soaring spirit winged aloft
On the plumes of agony and death—
Hear us. O hear
The dream still lives.
It lives, it lives.
And shall not die."

All across North Carolina last week friends called friends to relay the sad words that Guy Owen had died, and then each related some special memory of the much loved writer of stories and poems, his hearty laughter, and his own love for people and his North Carolina.

He was the victim of a cancer he had so valiantly fought. He was 56. Friends chose not to dwell on those final painful weeks, but to remember those years when he was so vibrantly alive—writing, talking, laughing, encouraging others.

We like to remember a friendship of 30 years, a friendship which began even before an exchange of letters when he was teaching at Stetson University in Florida, and continued with many shared experiences.

We went back and read last spring's *Pembroke Magazine* 13, edited by his good friend Shelby Stephenson, a special issue of tributes to Guy Owen, and a revealing interview conducted by Editor Stephenson. The 117 pages of that issue are filled with warm words of affection, appreciation and admiration from more than two dozen friends, fellow writers and literary critics.

We liked what Roy Parker, Jr. wrote two days after Guy Owen's death in the *Fayetteville Times:*

> In the sense that any good artist lives on, Guy Owen will live on as the special artistic voice of that part of North Carolina we call the Cape Fear Region, the land of slow-moving rivers, shimmering cornfields (more cotton when he was a lad), dusty crossroad villages, and tree-spangled small towns with Victorian houses and courthouse squares.
>
> This particular piece of geography was the special turf of Guy Owen. He wrote about it, talked about it, dreamed about it, cussed it, sang it. I think he would have gladly eaten it if someone handed him a fist full of good Bladen County loam.

But Guy's province was wider than the region. He was a writer of national stature. He struck a note of authenticity and just plain good fun in his bestseller, *The Ballad of the Flim-Flam Man.*

We will go back and read his books — *Season of Fear, The Ballad of the Flim-Flam Man, The Flim-Flam Man and the Apprentice Grifter, Journey for Joedel,* which was his favorite book and also mine, his books of poetry *Cape Fear County* and *The White Stallion and Other Poems,* and his essays and anthologies.

As Roy Parker said in his editorial column, Guy Owen "belongs to the ages."

Ragan, along with his words about Owen in *Southern Accent,* wrote a poem about Owen.

Guy Owen's Windshield Wiper

He was telling about a trip
With Guy Owen in Owen's car.
It was a day bright with sunshine
And we rode all the way
From Raleigh to Chapel Hill
With the windshield wiper going
Full blast, Guy at the wheel
So involved in what he was saying
He didn't notice.
I was new on the faculty, he said,
And I was so caught up
With that damn windshield wiper
I can't remember a thing he said.
Why didn't I tell him the wiper was on?
I didn't dare, he said.

We mourn the passing of Jonathan Daniels. He was one of the great editors of America, and a superb writer of many books. Our relationship went back a long way, and I treasured his friendship as much as I admired his abilities and skills as an editor and as a writer.

Jonathan was a tough-minded but essentially a gentle hearted man. As an editor, he had the ability to get to the heart of an issue in a few well-chosen words, and even in the day-after-day writing of editorials his prose had a freshness and a clarity which made his writing style stand out as a model.

His influence will live a long time in North Carolina, and his books will always be with me. But he will be missed.

Jonathan Daniels was a member of the star-studded class of 1921 at the University of North Carolina at Chapel Hill, and he more than held his own with such classmates as Thomas Wolfe, Paul Green, LeGette Blythe and other literary luminaries.

Jonathan had a two-edged career—as a journalist and editor of uncommon ability and as an author of nearly 20 books of distinction. He took pride in his profession as a writer, which he also regarded as a craft and a calling.

Once after I had told him that my wife, Marjorie, had exclaimed while reading one of his works, "He writes like a dream," he called her up to say, "that's the nicest compliment anyone ever paid me.

I worked closely with Jonathan for more than 20 years at *The News and Observer* and I learned a lot from him. He could become very much involved in the editorials he was writing, and he could become detached and calmly objective.

I recall the night of the Smith-Graham U.S. Senate election, in which Jonathan was emotionally and editorially involved, and while waiting for returns to come in he decided to write editorials for an upcoming edition. In scanning the Associated Press wire he spotted a four-line bulletin reporting the invasion of South Korea by the Communist forces of North Korea. He immediately saw the implications and the war so imminent made the election pale in significance. He sat down and on his old typewriter wrote one of the strongest editorials of his career. It should have won a Pulitzer Prize, but we didn't get around to sending it in.

More than any writer I knew, Jonathan had the facility for weaving facts into the fabric of the narrative he was writing and the reader learned a great deal while enjoying the story he was telling.

Jonathan Daniels loved writing and he also loved doing research. When he went out to Missouri to engross himself in the files of the *Kansas City Star*, when he was working on the biography of Harry Truman, *The Man of Independence*, he was reluctant to end the research and start writing. "It was all there," he said, and he couldn't understand why other writers, seeking to understand Truman, hadn't gone to the files of the *Kansas City Star*. Many historians have said *The Man of Independence* stands as a model for biography.

Jonathan couldn't stand what he called "thumb-sucking" in writing editorials. He wanted to get on with it, use your facts and hit the issue hard. He was a good editorial writer, and the writer of books with something to say and a fascinating way of saying it.

As always, Ragan published many poems sent to him by readers of *Southern Accent*. One particular poem sent to him by Maria Ingram Braucht surely reminded him of his growing up years on a tobacco farm in Granville County. The poem was called "One Story Beneath the Pin Oak."

Sunday afternoon we're sitting
in the backyard spitting seeds out
of bought watermelons and my
father says it's the worst
summer since 1930 when they had to
replant tobacco four times,
on into July, before it took hold.
Six and a half acres brought
a hundred and forty two dollars
at six cents a pound.
But there were some, he said,
Only brought a half, a quarter
cent a pound.
One old man from Stokes County
crated up a bunch of chickens
to bring with him.
The auctioneer's fee was more
than his tobacco brought,
so he took his chicken money
to get back out into sunlight.
They sat around the camp,
laughing to keep from not laughing
at the fine mess they were in:
young'uns needed saddle oxfords
and notebook paper.
Daddy asked the man from Stokes
was he going to raise tobacco next year.
Oh yeh, he said, that's the only
thing there's any money in.

Maria Ingram Braucht was one of five poets chosen for inclusion in the anthology *Thirtieth Year to Heaven: New American Poets*, published by Jackpine Press at Wake Forest University. She operated an international specialty foods and coffee roasting shop in Winston-Salem, called Maria's, for 33 years, from 1972 to 2005.

Journey into Morning, another collection of poems by Ragan, came out in 1981. Jonathan Daniels, his old friend from *The News and Observer* days, had this tribute about Ragan and his new book of poems. "Sam Ragan is North Carolina's poet-patron of all the arts. More than anybody else in our time — maybe any time — he has given much aid to the talents of others without ever diminishing his own rich store." *The Fayetteville Observer* had this: "Sam Ragan has hit his mark a double blow, touching the heart and the intellect."

Agnes McDonald taught English at several colleges and universities, including North Carolina State University and the University of North Carolina at Wilmington. A poet, she wrote a collection, *Quickest Door, Smallest Room*, and edited *Journey Proud: Southern Women's Personal Writings*. McDonald reviewed *Journey into Morning*.

> Sam Ragan is a poet for all seasons, a poet of all seasons. Ragan once again claims his place in that small but vital segment of writers who ignore the siren call of influence and trend, who simply are themselves, who simply write their hearts. The apparent ease of Ragan's lyrics belies the mastery accrued from years of hammering down the fog of feelings with the nails of words. These poems describe the seasons, their changes, the glittering panoply of autumn leaves, the chilly November of the soul. He simply lets the words do their work, reveal a mood, nostalgic, wistful, the bittersweet pull of memory, the pang of absence, the rich resonance of silence. Like his tale-teller in "The Story Teller," Ragan loves life and wants to pass it on, to take us "around the bend in the road." The next mountain, the next river, the next ocean. Telling us the wonders beyond. Of man's journey into those wonders. And the wonders of the human heart.

One of the best descriptions of the way Sam Ragan looked and dressed came from Agnes McDonald.

> Sam Ragan is everybody's picture of the Southern gentleman, comfortable mussiness, floppy bow tie which must be custom made since

no one else has been seen wearing one like his. Topping his wispy silver hair that is often worn at Byronic lengths is frequently worn the proverbial Southern planter's straw hat, brim riding high as a jack pine over the elegant expanse of forehead.

In one of the poems in *Journey into Morning*, called "A Moment Marked," Ragan brings to his poem his love of nature.

A Moment Marked

In this September sun
Before the last ding-dong of darkness
I watch this field of yellow daisies
Brought together in this cup
Of earth and sky
In one single tapestry of time.
What else is there to mark
Which would be so meaningful?
The earth, the sky, the daisies,
And you in mind walking naked
As sycamores against the field's far green.

In another poem from the book, "The Lilies Did Not Bloom This Year," Ragan perhaps is remembering his father back during his years growing up on the farm in Berea, in Granville County. Ragan believed in his poetry, as evidenced when he said this. "I feel that anything I publish stands up right well. It will last."

The Lilies Did Not Bloom This Year

He sits quietly in the late summer sun,
Brushing at a buzzing fly.
The trees are still green,
But it will soon be fall.
Something went wrong with the weather —
At first too much rain,
Then too much sun.
It's now too late for planting.

The seasons come and go.
For a little while everything grows,
But some things are now missing—
The lilies did not bloom this year.

Ragan never wasted words, once saying "I love language too much to waste words." Marie Gilbert wrote a poem that speaks to Ragan's poetry. This poem is excerpted below.

The Poem for Sam Ragan

The language must be bone and sinew
Saying what it means to say
Never leading down false paths
Or dead end streets.

There would be no place for pomposity—
what you'd see is what there is.

In 1981 North Carolina Poet Laureate James Larkin Pearson passed away. He was 102 years of age. Pearson had been Poet Laureate since 1953, a period of 28 years. Pearson had been appointed to the position by Governor William B. Umstead. The James Larkin Pearson Award is given for free verse poetry, presented annually by the North Carolina Poetry Council. The library at Wilkes Community College in Wilkesboro, North Carolina, is named in Pearson's honor, and contains many of his personal papers. An excellent book about Pearson was written in 2015 by Gregory Taylor titled *James Larkin Pearson: A Biography of North Carolina's Longest Serving Poet Laureate.*

10

Poet Laureate, "John Patrick's Walnut Trees," "Salute to St. Andrews," "The Kudzu Man"

Governor Jim Hunt appointed Sam Ragan in 1982 to the position of North Carolina Poet Laureate. It was a logical and good choice. Hunt knew Ragan and admired his work to bring the arts to as many North Carolinians as possible. Ragan had written prize winning books of poetry, was known throughout the state, was a committed Democrat, and so aligned with Governor Hunt, and Ragan was already becoming known as North Carolina's Literary Godfather.

Shirley Moody wrote a moving letter of support for Ragan to be named Poet Laureate.

> I first met Mr. Ragan in 1977 as a participant in the Sam Ragan Writer's Workshop. Mr. Ragan was most valuable in guiding myself and others throughout the workshop by example, lectures and the wisdom of his writing as well as life's experiences. Many of us became professional writers after his encouragement to mail out our poems, stories and novels. Some of my early poems were published by Mr. Ragan himself in his *Southern Accent* column of *The Pilot* newspaper in Southern Pines. The encouragement of Mr. Ragan helped me to decide to apply to the Artists-in-Schools program for North Carolina. I am now completing my fourth year as a poet in this program, and have conducted approximately 70 workshops throughout our state.

His influence throughout the state and the nation has been felt by hundreds and hundreds, just like myself. Mr. Ragan is truly a gift to all of us. Considering the importance he has been in my life, the least I can do is to go officially on record as a strong, devoted supporter of Mr. Ragan as our Poet Laureate. After all, in the minds and hearts of most North Carolinians, I believe he always has been.

The newly installed North Carolina Poet Laureate received many invitations to read his poems and share his vision of poetry and writing. The Friends of East Carolina University Library paid Ragan $200 plus expenses to speak to them, and a week later he spoke to the Randolph Arts Guild in Asheboro.

The North Caroliniana Society Award for 1981 went to Ragan. Nearly 250 people attended a banquet in the Carolina Inn in Chapel Hill to honor Ragan. The master of ceremonies was H.G. Jones, curator of the North Carolina Collection. Walter Spearman, Elizabeth Ives, former Governor Bob Scott, and William Powell gave tributes. Neil Morgan, who Ragan had hired at *The News and Observer* and had gone on to an outstanding newspaper career, was the main speaker.

Ragan received piles of mail each day, many pertaining to business concerning *The Pilot*, but also quite a bit of mail was of a personal nature. A lady from Clayton, North Carolina, wrote the following in 1981.

I would appreciate so much if you would send me your autographed picture. Please. I love your poetry and I wish you would sign one of your poems for me too. You are a great man, a great editor and poet. You are a favorite of mine. Best wishes to you and yours. Thank you and God Bless.

Heather Ross Miller wrote to Ragan in 1982 updating him on her projects as a writer and teacher. The letter shows how writers turned to Ragan for advice and encouragement, and also the letter shows some of the struggle writers went through to make a decent living.

I'm sorry I had to miss seeing you at the Blair thing. Clyde and I were at our first meeting of the Danforth Association in Raleigh and it went over on Sunday. I felt like I'd been dragged through hell backward, couldn't face the high-tone event in Winston-Salem.

In any case, I recovered enough to sneak down to Sandhills last Thursday and read a few stories to Stephen Smith's bunch. What a super person is Stephen Smith! I surely wish him the highest success in writing and teaching and publishing and laurel-crowning.

I will have my new book of stories from Moreland and Hogan and Briar Patch in September, I think. And also Moreland plans a reissue of *Confessions of Champeen Fire-Baton Twirler.*   People will have a chance to read that good little book in a decent binding.

The title of my new book of stories is *The Love Offerings of Jeremiah Coonrad Kirk.* I think these ten stories are ok, though they could all stand some improvement. Ain't it the truth.

James Boatwright took a new story for *Shenandoah*, though no word on when it will appear. I'll let you know more about the appearance of my new work as it develops.

Pfeiffer, suffering death throes, cut my pay by nearly $1000, and I am in a tailspin on how to make it up for the next year. Times will be definitely hard for me. If you hear of any readings, lectures, classes, etc. that pay at least $100, please suggest my name to same. I'll need every gig I can get now. Just like a struggling rock group.

I ran down to Converse College and took a look at Eudora Welty last month. I hope to become an old lady just like she is.

Do you know of any magazines that pay for decent in-depth literary articles? I have a couple of children's stories. What publishers do you recommend for such?

Teaching writing, as he had done for so many years at North Carolina State University, was one of Sam Ragan's favorite things to do. He loved to encourage people to write, whether it be for pleasure or to enter the profession. In 1982 he was appointed a Professor of Literature and Journalism at what is now St. Andrews University in Laurinburg, North Carolina. This was a part-time position, of course, because Ragan had so many other responsibilities. His payment was $1,000 per course that he taught. That first year he taught English 390B, Journalism and the Community. The course was held on Wednesday nights. Along with teaching writing guidelines,

Ragan told interesting stories to his students, related to writing or writers. These stories evoked vividly the craft of writing.

Ragan would always have a close affinity for St. Andrews after he started teaching there in 1982, and even before that through his close relationship and friendship with Ronald Bayes, among others. Bayes was a Professor of Literature and Creative Writing for many years at St. Andrews, and also founded the St. Andrews Press and the St. Andrews Review, and other literary magazines. I met with Mr. Bayes while writing this book, and not only did he help me a great deal with this book, but he is one of the nicest men one could hope to meet.

"Salute to St. Andrews" was written by Sam Ragan.

Salute to St. Andrews

The time, a place, a people —
The ingredients for a human experience,
A vision shared and growing,
Even before a young woman
Danced the Highland Fling
In the bright sunshine
Of an Open Field in Scotland County
There was a melding of the mists
Of time at a place
Where the voices of people were heard.

Have you felt it yet?
Yes, it is something to feel.
You can see the grass, the trees,
All the green and growing things,
And you can hear the voices,
Taste the sweetness of the air,
But you have to feel it —
The glow in the eyes,
The quickened step, the inner sounds
That take hold, and you know
It is the time,
It is the place,
And the people await,
Marching onward, always onward.

Another poem Ragan wrote was about a famous North Carolina author, O. Henry, whose real name was William Sydney Porter. Porter was born in Greensboro in 1862 and lived until 1910. One of his most well-known short stories is "The Gift of the Magi." Alcoholism is believed to have contributed to his death at the age of 47. Ragan wrote a poem about O. Henry.

O. Henry — Going Home

Did he really say it —
As they said he did —
There in that darkened room:
"Turn up the light,
I don't want to go home in the dark"?
The hard-drinking William Sydney Porter
(He called himself O. Henry) was nearing
The end of his story-telling.
He would soon be back in North Carolina,
And that popular tune of the time
Was ringing in his ears —
"I don't want to go home in the dark."

There were many things to keep this busy man busy. Ragan had established the Writers-in-Residence program at Weymouth, and for the first few years of the program the writers were selected simply by Ragan's invitation. Years later this process evolved into an application program. Margaret Graham wrote to Ragan in January of 1983.

Several friends have encouraged me to inquire about the possibility of using the facilities of Weymouth Woods for the writing of my present novel. As a teacher of long standing in this community, I naturally have too many interruptions to get anything done. It is with some temerity that I ask for the privilege of the place the first weekend in February with a view toward making more reservations if I find that I can write there. Grace Evelyn Gibson, Lil Buie, and others will recommend me. My book, *Katie*, is in its 3rd edition, published by Tyndale House, Wheaton, Illinois.

Ragan gave the commencement speech at Pembroke State University in

May of 1983. In the speech, Ragan touted many of the things he believed in, such as a good government, opposing censorship, praising the arts, and the value of a good education and following one's dreams. Some highlights of that speech follow.

> I have visited this campus on several occasions in recent years and I have been impressed with its fine facilities, the quality of the instruction, the dedication to learning by faculty, staff and students. I have been impressed with the excellence of many programs on this campus, and I cannot fail to pay tribute to one of the finest literary publications in this state and nation — *Pembroke Magazine.*
>
> It was Charles Dickens, I believe, who in writing about two cities, Paris and London, in the 18th Century said, "It was the best of times, it was the worst of times." The description might be apt in some parts of the world. Yet here in America — in spite of recessions, and a weariness of double talk — we are indeed in the best of times. The late Paul Green, one of North Carolina's great men, talked about how everyone has a dream and is entitled to see that dream realized. He knew that once dreams die, the human spirit and humanity itself had died.
>
> But I urge you to hold on to your dream, and as we move forward — and we must move forward — your dream will be realized.
>
> Several years ago I was a guest on the NBC Today Show, and we talked about our newspaper in Southern Pines and some of the editorial positions taken by the newspaper. I was asked what my editorial philosophy was, and I said that I have always felt that if you are on the side of humanity you won't go wrong. I urge you to be on the side of humanity, to be aware and be concerned about the well-being not only of yourself but of others.
>
> Human freedoms are precious things, and we must be dedicated to preserving them. We must resist the efforts of self-appointed censors who would tell us what to read, what to hear, what to see.
>
> There are people who rail against government, especially government with humanitarian instincts. I do not fear government — so long as it is humanitarian. Government is simply the instrument by which a people does things for people. We can use that instrument to make life better.

I would urge you to be as interested in the quality of our lives as in making a living. Making that living worthwhile should be a goal for all. One of the ways of bringing that extra dimension in your lives is through the arts. An interest in literature, in music, in drama, in painting will add immeasurably to the quality of life, will make the living worthwhile.

Ragan remembered that appearance on the NBC Today Show and wrote a poem.

Policy
There was this interview on television —
A nationwide network — and
The Editor was asked,
What is your editorial policy? And
The Editor said, "I have never
Thought about having a policy,
But I thought if I stood
On the side of humanity
I wouldn't go wrong."

Not everyone sent plaudits to Sam Ragan. As the writer of *Southern Accent*, Ragan received poems, stories, and books from readers of his column, which reached across most counties in North Carolina and into many states across the country. His column was even read in other countries. But a lady from Pinehurst took issue with Ragan in a letter to him.

About six to eight weeks ago, I gave you a copy of my husband's book, *How to Tell the Liars from the Statisticians*. I wanted you to have the book because you had been kind enough a year or so ago to give us advice in finding an illustrator. I now find I am quite disappointed that you didn't like it enough to give it a one line mention in *The Pilot*, or to let Bob know what you did, or didn't like about the book. I know that as Poet Laureate of North Carolina your chief interest is in the arts. You and your wife are always honored guests at all affairs, even when you are not active participants. Still, when someone visits her grandmother in Cameron on a Sunday afternoon, it can be reported in *The Pilot*.

Enjoying few things more than helping others to become writers, Ragan continued teaching writing and journalism. He was appointed Adjunct Professor of Literature and Journalism in 1983 to teach a course called Journalism and the Community at St. Andrews College, now St. Andrews University. He was paid $1,000 to teach the class for the fall semester.

Thomas Walters passed away in 1983. Walters received a Ph.D. in English Education from Duke University in 1968, when he was promoted to assistant professor of English Education at North Carolina State University in the same year. He had started teaching at NCSU in 1964 and would teach there until his death in 1983. Among his books was one of literary criticism, called *Southern Experience in Short Fiction*. In 1973 he was awarded a $5,000 creative writing fellowship from the National Endowment for the Arts, which he used to write a novel, *Always Next August*. Walters also wrote poetry, including a collection titled *Seeing in the Dark*. Ragan wrote about Walters in *Southern Accent*.

> Coming back from the memorial services for Tom Walters we picked up to read again his marvelous collection of poems *Seeing in the Dark* and went back with him to those days in his youth when he worked in a movie theater in Tarboro and
>
> > Kept his eyes on illusion
> > Memorized its names, its credits
> > Made it myth, lived its lore.

Tom Walters appreciated and understood myth and lore, but he was never lost in illusion and reality was something to be savored and seen close-up.

At the memorial services held at Pullen Memorial Baptist Church in Raleigh, his longtime friend and pastor, Bill Finlator, had quoted from an article written some months ago in *The Spectator* in which Tom had said:

Even in my illness the tension between dream and reality is very exciting to me. It sustains me that we don't have any guarantees of lasting anyway. Life—this wonderful adventure, this mystery we've been given—is a great gift. We shouldn't feel so proprietary about gifts. It wasn't given me forever, it's not always mine. You outgrow gifts and you give them to other people.

Tom Walters had a strong sense of place—so many of his poems and stories go back to his days of growing up on a farm near Conetoe in Edgecombe County where he absorbed so much from the land and the woods while reading voraciously about other lands.

There were many other qualities, too, in his writing and his life. We remember his keen wit, his strong laughter, his compassion for people, and above all that enduring devotion to his family and friends.

His friends were many, and they came from all parts of the state for those final rites after he had lost a courageous and valiant fight with cancer, and each one of them had a special memory of Tom Walters.

Many of those present at the church had been his students—he loved teaching and he had a special way of bringing excitement to learning. He had been a member of the English faculty at North Carolina State University since 1964, and he had been one of the pioneers in North Carolina's Poetry-in-the Schools program. At many towns and in country schools across the state they still remember him for the joy he brought into the classrooms as young boys and girls learned to fashion poetry out of their lives.

Tom Walters was a man of many talents—writer, painter, sculptor—and we remember the special rapport he established with young actors as a director of plays in the Raleigh Children's Theater.

We remember, too, the keen insight he brought to literary criticism. He had the scholar's touch, and the writer's ability to make a review as readable and as exciting as the book itself, and that is a special talent.

We loved to hear Tom read his poetry. There was a special flavor to it, his eyes would light up and the twinkle would be in them and in his voice. He could be earthy and he could make words soar.

Tom's friendships were strong, and he was a favorite at any gathering of writers. But what stood out was his love and devotion to his wife Linda and his young daughter Candace. They were at the center of his being.

Susan Katz is today an award winning children's book author, and the founder and Executive Editor of Connecting Authors, a national non-profit bringing authors into schools as role models of literacy and the arts. Susan wrote to Ragan in 1984.

I would like to tell you what a wonderful time I had last week at Weymouth. I can hardly believe that I once had been apprehensive about it, almost chickening out even up until the last minute before heading down Rt. 1. Leaving Southern Pines Friday, of course, teary-eyed, longing to stay. Well, part of that is because how thoroughly spoiled I had gotten. The whole place runs so smoothly.

In addition to the creature comforts of pre-arranged aloneness, I also loved the place. Oh, I know some people who've been there have written about the long leafs and the jonquils, and not being a garden-type poet myself, I wasn't sure what I'd find there. Purely and simply, just getting quiet allowed me to find all sorts of things. While at Weymouth, I wrote two one-acts, several essays, and a few poems. The warmest of thank-yous to you for allowing me to discover that energy and excitement.

About six months later Katz wrote to Ragan again, sending him a poem about Weymouth.

My time there this past spring was real important to me, I knew beforehand that it would be, and I continue to harvest from those same fields cultivated that week. Hope I will be able to give back some of what I got during my stay there. Heard you were looking for some Weymouth poems and wanted to send you this one.

Weymouth

Funny,
I had thought this place
to be a retreat
silent
the only sounds
perhaps that of
magnolias dripping,
or longleaf pines
letting loose their needles.
What I hadn't counted on
was the nightly clacking,
the ghost of Jim Boyd
alive at the typewriter.
Hailstorm of poems
falling from the sky.

Sam Ragan was elected into the North Carolina Journalism Hall of Fame in 1984, along with Burke Davis, Gerald Johnson, William Lassiter, and Eugene Robinson. By this time, Ragan had been working for newspapers since the 1930s, well over 40 years. The University of North Carolina at Chapel Hill School of Journalism had established the Journalism Hall of Fame in 1981, recognizing persons born in North Carolina, or persons born elsewhere who became identified with the state.

John Ehle wrote to Ragan in 1984. The two were good friends and frequent correspondents.

My newest novel, *Last One Home*, comes out soon, and the publisher, Harper and Row, is supposed to send you a copy. I'm pleased with it. Years ago I wrote *Lion on the Hearth*, set in Asheville, a novel patient with its own pace and characters, and this one, also set in Asheville, has taken on some of the same assurance. Anyway, it is done.

Manly Wade Wellman wrote to Ragan in 1984 from Chapel Hill, touching on several subjects. The book he mentions is one of his many books, called *The Story of Moore County,* which was a history of Moore County, where Southern Pines was located.

> If you aren't satisfied with this, neither am I. You said 2000 words. I had to figure out what I must omit, events and people really belonging in history. I did emphasize three men who must be remembered — Page, who founded Aberdeen, Patrick who founded Southern Pines, Tufts who founded Pinehurst. More or less, they made Moore County what it is today. Do whatever you like with it. You have to revise lots of country correspondents. The only news here is the same. I'll be 81 in May, and by the end of the year my 81st book will be published by Doubleday. Then another next year, while I work like hell on what I hope will be my best book so far. It happens in North Africa around the end of the 7th century. After that, we'll see.
>
> I didn't even mention you, who just might be the most admirable and interesting man in the county. That sort of thing happens when a history is reduced to generalities.

As usual, Ragan continued to speak to organizations around the state and country. In late 1984, Nancy Mann, Vice-President of the Poetry Society of Virginia, read an article about Ragan in the *Norfolk-Virginian Pilot.* Mann invited Ragan to read his poetry in Virginia Beach. Mann offered a fee of $150, and then enticed him with these words, knowing of Ragan's love of nature. "May is a lovely time of year at Virginia Beach. If you drive into the Bay Colony area, the dogwood and azalea are usually in full bloom, and local gardens are colorful with daffodils and tulips. I do hope you and Mrs. Ragan will be able to come." Ragan accepted Mann's offer.

In 1985 Elwyn Brooks White, better known as E.B. White, passed away. White contributed to *The New Yorker* magazine for more than 50 years, and was co-author of *The Elements of Style.* White also wrote many children's books, including *Stuart Little, Charlotte's Web*, and *The Trumpet of the Swan.* Ragan wrote about White in *Southern Accent.*

> "He never wrote a mean or careless sentence," William Shawn, *The New Yorker* editor, said last week of E.B. White, who died October 1 at his home near Ellsworth, Maine.

As a writer, E.B. White was indeed the master craftsman of his time. He wrote with grace, and wit, and charm, and his essays whether read the first, second or third time, were always a delight.

His name was Elwyn Brooks White, and he was born in 1899 in Mount Vernon, N.Y. His friends called him Andy, a nickname he acquired as a freshman at Cornell. Among those friends was Francis Gray Patton of Durham, also a writer for *The New Yorker*, who often visited in the home of Andy and Katharine White.

White joined the staff of *The New Yorker* two years after its founding in 1925 and established the "Talk of the Town" column as a special form of reporting. He was followed in the "Talk of the Town" by two natives of North Carolina, Joseph Mitchell of Robeson County and St. Clair McKelway of Cumberland County, and both have a grace of style that is their own.

I first came upon White in *The New Yorker*, and then found special pleasure in his books, *One Man's Meat* and *The Points of My Compass* being especially appealing. The anthology which he and his wife edited, *A Sub Treasury of American Humor,* is an American classic. All of White's books are classic, and he has had a tremendous effect on other writers.

William Shawn said, "Because of his quiet influence, several generations of this country's writers write better than they might have done."

White found his own world on his Maine farm where he had lived for many years, and he wrote about his world with an appeal which was universal.

He remained an optimist, although he saw the world and the human condition with realistic eyes. A few years ago he wrote to a friend, saying, "As long as there is one upright man, as long as there is one compassionate woman, the contagion may spread, and the scene is not desolate."

Kudzu was the topic in Ragan's *Southern Accent*, and also the subject of a poem he wrote.

A few days ago *The Pilot* published a picture by Chief Photographer Glenn M. Sides of a rural scene covered by kudzu. It was titled "Captured By Kudzu" and indeed it was. There was kudzu everywhere, on the grounds, the trees and the roofs of two old tobacco barns.

The large-leafed, indestructible vine is one of the leading characteristics of the Southern landscape. The plant was imported last century from Japan, where it is used as a jelling agent, cushion stuffing, mosquito repellent, tofu ingredient and medication.

Southern men and women of a certain age will sometimes confide—if they know and trust you well—that in their youth they planted kudzu along eroding banks to conserve the soil. But in this section of warm winters and robust summers, kudzu has become the Secretariat of fast-growing vines. It leaves the rapacious wisteria and honeysuckle in the dust.

It is difficult for anyone who has seen kudzu consume houses to talk about it without using verbs like "devour" and "enshroud."

The Kudzu Man

She called him the kudzu man,
And there were similarities in the two.
Kudzu comes on quietly,
Giving its greenness to the gully-washed land,
Covering the raw erosion, providing food
For cattle, shade for a sun-washed porch.
In its early days it is gentle,
Caring and kind, but then—
Before you know it, before you
Are really aware it has taken over,
Covered everything, swallowed up
The land, the trees, telephone poles,
And even the house.
Kudzu is the overpowering king,
It takes everything.
He did, too.

Louis Rubin, who founded Algonquin Books of Chapel Hill, wrote to stockholders of the company in 1986. Algonquin was in a financial crisis. Sam and Marjorie Ragan were already major investors in Algonquin when the letter from Rubin arrived in Southern Pines.

It has been almost five years since we set out to establish a small but full-fledged trade publishing house in the South. We wanted to publish good books, and eventually to make a reasonable profit doing it. We knew it would take a while, we would have to develop our own authors, develop a sustaining backlist, and create a national reputation. Now, just when we are in sight of our goal, we seem about to lose control of our company.

In the absence of sufficient capital to handle our outstanding indebtedness and see us through this winter and spring, we must either sell the company or face bankruptcy. We have only enough money to keep going for two more weeks.

Two publishing houses have expressed a strong interest in buying us. Neither has made a firm offer. What both would probably do is to assume our debts, retain our name and our Chapel Hill address, retain our editorial staff; Shannon Ravenel and I would receive a salary for the first time in our five years of operation, but our stockholders are likely to receive little or nothing.

So it comes to this. If our stockholders are willing to increase their investment so that we can pay off our pressing debts and keep going, it seems likely that we can turn everything around.

The latest update on our fall orders not only shows frontlist orders for 23,279 books, but backlist sales of 5,726 books since July 1. This is much better than ever before. Avon Books has bought paperback rights to William B. Hopkins' *One Bugle No Drums*. Both Canadian book club and trade edition rights to *The Complete Pregnancy Workbook* have been sold. But it is our spring list which really holds the promise. Clyde Edgerton's new novel has been made a Book-of the-Month Club alternate selection, thus ensuring it of enormous publicity. We should probably print 50,000 copies of the initial printing. Another novel, by Kaye Gibbons, shows signs of being a hit; we have rave reviews from Eudora Welty, Walker Percy, Elizabeth Spencer, Alfred Kazin and Gordon Lish to use in advertising it. We have an almost certain hit in a baseball book for young people, *Ask Dale Murphy*, the Braves all-star centerfielder.

That was the form letter sent to all of the investors. In a side note to Sam Ragan, Rubin wrote, "Sam, you invested very recently, and I do not feel you ought to do so again, you've done your part." But, as usual, when a literary entity in North Carolina was in trouble, Ragan always did what he could. Within days of getting the letter asking for more investment in Algonquin Books, Ragan invested more. Ragan received another letter from Rubin, "Sam, thank you for your splendid investment in our company."

Acquired by Workman Publishing from Louis Rubin in 1989, Algonquin Books now has offices in Chapel Hill and New York City, and has published authors such as Dan Rather, Tayari Jones, Sara Gruen, Robert Goolrick, Lee Smith, Jill McCorkle, Clyde Edgerton, and Robert Morgan, among many others with national reputations.

Louis Rubin retired from Algonquin in 1991 as chief editor and publisher. From Algonquin's start in 1982, when its office was in Rubin's garage in Chapel Hill, to today having a nationally recognized publishing company, Algonquin has come a long way, to say the least. Rubin was given the Ivan Sandrof Lifetime Achievement Award in 2004 by the National Book Critics Circle for his work at Algonquin and his work as a writing teacher. He was selected into the North Carolina Literary Hall of Fame in 1997, the same year his good friend Sam Ragan was. Rubin passed away in 2013.

Another person who came to Sam Ragan for help in 1986 was Charleen Swansea. Swansea founded *Red Clay Reader* in 1964, an annual magazine that published mostly Southern authors. She also founded Red Clay Publishers. Swansea had turned to Ragan for funds for the magazine, especially during Ragan's tenure as chairman of the North Carolina Arts Council in the late 1960s and early 70s. In April of 1986 her husband was killed in a fire that destroyed their house in South Carolina. Swansea and her husband had separated, so it was not sure why her husband was in the house. He had moved out, and the house was for sale as part of the pending divorce settlement. Swansea, in her letter, is pretty sure who set the fire. And after the fire, she would go on to publish her book "about the human mind," *Mindworks: How to Become a More Creative and Critical Thinker.* Ragan, along with other writers who knew Swansea, did provide some aid to one of their fellow writers in need.

In June Swansea sent Ragan a letter.

On April 23rd my house and office for writing, teaching, and publishing burned to the ground. I lost everything I ever owned, all my library, and cherished manuscripts by mentors like T.S. Eliot, Conrad Aiken, and Ezra Pound. Because the fire was set, there is little insurance. I am devastated by the loss of my husband, but his violent and irrational act has doubled my dedication to the research and writing of a book I was working on about the human mind. I am currently teaching young scholars at the Governor's School in Charleston and I intend to continue writing and giving seminars. Do you suppose that the N.C. Writers Conference could find a way to help me? I have worked long and hard on the behalf of writing and publishing in the State of North Carolina. To continue working, I need basic books like Shakespeare, Dante, Tolstoy, the poets we all loved, Frost, Whitman, Dickinson, the novelists like Hemingway and Faulkner, the Southerners, Eudora, Tom Wolfe, and Bill Styron. It would cost $2,000 to replace the 200 books that I need.

By this time, Ragan was several years into his poet laureateship. He spoke about his position.

I have a duty to promote and encourage the reading and writing of poetry, so I have made public appearances, at least 25 or 30 each year, since that time. I recall at the press conference when Governor Jim Hunt announced my appointment and someone asked what a poet laureate does and his reply was that "He does what Sam Ragan has always been doing." At the North Carolina Poetry Festival, held each year at Weymouth, all poets in the state are invited to come and read. For the past couple of years, we've had about 150 poets and everybody gets a chance to read their poetry. It's an all-day affair, but not formal or highly structured. We try to keep it informal and make it an enjoyable occasion. I also work with other groups such as the North Carolina Poetry Society and the Poetry Center of the Southeast at Guilford College and the North Carolina Poetry Council in Asheville. The development of poetry in North Carolina has been remarkable. I can remember 30 years ago, you could count the practicing poets in the state on the fingers of your hand. Now if I were getting together an anthology of North Carolina poets in the state, the number would be in the hundreds.

Ruth Moose is a winner of the Sam Ragan Fine Arts Award and the Robert Ruark Award for Short Story. She has published collections of short stories and collections of poetry. She was on the Creative Writing faculty at UNC-Chapel Hill for 15 years. Recent books include *Doing It at the Dixie Dew* and *Wedding Bell Blues*. She wrote to Ragan in 1986, catching him up on events in her life.

A note to say I was sorry to miss Poetry Day at Weymouth. Flew to Texas to do a short story workshop and took a few days afterwards to tour. Went to Waco and Baylor where the Armstrong-Browning Library contains the world's largest collection of Eliz and Robert Browning letters and manuscripts. A find! In August I've been accepted at the Robert Frost Symposium held in the Frost home in Franconia, New Hampshire, for a week of workshops, study, readings. And I got a PEN award for a short story recently. So it's been a busy summer. I continue to enjoy *The Pilot*. Always your column and the book reviews. Keep 'em coming. Yesterday we had a celebration and autograph session for *Signs Along the Way* in Charlotte. Didn't that book turn out well? Looks and content. Your poem was read as an opener. A fine afternoon and some books sold. Is someone reviewing *Cardinal* for *The Pilot*? Dick Krawiec did such a good job with that collection that it deserves some banners. Steve Smith would be a good one to do a review. Tell him I said so, as if he isn't up to his ears in enough stuff all the time anyway. And thanks for reprinting anything from *Arts Journal*. We hang in and any attention is welcome.

Weymouth, the former James and Katharine Boyd home now called Weymouth Center for the Arts, was well into its writers-in-residence program by this time, 1986. Many writers had been invited, mostly at the invitation of Sam Ragan, to spend a week or two at Weymouth to work on their craft. The rooms were cozy, and there were beautiful grounds, woods, and flowers to enjoy while roaming outside. Many programs were held at Weymouth, other than the writers-in-residence program. For example, the 1986 schedule included Bill Neal talking about his new cook book, Clifton Matthews gave a piano recital, and in November a book agent, Rhoda Weyr, gave a lecture about how books get published. In January of 1987, a saxophonist, James Houlik, and Nelson Padgett, a pianist, gave a concert.

Sam Ragan was honored with a big gathering in early 1986 when there was a ceremony at Davis Memorial Library at Methodist College in Fayetteville for a presentation of his poetry being recorded. Spoken Arts, the company that did the recording, titled the record *Poems of Sam Ragan Read by the Poet*. Ragan signed the copies for distribution to over 1,000 libraries around the state.

Roy Parker introduced Ragan as "a distinguished editor earlier in his career at *The News and Observer* and more recently at *The Pilot* in Southern Pines, as a distinguished bureaucrat as the first Secretary of the North Carolina Department of Cultural Resources, and as a mentor to hundreds of creative people in the state, the writers and historians, not to mention his own poetry that got him named Poet Laureate." Former Governor Bob Scott made remarks about his old friend, Sam Ragan, who he had appointed as that very first Secretary of Cultural Resources. William Friday spoke, James Hemby, who was president of Atlantic Christian College, Ragan's alma mater, was on hand, as was Sally Buckner, a former student of Ragan's at his Writers Workshop class at North Carolina State University. Buckner was teaching in the English Department at Peace College in Raleigh and was an accomplished poet herself. Hemby remarked that Ragan "was a gentle man, clean of spirit, clear of mind, who knows from whence he came." Friday, with a nod toward the then President of the United States, called Sam Ragan "a bona fide Southerner with his longing for place, for roots and ties, one Ragan I can really cheer about." Buckner asserted that Ragan was the literary godfather who "has made generosity part of the job description for a North Carolina writer."

The Town of Southern Pines started to prepare to celebrate its Centennial in the early 1980s. Southern Pines had been founded by John T. Patrick. Patrick was born in Wadesboro, North Carolina. Even at a young age, Patrick started making money. He traveled around the country as a retail confectioner and also gave magic lantern shows. He became the owner and editor of the *Pee Dee Herald* newspaper in Wadesboro. Patrick also owned a general store and was a captain in the State Guard. Along with all of this, he sold building lots in Wadesboro, located in Anson County. Patrick then got the idea to distribute to northern newspapers information about the inexpensive and fertile land in Anson County. The governor heard about this plan and named Patrick head of the State Department of Immigration in 1883. Patrick had relatives who lived in Moore County, and he became aware of the healthful qualities of the Sandhills area. He purchased 675 acres in Moore County and laid out a town first called Vineland but soon renamed Southern Pines. When James Tufts of Boston came to the Sandhills in 1895, Patrick showed him the area and Tufts chose the site of what became Pinehurst.

So as Southern Pines began preparations for its Centennial in the early 1980s, Sam Ragan's love of history and trees resulted in a standoff between the town of Southern Pines and him, and also produced a new poem by Ragan. Ragan wrote about this experience in *Southern Accent*.

> There is an irony in the fact that as the Town of Southern Pines prepares to celebrate its Centennial it cuts down four large black walnut trees planted by the town's founder on one of the town's main avenues.
>
> Those walnut trees were in front of *The Pilot* and we had resisted their destruction for more than a year. It had been determined that they were planted in the early 1880s by John T. Patrick, that man of vision who founded Southern Pines. Patrick had owned a house located on the Pennsylvania Avenue site where *The Pilot* now stands.
>
> There had been five walnut trees, but one of them had died a few years ago and was removed. The four remaining were healthy, however, and upwards of 18 inches in diameter at their base. They were ungainly, but they provided some shade in summer, a sizeable walnut crop, and their stark, bare branches in winter had a certain beauty and a strong appeal.
>
> We finally gave in when it became evident we were the only holdout in the block and the Town of Southern Pines agreed to remove the old walnut trees and plant about a dozen red maples. Those red maples will look beautiful when they grow a little more.
>
> The town also agreed to cut the walnut trees into suitable lengths and to store the wood on town property. The plan is to use the walnut wood for such things as commemorative plaques, gavels, carvings and art works as the town enters its period of celebration of its Centennial.

There was a surprise development out of the demise of the walnut trees. Tony Parker, the hardware man and *The Pilot's* next door neighbor, came visiting a few days ago. He had salvaged eight walnuts from the gutters of our building, and had rooted them in small clay pots. He kept a couple and brought us the rest of the newly sprouted walnut trees.

"You can still have a Patrick tree," he said.

We brought one home with us, and in the past two weeks it has grown two inches. That little green sprout has a special meaning for us.

We hope to get our stone bench which sat under one of the walnut trees back within a few days.

We know the street will be beautiful in the future. Those red maples will put on a good show. But we still miss our old black walnuts.

Sam Ragan, as he often did with his poems, held on to memories by writing a poem about his beloved old walnut trees.

John Patrick's Walnut Trees

The founder of the town had planted them —
Five black walnut trees had survived
More than one hundred years.
One had died at the century mark,
But the others still had their ungainly beauty,
The bare stark branches against the sky
Had a special appeal, and the avenue
Along which they stood was enhanced
By their presence.
But the town fathers knew they were old
And perhaps would soon die,
So they were ordered cut down.
He resisted them for more than a year,
But finally gave in after promises were made
That new red maples would take their place,
And their timber would be saved
For historic artifacts. But he stayed away

The morning they came down. It was too much to watch.
And then, a neighbor came with a pot
In which a seedling grew—he had saved
Some of the walnuts and they had sprouted.
Now that seedling is more than two feet tall,
It will be nursed to manhood,
And a link to John Patrick.

11

"Let Us Walk into April," "Not just a newspaper but a work of art"

The Pilot had been growing in both number of pages and in subscriptions since Ragan had bought the newspaper in 1968. The circulation was over 14,000. Ragan made the decision to go bi-weekly in 1986, to be published each Monday and Thursday. In 1986 Talmadge Ragan was listed as a Consultant, Norris Hodgkins as Treasurer, Florence Gilkeson as Managing Editor, Sara Lindau, Claudia Madeley, and Brent Hackney as Reporters, Mary Evelyn Nissoff as Pinehurst Editor, Woodrow Wilhoit, Carthage Editor, Charles Weatherspoon as Circulation Manager, Kathy Lawrence as Office Manager, Faye Dasen as Editorial Secretary, and Glenn Sides as Chief Photographer.

In an interview he gave during this time, Ragan commented on running a newspaper.

Every day I come to work with a sense of excitement. I like to take the raw material of news and shape it into a newspaper. I like to think of each issue as a work of art. *The Pilot* serves a unique community, a resort area and retirement center. Many of the residents are retirees. They're from top level management, the military, the U.S. State Department and educational fields. They don't want to play golf all the time. They want to be involved.

The measure of any paper, whether it's the *New York Times* or *The Pilot*, is how well it covers its community. Good newspapers can have as much influence for good as a university, the church, the school system. As one learned person said, "the newspaper is the university of the people." We try to be comprehensive. We try to cover everything, from potholes in the street to what happens in Raleigh and Washington. I believe in complete news coverage of a community, and there should be no censorship.

Every editor has his own standards, of course, and I believe objectivity is at the heart of those standards. A true newspaperman is taught and learns by experience that it is his duty to objectively inform people of facts to the best of his ability. The whole basis of our democratic society is that an informed people can be depended on to make the right decisions about their lives.

We also believe, as did Thoreau, that one should "never ignore a fact, it may flower into a truth."

Ragan's poem, "The Editor," contains some of his viewpoints of running a newspaper and the job of an editor.

The Editor

I like to take the raw news
And shape it into a newspaper,
And on a good day it becomes
Not just a newspaper
But a work of art.
I like to think of it that way.
It is a mirror of my town—
The good, the bad, the reality
Of living and dying.
What people do, what they say,
What they think—it's all there.
I believe that an informed people
Can make the right decisions
About their lives.
That is why we are here,
And we are the record of those lives.

A long time ago a wise old editor said
The function of a newspaper
Is "To print the news and raise hell."
I haven't been able to improve upon that definition.

In 1968, when Ragan bought *The Pilot*, the newspaper was doing just over $200,000 in business a year. In 1986 that number was over $1.1 million.

Ragan wrote most of the editorials, and there was no question that when it came to politics, he leaned Democratic. In the 1984 presidential election of 1984, when Walter Mondale opposed Ronald Reagan, Ragan wrote, "An examination of individual contests points to Democratic choices from the presidency on down." A Republican reader took issue. "It's a shame that area readers are not provided with a fair and truthful analysis of the candidate's overall qualifications to hold office rather than with a pure party line demagoguery, which by this time we really have had a belly full." After Moore County voted Republican in the election, Ragan acknowledged the popularity of Reagan in an editorial. But a reader sent a letter to the editor. "Your editorial tries to rationalize this great victory by lamely stating that it occurred because the public wished to elect 'an affable and aging actor who has proven himself to be a master of rhetoric.' Mr. Ragan, have you so little faith in the American people?"

The Pilot, under Ragan, sometimes devoted an entire page to letters to the editor. Ragan printed them, whether they were in agreement with something in the paper or not, whether they agreed with his editorials or not. He firmly believed in a newspaper being an instrument for dissent and opposing ideas, to give readers a voice in their community. All he asked was for the letters to be decent and not too personal.

After Velma Barfield was executed in North Carolina for murder in 1984, Ragan wrote an editorial against capital punishment. He used only 16 words to make his point, the 16 words were the entire editorial, surrounded by heavy black border. "Is North Carolina a better place today for its killing of Velma Barfield last Friday morning?"

Following are some excerpts from Ragan's *Southern Accent* in 1986.

Harness race training is in full swing in Pinehurst this month, and before the fall and winter training season is over and the horses head for northern tracks more than 500 will have been in the area.

The training of horses for harness racing long has been identified with Pinehurst, and many people like to get up early to watch them run.

One of those who visited the Sandhills some fifty years ago and who wrote about harness racing in his novels and stories was Sherwood Anderson. He was a true devotee of the sport.

Anderson was a visitor at Weymouth of James and Katharine Boyd, whose daughter, Nancy, recalls that he had a daily ritual which revolved around the harness race tracks. She said that Anderson would have someone make him a sandwich the night before, and he would arise early, long before dawn, put the sandwich in a jacket pocket, and have a driver take him to the track on Midland Road. There he would lean on the fence and watch the horses run, munching on his sandwich. When the running stopped he would return to Weymouth for a full breakfast and then a period of writing.

One of Anderson's most famous stories about horses was "I'm a Fool," and at least one story, and maybe two, were written while he was a visitor with the Boyds at Weymouth.

Anderson is best known for his American classic, *Winesburg, Ohio*, but he won the Pulitzer Prize in 1925 for his novel, *Dark Laughter*, and his collection of stories *The Triumph of the Egg* also is a classic.

He was an original on the American literary scene. William Faulkner said of him, "He took us to the top of the hill and showed us the vistas beyond. He showed us the way."

❊

Robert Penn Warren is a splendid choice for America's first Poet Laureate. He is indeed a master in both poetry and prose, the only person to win the Pulitzer Prize in both fields, twice in poetry, and he brings honor to the title.

We met Red Warren several years ago, and one of the most stimulating evenings we have ever enjoyed was in his company. Our talk continued until 4 o'clock in the morning, and every minute was an experience. Warren and I sat around and drank a little and talked a lot. We mostly talked about poetry, but also his folks, how they grew tobacco — burley tobacco in Kentucky. We also corresponded. He was a remarkable talent.

Other poets in the 20th century may have been technically more inventive, a few have been more influential in academia, but surely none has spoken more authentically to the soul of American life. Like his justly celebrated novel, *All the King's Men*, the verse of Warren's mature years inquires into man's deepest moral concerns, especially the nature of evil and the individual's search for freedom and order.

For Southerners, Warren's elevation to Poet Laureate is particularly gratifying. Warren has taught at Yale University since 1950, but his themes are inseparable from the South's history and heritage. He was one of the leaders of the group at Vanderbilt University whose members called themselves The Fugitives, young writers who championed the spiritual values of the agrarian South.

In the poetry and prose of Robert Penn Warren, the South has risen triumphant, and a nation's conscience has risen with it.

Ragan wrote a poem with Robert Penn Warren in mind, and also showed that poets minds wander, just like others. Ragan once said, "Poems are compiled from fragments of living."

The Poet

The poet stood in front of the class
And talked about his poems.
My poems are fragments, he said.
All my life I have gathered fragments.
I try to put them together.
He talked on and on, telling
Pleasant stories — about what
Red Warren said about writing a poem:
Erecting a public monument
From a private itch — and of others
Who also talked about their sullen art.

His talk was in fragments,
And then the girl in the front row
Uncrossed her legs
And his mind wandered to other things.

※

Manly Wade Wellman was an old friend who had turned from a career in journalism to an incredibly productive career as a professional writer of fiction, history and biography.

Several years ago he had confided to us that he wanted to publish a number of books equal to his age. This he had done a couple of years ago and when he died a few days ago at the age of 83 he was at work on his 84th book.

There were in addition more than 500 short stories and innumerable articles. He was indeed a professional writer and very proud of it.

We first met Wellman many years ago when he was living in Pinebluff and had published a first-rate biography of a man for whom he was named—General Wade Hampton of South Carolina. He called it *Giant in Gray* and we had given it a favorable review. There came a note of appreciation from him, and shortly thereafter we were asked to introduce him at a gathering in Raleigh where he spoke on Hampton and other aspects of his work.

There were correspondence and meetings over the years, and we were privileged to speak about him and his career when he was honored a few years ago by the North Carolina Writer's Conference. Sometimes he would drop me a note of inquiry about some fact in regard to a book he was working on. He was a careful researcher, and his journalism background made it second nature for him to be sure of his facts before he wrote anything down.

We worked with Manly in the writing of *The Story of Moore County*, that superb history.

Manly Wade Wellman encouraged many young writers. He had taught creative writing at Elon College and the University of North Carolina Chapel Hill, and he used to bring some of his students to the annual meetings of the N.C. Writers Conference. He wanted them to meet other writers and perhaps find the enthusiasm for writing which he had and wanted to share. He had a great respect for the written word, and he was a prolific practitioner of the art. To him writing was a craft, a profession, and a calling.

※

The 37th annual gathering of the North Carolina Writers Conference was held this past weekend at the Mission Valley Inn at Raleigh, and more than a hundred writers from all parts of the state were on hand for some lively discussion on the literary arts and the craft of writing.

We joined with several others in trying to answer the question of "Southern Writers: Why Are There So Many Of Us?"

Mary Snotherly, who is the incoming chair of the conference, posed the question and presided. Seeking an answer were R.T. Smith, formerly of Appalachian and now at Auburn University, Jack Roper of St. Andrews College in Laurinburg, Stephen Smith of Southern Pines, and Margaret Baddour of Goldsboro.

We recalled the old story of the visitor to Hannibal, Missouri, who came across an old timer and asked him if he knew Mark Twain. The old timer said, "Sure, I knew Sam, and I knew just as many stories as he did. The only difference was he writ 'em down."

Steve Smith, who is one of the best story-tellers in the literary realms today—a story-teller of great humor and wit—said that Southerners like to embellish upon a tale. "Some call it telling lies," he said. He gave some examples of what he was talking about.

All agreed that a strong sense of place is a dominant factor in the best of Southern writing, that Southerners feel close to nature because most of them felt close to the land. There was a mystic quality to the land, and that entered into the literature.

Ragan published his fourth book of poetry in 1986, titled *A Walk into April*. As always with his poems, Ragan employed a lean and spare phrasing, with many of his poems describing the change of seasons. The "Let Us Walk into April" poem is displayed on one of the walking trails on the grounds at Weymouth.

Let Us Walk into April

It was a pear tree in bloom
That lit up your eyes.
You came at blossom time—
Dogwoods and lilacs,
The camellia and azalea,

And the glow of the redbud tree—
Thousands of wildflowers run before your feet,
And a faint green hovers in the woods.
Here we are just before the coming of April,
When the whole world is new
And each day is a beginning,
A time of sunlight and splendor—
Come, let us walk into April.

In "Morning Collection" Ragan tells us to not take things for granted, to savor each moment, to store good memories to help us get through not so good moments. Remember the good morning for perhaps the afternoon might not be as agreeable.

Morning Collection

I was awake early
To the innocence of morning,
Collecting that innocence,
The colors and sounds
And storing them away
For noon time, afternoons and nights.

Also included in *A Walk into April* was "The Leaving," a poem that speaks to the expectancy of marriage and new relationships and all that they would bring, but sometimes it just doesn't work out.

The Leaving

It wasn't what she expected at all—
It was no mansion, it was a hovel,
And he wouldn't, or couldn't,
Talk to her.
After eight months she had had enough,
She would go back to Richmond,
Back to her friends, tell them something.
She packed her bag,
And on that May morning

She walked out to the field
Behind the house where he was plowing.
She waited at the end of the row
Until he had pulled the horse to halt.
"I'm leaving you, Will," she said.
He did not say anything.
His eyes said it all,
And he slapped the horse with the line
To start a new furrow.
She did not look back.

One of Ragan's favorite ways to relax was to sit in his back yard at his home in Southern Pines, look at the pine trees and flowers, and read a good book. Other times he would sit with Marjorie, or daughters Nancy and Talmadge, or Robin and Eric, the grandkids. In "Done with Apple Picking," he is reading one of his favorites, Robert Frost.

Done with Apple-Picking

I put down the book
And see the September moon
Rising slightly red
Beyond the stilled pines.
I have been reading the poet
Who talked of apple-picking,
And mending walls, the bending of birches,
Of pasture springs and other things...

But I am done with apple-picking now.

The moon has gone higher.
And far off in the night,
In the valley of Aberdeen
A dog is barking.

Approaching almost 50 years of marriage by the time *A Walk into April* was published, Sam's and Marjorie's love for each other continued to grow. Ragan thinks of his beloved wife as he wrote "Face Sleeping."

Face Sleeping

I was awake early,
But before I arose,
I watched your face sleeping.
I cannot remember when your face
Has not been there.
I drink coffee and watch
The sun come up.
I feel a warm glow.

Paul Kresh, in reviewing *A Walk into April,* said, "Everywhere the reader will encounter an absolute clarity, not only in Ragan's sharp-focused imagery, but in point of view unwaveringly and entirely his own, stringent and economical with language, but open-hearted and unstinting in compassion for human suffering." Tom Wicker of the *New York Times* wrote, "This is poetry sensitive to the seasons of life, the sureties and contradictions of living, the elements in which we exist. And it could only have been written out of a Tar Heel's sense of place."

Along with "Let Us Walk into April," "Return to April" and "The Tally of Our Days" all included references to April. These April poems were part of *A Walk into April*. April was perhaps Ragan's favorite month, along with October. He wrote about the month of April in *Southern Accent.*

Chaucer wrote that when April comes folks start thinking about going on pilgrimages. The Latin name for April is Arilis, and the ancient Romans considered this fourth month as being sacred to Venus, and some believe that its name comes from Venus' Greek equivalent, Aphrodite, the goddess of love and beauty. There are others who believe the name comes from the Latin "aperire," meaning "to open," and that is consistent with the time of the year when there is an unfolding of buds and blossoms.

In our land we see this opening, this unfolding, in a rhapsody of blossoms — the dogwood, the cherry and the pear, the millions of field violets, lilacs, wisteria, a riot of azaleas, the camellia, and hundreds of other flowers, both wild and domestic.

Even before April arrived we had seen the subtle colors of the woodlands emerge, and all our senses were becoming attuned to a world almost suddenly alive with new sights and sounds. And the smells of Spring, of new turned soils, the growing grasses, and the sweetness in the air from the flowering of the earth.

T.S. Eliot said "April is the cruelest month," because it awakens old desire, but other poets see it as a time for rejoicing. As paeans to Aphrodite the themes of love and beauty are found in much of the English and American poetry of earlier times and even today.

Ragan also included "An Evening of Talk" in his new book of poetry. Gerald Johnson was in the poem and Ragan wrote about Johnson when he passed away in 1980.

Gerald Johnson had lived in Baltimore for more than 50 years, but he kept his roots in his native North Carolina. Until ill health intervened a few years ago he came back every summer to Riverton, where he was born in Scotland County, and spent several weeks at Spring Hill. Those weeks were times for rejuvenation, and he would return to Baltimore for work on another book, and during his illustrious career which ended a few days ago when he died at the age of 89, he published more than 30 books.

There was grace and charm as well as tremendous erudition in his writing, whether it was an editorial in the *Baltimore Sun*, a biography of a president such as Andrew Jackson, an essay, or a work on the American people. He was a keen observer and he wrote with an understanding heart. Whatever he wrote was a pleasure to read.

Some years ago we invited him to talk at a meeting of the North Carolina Writer's Conference. We met in Charlotte and when he arrived he had lost his baggage, but he was not concerned about it, and he immediately sought out some old friends for reminiscing and talk about the present and the future. We sat fascinated as Gerald Johnson, Paul Green, and Jonathan Daniels talked until 2 or 3 o'clock in the morning. His talk the next day at the Writer's Conference was excellent, but we remember that night of conversation as a treasured time.

Gerald Johnson will be long remembered. He was a native son who brought luster to the state.

An Evening of Talk

They were in a room together,
Alike and unalike —
Paul Green, Jonathan Daniels, Gerald Johnson.
A little bourbon and branch,
From time to time, loosened them
And they talked until morning.
They talked and I listened.
It was a splendid evening.

In 1987 Ragan edited the book *Weymouth: An Anthology of Poetry.* Anna-Carolyn Stirewalt Gilbo was the Coordinating Editor and Marsha Warren was Consulting Editor. Many writers contributed poems to celebrate the former home of James and Katharine Boyd which at this time was called the Weymouth Center for the Arts and Humanities. Anne Russell wrote "The Herb Lady of Weymouth." Anna-Carolyn Stirewalt Gilbo wrote "Beneath the Slate Roof."

The Herb Lady of Weymouth

She dug her bony fingers into winter hard earth
I'll plant alyssum here, she said
And there I'll plant some marigolds
You can't see it, but beneath these weeds
There's a garden waiting to be reborn
I'll put a border of bricks around it
You won't recognize this place next spring
I'm just an old woman who lives alone
Not much good to anyone
But I love to make things grow.

Beneath the Slate Roof

At night
I close my eyes
and see

the hounds of stone
leap down
desert their posts.
They chase
through virgin pines
to bay at shadows
in the fields
while in my room
beneath the slate
I summon Wolfe, Fitzgerald, Boyd
and all the spirits
of the house:
  Come, touch
   my dark,
    my waiting pen.

Ragan continued *Southern Accent*. Here are some topics he wrote about in the late 1980s.

It was back in the early 1950s that we struck up a correspondence with Guy Owen, who was at that time teaching at Stetson University in Florida. We had printed one of his poems in this column a few years earlier.

Later we encouraged Guy to apply for an opening in the English Department at N.C. State University and set up an appointment with Lodwick Hartley, then chairman of the department. Guy was hired and within a few years became an institution himself at N.C. State. He brought with him to State the *Southern Poetry Review* which he had founded under the name of *Impetus* at Stetson, and the magazine soon acquired a national reputation for excellence.

Guy Owen continued to write both poetry and prose. A collection of his poetry, *Cape Fear Poems*, had appeared earlier, and that was followed by *The White Stallion*, published by John F. Blair. It was as a novelist, however, which gained him national attention. *His Ballad of the Flim-Flam Man* was a bestseller and was made into a movie, which is still being seen on television. There followed a sequel to the *Flim-Flam Man* and then a novel which we regard as a North Carolina classic, *Journey for Joedel*. There also were short stories published, and Guy was much in demand as a speaker all across the country.

He gave his time and talent to many good causes, including the establishment of the Weymouth Center in Southern Pines. He was the first writer-in-residence at Weymouth when that program was started in 1979.

"The Reader" by Fred Chappell of Greensboro is from the Spring issue of the *St. Andrews Review*:

Beside the floor lamp that has companioned her
For decades, in her Boston rocking chair,
Her body asks a painful question of the books.
Her fingers are so smooth and white
They reflect the pages, a light
The color of cool linen bathes her hands.
The books read into her long through the night.

There is a book that opens her like a fan, and so
She sees herself, her life, in delicate painted scenes
Displayed between the ivory ribs that may close up
The way she claps the book shut when she's through
The story that has no end but cannot longer go.
It doesn't matter what the story means,
Better if it has no meaning — or just enough
For her to say the sentence that she likes to say,
Why do these strange folks do the way they do?

And yet they comfort her, being all
That she could never be nor wish to be,
They bring the world — or some outlook of its soul —
Into her small apartment that is cozy
As the huddling place of an animal
No one is yet aware of, living in
A secret corner of a secret continent.
An animal that watches, wonders, while the moon
Rides eastward and the sun comes up again
Over a forest deep as an ocean and as green.

*

Richard Walser, who died Saturday night at the age of 80 in Raleigh, was always collecting bits and pieces about North Carolina writers and their work. He wrote thousands and thousands of words, including many books, about them. He was hard at work when a stroke brought on his final illness, and his last conversation with a friend was about work he still wanted to do.

Dick Walser loved North Carolina, and he decided many years ago that the best way to express that love was to call attention to its literature. He called himself a "literary historian," and there are several monuments to his accomplishments — biographies of such writers as Inglis Fletcher, Bernice Kelly Harris, Paul Green, John Charles McNeill, and the list could go on and on. One of his monuments is *Literary North Carolina*. It is a monumental work, and in 1987, in collaboration with E.T. Malone Jr., an updated edition was issued.

He was the foremost literary scholar of Thomas Wolfe, whom he considered the greatest North Carolina writer and his books on Wolfe will be studied by students and scholars for many years to come. He had a special fondness for the work — the plays, essays, stories — of Paul Green and in a television interview several years ago he exclaimed, "he was the daddy of us all."

*

For many years, *The Pilot* received plaudits for the splendid photography, especially his landscapes, of Chief Photographer Glenn M. Sides.

Artist Talmadge Moose of Albemarle has called Sides' pictures "real art," and others have commented on his artistry in photographs of the Moore County landscape, in which he captures not only the details of a scene but the mood of the place and time. Moose talked of the composition of the photographs and it is something which Sides has learned from experience — he can see the picture before he snaps the shutter of his camera.

Good photography is indeed an art, and we can think of many photographers whose work was elevated to art, along with Sides. In North Carolina we have worked with many excellent photographers, people such as Hugh Morton, Ken Cooke, Lawrence Wofford, Emerson Humphrey, Aycock Brown, and the list could go on and on.

✻

We thought about reminiscences of Bernadette Hoyle last week when Betty Hodges called to tell us that Hoyle had died after a long and courageous battle against assorted illnesses over the past few years. She was 77, and lived in Smithfield, where she had returned to the home she had built many years ago and after living in Raleigh for years and engaging in a variety of public relations jobs and in promoting creative writing in North Carolina.

Bernadette Hoyle, who also was an excellent photographer, had made pictures of nearly every Writer's Conference since the early 1950s. In 1956 John Fries Blair of Winston-Salem had published her book, *Tar Heel Writers I Know*, which contained insightful interviews with several North Carolina writers. She had her own observations, but she let the writers tell in their own words what they sought to do in their writing, and the vision they had for their state. It was a recognition of the importance of literature in North Carolina and its significance in the cultural life of the state.

For many years after that Bernadette organized and conducted her "Tar Heel Writers Roundtable" in Raleigh, and she persuaded the top writers in the state and region to come and talk about their craft and art. The Roundtable drew aspiring writers from all parts of the state and from other states, with many coming back year after year and establishing a special camaraderie which marked the sessions.

Ill health forced Bernadette to cancel the "Tar Heel Writers Roundtable" a few years ago, but she always was planning for the next one.

We talked with Bernadette on a visit to Smithfield this past spring, and although we could see that illness had taken its toll we were struck by her eagerness to know about old friends in the writing fraternity and her positive views on the future.

Her passing is a loss to the North Carolina writing community. Her friends were legion, and she will be greatly missed.

﹡

It was my daughter, Talmadge, who first told me about Wynton Marsalis, the trumpet player. She had heard him play in New York several years ago and immediately said he was the greatest of the times and would be even greater as time went on.

A few days ago I read that he was conducting master classes at the Eastern Music Festival in Greensboro and was quoted in the Greensboro *News and Record* as saying that he is now devoting most of his time to jazz rather than to classical music. He explained why as follows:

> Jazz is to classical music what America was to Europe back in the early days of American independence. Democracy in America, with some obvious exceptions, meant freedom and the will to act for the benefit of all rather than for just a privileged few. Although jazz gives the performer freedom to improvise, it also demands that the performer listen to every other performer in the group and know what each is doing. The point is to create music together.

Beautifully said.

My list of the best books that show the breadth and depth of North Carolina are these.

Tar Heels by Jonathan Daniels
Southern Accent by William T. Polk
Journey for Joedel by Guy Owen
Collected Poems of Carl Sandburg
Entries from Oxford by Thad Stem
The North Carolina Gazetteer by William S. Powell
The Lost Colony by Paul Green
The Weymouth Anthology of Poetry
Contemporary North Carolina Poetry by Owens and Williams
Jackson Mahaffey by Fred Ross

These top ten would be closely followed by this next ten.

The Ragged Ones by Burke Davis
The Generous Man by Reynolds Price
The Wedding Guest by Ovid Pierce
Literary North Carolina by Richard Walser, with Ted Malone
Incredible Tale by Gerald Johnson
They Don't Dance Much by James Ross
Four North Carolina Women Poets by St. Andrews Press
Of Time and the River by Thomas Wolfe
Collected Poems of Fred Chappell
The Wind Southerly by Heather Ross Miller

12

Collected Poems, "Tree Lover," "Markings," "A great economy of language," "On the side of humanity"

S am Ragan's fourth book of poetry, published in 1990, *Collected Poems of Sam Ragan,* was edited by Marsha Warren and designed by Georgann Eubanks. It was published by St. Andrews Press. This book was his second that had been nominated for a Pulitzer Prize. Paul Green wrote of the book, "No voice has been stronger or perhaps more persuasive than Sam Ragan's." Heather Ross Miller wrote, "I've said it before: Sam Ragan is a North Carolina natural resource. These poems remember, dream, and celebrate." Ronald Bayes wrote, "His respect for the human condition and his ability to capture that condition in quiet, meaningful, courageous ways has always aroused my admiration. Sam Ragan is a poet of affirmation."

Collected Poems of Sam Ragan also won the prestigious Roanoke Chowan Award for Poetry. At the award ceremony in the Old State Capital Building, E.T. Malone, of the Historical Publications Section, North Carolina Division of Archives and History, had this to say about Ragan.

His poems have a striking directness and simplicity, a great economy of language that gives him a style all his own among North Carolina poets. He speaks honestly and briefly, sometimes confining the content of his poems to depicting a single image, in a manner almost as condensed as the Japanese haiku but without its formulaic restrictions. Yet this lean, no nonsense language is rich in its amazing ability to evoke with a few strokes the true portrait of his native land, the North Carolina of past and present.

Sally Buckner, a former student of Ragan's writing class, wrote the preface to *Collected Poems of Sam Ragan*. Excerpted, she wrote,

His poetry has focused on phenomena which never rate a headline: ordinary people, small incidents of daily life, quiet unfoldings of nature. Most of the poems are short. Each is candid. We view ordinary folk—a traveling salesman, an itinerant evangelist, a night watchman, a teacher—doing ordinary things on ordinary days. And yet nothing and no one is ordinary. Many of these poems move beyond purely human concerns to concentrate on nature. Again, Ragan draws our attention to the small, the seemingly ordinary: plum blossoms, the call of a whippoorwill, the blaze of maples in October. With his words, Sam Ragan has made genuine meaning of the daily and the plain: the tag end of our days, the private corners of our lives, the flowers and bird flights at the edge of the woods. Sam Ragan's poetry is understated—and utterly true, and therefore utterly beautiful.

"Markings" tells us to remember beautiful images, mark them in our memories, so we can use them to make our time on earth more enjoyable and worthwhile.

Markings

These are the markings that I make—
The trees now gold that will be green again,
The stone which brings the horse to halt when
Plowing furrows which must be begun again,
The slope of land to where the willows grow
Along a stream that flows to woods
Where birds now fly.
I make the markings with my eye.
For I have not traveled this road before,
And the markings I make are to remember it by.

"The Writer of Songs" is a poem in *Collected Poems of Sam Ragan* that tells readers that writing can be a lonely pursuit, and that writers like to share their art, their words, their poems, with others.

The Writer of Songs

He writes strange words
And sings them to himself,
All alone there by the window.
The words are like candy
To be tasted, to be tested on the tongue
Before the placing on the paper.
They are his songs, his poems.
He will carry them in his notebook
And if anyone will listen
He will sing to them
Just as he sings now
To himself.

"The Collector" is a poem where Ragan tells us to appreciate what is around us every day; the ordinary can be extraordinary.

The Collector

I have collected mornings,
Sunsets and stars,
Roses and wind's whisper,
Sounds and silences
Of days and nights,
The fragrance of lilacs,
Your smile, the shadows of moonlight,
Warm shadows in which to hide, and…
Yes.

Elizabeth Spencer, 98 years of age at the time of this writing, lives in Chapel Hill. Spencer wrote her first novel in 1948, *Fire in the Morning*. She has now written nine novels, seven collections of short stories, a memoir, and a play. Her book *The Light in the Piazza*, written in 1960, was adapted for the screen and made into a Broadway musical. Spencer is a five-time winner of the O. Henry Award for short fiction. Among her many other awards, she won the North Carolina Governor's Award for Literature, the Thomas Wolfe Award for Literature, and the William Faulkner Medal for Literary Excellence. She was inducted into the North Carolina Literature Hall of Fame in 2002.

I visited Elizabeth Spencer in her home in Chapel Hill for several visits in 2018 and early 2019. Following is some of what she told me about Sam Ragan.

> I remember Sam Ragan very well. He was a terribly sweet man, who always encouraged other writers. When I was at Weymouth for my writers-in-residence, he would stop by and talk to me. We talked about writing, books, his newspaper, and many other things. I told him how much I enjoyed the garden and flowers on the grounds outside the house. When I got tired of writing, I would walk outside in those beautiful gardens and woods, clear my mind, and go back to writing. I was working on my novel, *The Salt Line*, while there, and I got a lot done during those two weeks. It was a wonderful place to go and relax and get a lot of work done.
>
> I think Sam Ragan deserves the title "North Carolina Literary Godfather," I do. He didn't care who you were, a writer, an artist, he was always there for you, offering kind words, publicizing your work, giving you a room at Weymouth to write in peace. Just a wonderful man. He certainly is deserving of this biography.
>
> One of my favorite poets is William Butler Yeats. [Mrs. Spencer reached to her side and held up a book of poetry by Yeats.] I also like Walt Whitman. I think I am remembered mostly for my book, *Light in the Piazza*, but I really think I have written better books than that one. But somehow, that is the one people talk about, I guess, because of the movie and play that came from it.

In 1990, Spencer wrote to Ragan, once asking to come to Weymouth to write and reflect, and then after spending time at Weymouth, she wrote him again. She was teaching creative writing at UNC-Chapel Hill at the time of these letters.

I remember once you told me that if I wanted to get away from home to work on my fiction, there was a possibility I might be able to put up at Weymouth. I have term break here from March 10–19, and wondered if by any chance you had room for me then. I am far into writing a novel, but it is hard to work and teach too so have gotten somewhat behind.

It was a very fine week I spent at that superb house. I still close my eyes and see the garden. Also got some ahead on my work. Many thanks for allowing me the privilege. Best to Marjorie.

In *Southern Accent* in 1990, Ragan wrote about many topics. *Southern Accent* was now in its 42nd consecutive year, having started when he was with *The News and Observer* in 1948.

Even as a teenager Ava Gardner had that certain quality which made her stand out and which led to her becoming a star in the world of movies.

That quality has been called "It" and maybe that's the only word for it. She had a beauty which attracted attention, and she was far greater as an actress than she herself realized.

Ava didn't think of herself as a movie star, in her mind and in her own words she was just a "country girl" from Johnston County. But there are many of us who remember her sultry beauty on the screen and think of her as a star — North Carolina's only real movie star.

We first saw Ava when she visited her sister at Atlantic Christian College, which she later attended as a day student taking a business course. At the time she lived at nearby Rock Ridge, where her mother was director of the school's teacherage.

A few years later when she had gone to Hollywood she would come home on visits and her first stop would be with a sister who then lived in Raleigh. Tony McKevlin, the then managing editor of *The News and Observer*, was a friend of Ava's sister and the two of them would come calling at the newspaper office late in the evening. There would follow a party at someone's house, and once we recall Ava coming along for the ride as Neil Morgan and I went out for hamburgers. She startled everybody in the place by pulling off a wig and hanging it over the napkin container at the counter. She already had taken off her shoes—she was back home in North Carolina.

We remember when she brought her first husband, Mickey Rooney, to the newspaper office one night, and she stood aside as he tried to impress everybody in the newsroom. Ava was 19 or 20 at the time and all eyes were on her, and not on Mickey.

Ava did not like the bright lights of Hollywood and New York, and after her marriage to Frank Sinatra went on the rocks she moved to Spain, where she lived for many years before moving to London several years ago, and it was in London where she died last week.

On Monday of this week Ava came home to Johnston County for the last time, and more than 3,000 people turned out for her burial in the family plot at Smithfield.

❋

Our friendship with Clifton Blue dated back to the 1930s and we shared a warm and friendly relationship down through the years.

We met Cliff in the latter part of 1936 shortly after he had moved to Aberdeen after merging *The Captain*, which he had started at Vass, with the *Sandhill Citizen*. We were at that time living in Hemp (now Robbins) where we had joined Stacy Brewer in starting a newspaper, *The Plain Dealer*, and were having problems with our printer and someone suggested we call Cliff Blue in Aberdeen. Cliff had gotten his paper out, and he said to come on down, he would be glad to print our paper.

Later when we were in Raleigh with *The News and Observer* and Cliff Blue was a member of the Legislature from Moore County he often would drop by the newspaper to chat about affairs of the day and report on mutual friends.

We watched him rise in influence in the Legislature and shared the pride held by many of his friends when he was elected Speaker. As Speaker, Cliff was responsible, more than anyone else, for the enactments of the laws establishing the statewide community college system.

When we moved to the Sandhills as editor and publisher of *The Pilot* one of the first persons to welcome us was Cliff Blue, who was our next door neighbor as editor and publisher of the *Citizen*.

We think of the word integrity when we think of Cliff Blue. His friendly personality was persuasive, and his word was his bond. It was a privilege to call him a friend. He was a good man, and we shall treasure his memory.

During the recent meeting of the North Carolina Poetry Society at the Weymouth Center, the Poet Laureate Award was presented to Anne Furnas Stock, who lives near Banner Elk, for her poem, "Obituary—'89." The winning poem was as follows:

Edward Clayton Pitt died
Tuesday afternoon at 4:00 p.m.
after his chores were done,
the goats grained, the hives tended to
and when there was time
to porch-sit till supper.

Born 1906, in Ashe County
to Raymond and Delia Pitt, he was
a farmer. Jack of all trades like
any mountain man who makes a
living off the land. At the last,
a grey man in a small rocker
one his daddy built
his blue eyes and wide grin
all the light in him.

Ed got grey from fading.
Like his overalls. Like the
unpainted house. Not the homeplace
that lightning took
but the one Ed built
with lapped board, right-angled
corners, straight at
the ridgepole as the builder.

He was preceded in death
by his wife Mae
for whom he'd picked roadside daisies

and he is survived
by three sons and a daughter who
live here in town, so the
interment is in the
Good Hope Gardens perpetually
mowed to naked like a shorn lamb
where the Reverend Stayfinch officiates
in a long gown
where bronze plaques
decorate each chest the same
the names so hard to find
in this flat field where
in the rows of urns
the plastic poppies sprout.

Up on the ridge
his daddy lies
beneath the brambles reaching
for the fence Ed built
to keep the cows out.
Under a piece of mountain
bone set upright.
Where the white morning glories climb
and the birds sit singing
daylong.

※

Walker Percy died last week at the age of 74.

We met Walker Percy several years ago when he returned to Chapel Hill for a reunion of his UNC class. He and my wife, Marjorie, were in the same class at UNC, and it was one of his first trips to the university where he obtained an undergraduate degree before going on to Columbia for a degree in medicine.

He was somewhat reserved, but easy to talk to, and although he was an acclaimed novelist there was no sign of an ego which needed massaging. Our impression was of a man who was polite and courteous, somewhat shy, but with an interest in people.

He had said his career in Chapel Hill was undistinguished, and someone asked him about his most enjoyable experience at UNC. He replied that what he most enjoyed was "sitting on the verandah at the Carolina Inn and watching the people go by."

Of his novels we liked *The Moviegoer*, which won the National Book Award, and *The Last Gentleman*, the best, followed by *Love Among the Ruins*. We have noted before that there are nuances in *The Last Gentleman* that only a Southerner could express, and there are other Southern distinctions in his writing, which have not been touched upon by most critics of his work.

The year of 1991 was a busy one for Sam Ragan. He was 75 years old, but still working hard, running *The Pilot*, writing *Southern Accent*, speaking, offering advice and encouragement to writers in North Carolina, still serving as North Carolina Poet Laureate, which at this time was a lifetime appointment. He moderated a panel discussion on "Poetry and Human Values" at North Carolina State University. He was active locally, being a member of the Southern Pines Kiwanis Club and the Moore County Historical Association, just to name a few organizations he participated in.

He believed in a strong and forceful editorial page, and he wrote many of the editorials that appeared in *The Pilot*. In the editorials he stated what he believed in, a progressive agenda, support for the disadvantaged, support of the Democratic Party, opposition to the death penalty, arts for everyone. He received opposition to these editorials from some, of course, but it did not deter him one bit. He once said, "I am a strong believer in having a really strong editorial page. I get people who come in here and chastise me. One man used to write letters every week. He comes in now, stops by my door and just shakes his head. I was once interviewed on the 'Today Show' and was asked why I take strong editorial stances in a community newspaper. I said, 'Well, I have always felt that if you are on the side of humanity, you won't go wrong.' That was off the top of my head, but that sort of sums up my philosophy of the news business."

Following are some excerpts of editorials written by Ragan while with *The Pilot*. In some he takes stances, but in others, he writes of things that please him. (Note: Jim Holshouser was Governor of North Carolina from 1973 to 1977.) These editorials were written over a number of years.

It is inconceivable to us that the Pee Dee Council of Governments, and especially those from Moore County, would be so callous as to turn down the funds available for the Senior Citizens Nutrition program. Taking the initiative in rejecting the plan to provide decent meals for old people were two members of the Council from Moore County, and the excuses for turning down the funds are weak. It's true that the $138,000 in federal funds to feed old people would have to be matched with 10 percent of local funds, but that is a small amount in local money. People in power should have some compassion and common sense, and not forever assume an arrogant know-it-all attitude. This rejection of a program to feed old people was a mistake. There should be some effort to correct it.

❋

We are not sure we understand the full implications of the Holshouser highway agenda, but one of the announced policies disturbs us very much. That policy is the one which says the state is going to stop paving rural dirt roads, and to our mind this is a policy which is not only unfair but cruel and unreasonable.

The best we can figure the new highway policy to be is that it frankly follows the cynical philosophy of "them that has gets." It rejects and downgrades the State's secondary road system, a system which has been a primary cause of the State's advancement, and concentrates the State's highway dollars and commitments into the concrete jungles of our urban areas. Some people may applaud this new policy, but we see it as a step backward, and unfair to thousands of mud-locked citizens of the State.

❋

There is much beauty in November even if we think of it in terms of cold weather, bare branches, dead flowers and, indeed, the dying of the year. In our part of the country there is still color remaining in the woods. Those fall winds and rain have not yet taken all of the leaves away, and bright swatches of color greet the traveler along Tar Heel roads.

In America, of course, it is the month of Thanksgiving. A genuinely American holiday, it has a significance beyond the orgies of eating and the first of the huge televised Christmas parades. It is, or should be, a real time of thanks giving.

It doesn't hurt anyone to occasionally stop to count his blessings and be grateful for them.

✳

We would like to see a renewed effort to abolish capital punishment in North Carolina. The experience in other states and countries—and even in North Carolina—has proven that capital punishment is no deterrent to crimes such as murder.

A further point which should be made against capital punishment is that it never has been evenly applied. Almost always it has been the poor, the black and the friendless who have been put to death. Few rich men have ever been gassed to death or electrocuted in North Carolina.

At any rate, North Carolina's harsh and inhumane capital punishment laws should not be allowed to stand further to disgrace our state.

✳

Many football teams could probably use the talents of women. But Secretary Joseph Califano Jr. of the Department of Health, Education, and Welfare doesn't see much future for women in football, and for that reason he is softening the regulations against sex discrimination in intercollegiate athletics.

Last week Secretary Califano said, however, that football is unique because of the size of its teams, support staffs and facilities and the volume of revenue it generates. Therefore, schools with football teams do not necessarily have to adhere to the HEW guidelines on anti-discrimination.

Football may be a mitigating factor insofar as HEW is concerned, but that doesn't mean women athletics will be any less. There will be a day when the girls Wolfpack and the female Tar Heels will be drawing as many spectators at basketball games as the men.

✳

It was something of an embarrassment for Wilson to discover a few days ago that the city council had outlawed rooster crowing in the city.

The reason was Wilson's slogan and symbol. "Wide Awake Wilson" the city is called and a crowing rooster is the symbol. There's a huge rooster mounted on top of the city's tallest water tower.

Wilson isn't the only city or organization which has adopted the rooster as a symbol. A crowing rooster is a proud, exuberant fellow who fits in well with a feeling of satisfied ebullience. Moreover, his clarion call at dawn for all sleepy heads to wake up is also a call to join in the cheering.

Many old time Democrats preferred the rooster as a symbol for their party over the donkey. All through the years when Josephus Daniels and Jonathan Daniels were editors of *The News and Observer* a crowing red rooster greeted readers the day after election if the Democrats won the presidency. Josephus Daniels often wrote about the virtues of the rooster as a party symbol.

On countless barns throughout the country the rooster stood atop the weathervanes, giving a sense of security to the old home place.

As far as we know, there is only one church in America which has a rooster on its steeple. That is Christ Episcopal Church in Raleigh.

The rooster figures in the folklore and folk tales of America, and many are the stories of historic cock fights. Though now illegal, cock-fighting used to be a major sport in the rural South. One of the best books about cock-fighting is that classic of North Carolina humor, *Jackson Mahaffey* by Fred Ross.

❊

Time is running out for the Equal Rights Amendment, and it will be to the shame of America if it is not permitted to pass. The Equal Rights Amendment is such a simple one that it is inconceivable that anyone would object to it. It says simply that the rights of no person shall be abridged because of sex.

ERA should be ratified.

Marjorie Ragan served for many years as associate editor of *The Pilot*, even running the newspaper during the early 1970s when Ragan was appointed Secretary of Cultural Resources. Ragan drove to Raleigh for work as Secretary and would spend much of the day there, so Marjorie sort of took his place and they would discuss things after Ragan got back from Raleigh. She also did book reviews, and one author was well pleased with her review of his work, evidenced by a letter sent to *The Pilot*. "I especially want to thank Marjorie for her very beautiful review. Not only was it original in its approach and phrasing, but it went right to the heart of my books, and it really delighted me that she responded to the 'shaft of light in a lonely room' and detected so perceptively and sensitively the 'secret symbols' which tie the book together and are, in fact, its essence. It is a lovely piece of critical interpretation, and I do very much appreciate it."

Marjorie Ragan started the column "It Says Here" in *The Pilot* that was later continued by her daughter, Talmadge. Marjorie won first place honors for news writing and feature writing for articles she wrote from the North Carolina Press Institute.

Marjorie would always be the love of Sam Ragan's life. By 1991, they had been married 54 years. Marjorie was a well-respected journalist and newspaperwoman in her own right, a loving wife and mother to Nancy and Talmadge, and grandmother to Robin and Eric. She was active in the Southern Pines and Sandhills communities also. She was also an enthusiastic grower of roses, even writing about roses and their care. She loved to read, and she loved cats.

Sam Ragan wrote many poems to and about Marjorie. Two are touching and shows his love for her:

For Marjorie
(March 31, 1991)

Spring came early this year,
And the explosion of the yellow flowers
Of March was quickly accomplished,
Followed by the full flowering
Of peach and pear, the delicate white
Of apple blossoms, the bold red
And softer pink of the camellia,
The redbud trees suddenly appearing
In the first whisper of the greening
Of the woods, now dappled
With the dogwood—and the azaleas
Of all colors are everywhere.

It is spring at its fullest,
And I think of you
As the full blossoming
Of this season of magic
And memory—A time of wonder.
I kneel to you.

For Marjorie

(March 31, 1992)

The days, months and years
Have been brought together
Into one bright and shining
Sun speckled morning—
A morning of flowers and bird song,
A red rose I give to you.
You are that rose,
And I warm to the touch of you
In this glow of the morning.

Writers across the country continued to turn to Sam Ragan to be invited as a writer-in-residence at Weymouth. Laura Anderson wrote to Ragan in 1991.

Would you consider allowing me to come to Weymouth to work on my fiction around the Christmas holidays? I have a rare break from December 22–26. I know it may seem unusual to want to spend Christmas alone, but to me it would be a gift.

You'll find enclosed a chapbook of my poetry. Also a clipping from the Canberra *Times* in Australia when I covered the Poet Laureates Conference, where I had the pleasure of meeting you and hearing your work.

Yes, I work both sides, non-fiction and poetry. And now short stories, for which I greatly desire the solitude of Weymouth. My undergraduate degree is from Chapel Hill, where I studied honors poetry with Carolyn Kizer. My graduate degree came a dozen years later, from Hollins College in Virginia. In between I had the good fortune of working, in the early 70s, for Robert Mason at the *Virgin-ian-Pilot*, whom you may know. For the past 3 years, freelancing has provided bread and overhead for me and my 9-year-old daughter. I live in Raleigh.

Also that year, 1991, Ragan gave a very nice donation to St. Andrews University Press in Laurinburg. St. Andrews Press was started in 1969, and since that time has published over 200 volumes of poetry, fiction, and non-fiction. St. Andrews published the *Collected Poems of Sam Ragan,* and books by Shelby Stephenson, Anthony Abbott, and many other noted authors. St. Andrews Press also published a nationally recognized literary magazine, *CAIRN: The St. Andrews Review,* and *Gravity Hill,* a campus literary magazine of St. Andrews University. Ronald Bayes is the founder of St. Andrews Press, *CAIRN,* and *Gravity Hill.* Bayes has won many awards for his poetry and writing, and is now enshrined in the North Carolina Literary Hall of Fame. Bayes was a good friend of Ragan. While director of the North Carolina Arts Council in the late 1960s and early 1970s, Ragan had granted money to St. Andrews Press to help it get started and to build itself in those first years of its founding in 1969. Bayes wrote the following note.

When I met with Sam Ragan earlier today he presented me with a check for St. Andrews Press, in the amount of $5,000. Sam asked that $1,500 of the gift be designated for the production of Agnes McDonald's book, *Quickest Door, Smallest Room,* and $3,500 go toward the St. Andrews Press Endowment. His wonderful largesse puts us awfully close to the goal for the Haines match!

But, as always, not everything went okay. Running a newspaper required Ragan to wear many hats. He received this letter in 1991, and he responded.

This letter is to notify *The Pilot* of a cease order for all Richmond Federal Savings Bank advertising. We are extremely upset over the lack of consideration you have shown our client. We hand delivered a press release along with a photograph. You chose not to run the photograph.

I am perfectly aware that in the view of newspaper people, editorial and advertising have no relationship to each other. I do feel, however, that a certain consideration should be given to clients who run a good and perpetual advertising schedule. So, until further notice, Richmond Federal will not be running in *The Pilot*.

What is this all about? We ran a news item but I do not recall a picture sent. I will still use a photo if one is provided.

In the early 1990s the Marjorie Usher Ragan Scholarship was established at the University of North Carolina at Chapel Hill School of Journalism. Marjorie was a journalism graduate of UNC in 1937. "Marjorie has always been a pioneer, in journalism and in life," said Dr. Richard Cole, dean of the journalism school. "She was among the first half-dozen women newspaper editors in the state, one of the first women to cover the U.S. Senate and the first female radio news directors in North Carolina. We've always been proud of her as an alumna of our school, and now we're delighted to have this scholarship that will cement her name with the school from now on."

Heather Ross Miller was a good friend and corresponded with Ragan on a regular basis. Miller was born in Albemarle, and grew up in Badin, an aluminum-smelting town. She was part of a well-known Southern writing family, which included her father, Fred Ross. Miller studied with Randall Jarrell at what is now UNC-Greensboro. She wrote over a dozen books of poetry, fiction, and non-fiction, and taught creative writing at Pfeiffer University, the University of Arkansas, and Washington and Lee University. Her book, *Friends and Assassins*, which she refers to in the following letter to Ragan, was published in 1993.

I was pleased to be asked to submit something to the special Sam Ragan issue *of St. Andrew's Review*. Since everybody in the world will send poems, I plan to send some stories. Steve can pick the one he wants.

The University of Missouri Press accepted a second collection of poems from me this month. It is exciting to have this book follow so soon upon the heels of the other. Called *Friends and Assassins*, it should appear in early 1992. You are the first person I'm telling. You may announce it in your "Southern Accent" if you like. You will get one of the first copies.

Did you ever get the Kelly Cherry book called *An Exiled Heart* from LSU? If you do, I will review it for you. Just send it here.

In the meantime, I am teaching two graduate classes in summer school, Classical Children's Literature (we plowed into *Huck Finn* yesterday, I like ole Huck, so warm-hearted and blunt) and a writing workshop. They are enjoyable and move briskly along. I was glad to get back into teaching. The students are good medicine for me.

Arkansas matched Washington and Lee's offer, so I will probably stay here because I like teaching graduate students so much.

Love to Marjorie and all the best to you.

Southern Accent continued with many topics covered.

A couple of years ago James J. Kilpatrick, the syndicated columnist and former editor of the Richmond *News Leader*, spoke to a group of us at a Chapel Hill press meeting about the need for better writing.

He opened up by saying he had had breakfast with the great novelist Lee Smith and he said, "Do you know what makes Lee Smith a great novelist?" and he answered his own question by saying, "she sees intently and she hears intently."

Those of us who on Sunday at Weymouth listened to Lee Smith talk about her writing and read a selection from the novel she is working on now know exactly what Jack Kilpatrick meant by that observation. She knows what people do, what they think, what they say and how they say it and it is marvelous.

Lee Smith, who was accompanied to Weymouth by her father who lives in Grundy, Virginia, where she grew up, and where she listened to tales told by her father and started writing stories on her own when she was in grade school. She later attended and graduated from Hollins College and went on to work on newspapers as a reporter, including work with Kilpatrick on the Richmond newspapers. She has published seven novels and two collections of short stories, and won awards for her writing. She says she writes out of her Appalachia background, but there is a universal quality about her work, and of it a reader will surely say, "that's the way it is." In other words, her credibility is unquestioned.

For instance, when she was writing about a beauty parlor operator in one of her novels she got a job in a beauty parlor and worked for several weeks so that she would know what she was writing about. Her new novel will deal with country music (she has written several country songs to go along with her prose) and to know what she is writing about she has spent a great deal of time in Nashville, with the Grand Ol' Opry, and has visited with and talked with dozens of country music legends. Recently she went to Clayton on a Saturday night to hear the legendary Kitty Wells perform, and later to talk with her about her early and current career.

Lee Smith joined poet Agnes McDonald of Wilmington at Weymouth Center here this past Sunday to launch the 1991 Writers and Readers Series, a statewide literary event which is now sponsored by the North Carolina Writers Network with a grant from the Blumenthal Foundation. Marsha Warren, the executive director of the network, was present and was given recognition for reviving and keeping the series going.

✳

When Dr. McLeod Bryan recently opened the 1991 Ruth Pauley Lecture Series at Sandhills Community College he cited a special irony about the recent celebration of the 50th anniversary of the publication of *The Mind of the South*, the monumental work by W.J. Cash.

The celebration and a five-day symposium on the Cash book was held at Wake Forest University in mid-February. But when it was published and won the Mayflower Cup in 1941 as well as considerable nation-wide critical acclaim, the book and its author, who was an alumnus of Wake Forest, received no attention at all on that campus. Dr. Bryan was there at the time and continues to serve on the Wake Forest faculty as the highly regarded professor of ethics. He remarked in his lecture on ethics at Sandhills that it was more than passing strange that Wake Forest University went all these years without taking note of Cash and his book. There was, indeed, an irony in that incident.

At Wake Forest, Cash, who was born in Gaffney, S.C., and grew up in Boiling Springs, N.C., was called "Sleepy" but among Charlotte friends he was known as "Jack." He had received a fellowship after publication of *The Mind of the South* and got married and went to Mexico to work on a novel. A few months after the book was published and a few days after arriving in Mexico City Jack Cash hanged himself with a necktie in a hotel room. That act itself has added to the Cash mystique.

There are many flaws in the book. Cash was very enamored of the style of H.L. Mencken, and he was given to a flamboyance which led to over-statements and a lambasting which the South may or may not deserve. The book also is limited to a small portion of the upper Piedmont of North and South Carolina, and the coastal plains, as well as women and blacks, are ignored. One critic has said that as far as Cash was concerned, they did not exist.

The most serious flaw is that he regarded the South as monolithic, when most observers long ago concluded that there are many Souths, some in strong conflict with others. We think there are probably forty Souths, instead of the one which Cash saw.

All of this may be beside the point, however, as it should be pointed out that *The Mind of the South* never has been out of print since it was published by Knopf in 1941, and it is essential reading in many graduate courses and for any serious student of the South.

Ragan was 76 years of age in 1992, but he still enjoyed working. It was in his later years that he stopped smoking, almost doing it "cold turkey," after a lifetime of the habit. Many photographs capture Ragan with a cigarette in his hand, ready for another puff. He knew it was affecting his health. Peppermint candy, the hard-sucking variety, was his weapon. When he got the urge to smoke, he popped a candy in his mouth instead. It worked, along with his strong will power and discipline, and he gave up smoking his longtime beloved Salem and Camel cigarettes.

Marjorie was having some health problems, so this took more of Sam's time to help look after her. But he was still serving as Poet Laureate, which came with many requests to speak around the state. The Randolph Arts Guild in Asheboro invited him to speak about "Experience the Arts" and paid $100 for the lecture.

By 1992 over 550 writers had come to Weymouth as part of the writers-in-residence program that had been started by Ragan in 1979. David Rigsbee, an English professor at Virginia Tech, came during 1992, and wrote to Ragan afterwards.

Thank you for making last week's time possible for me. I think I was able to use it to good effect, writing nine new poems—a lot for me. Weymouth is a lovely place to work, and you can get serious there. I hope I'll be able to find the time to return. Once a place works the first time, its charm is good in perpetuity, as far as I'm concerned.

One of my unpublished collections, a book of long poems, was accepted by Edwin Mellon, a Canadian publisher with a branch in the U.S. I had been partial to this book, but I figured that nobody read long poems, let alone a book of them.

It's hateful to be back in the hot classroom, but at least it's with a strong feeling of rejuvenation. It was good to visit with you last week. And thanks, in advance, for running Shelby's review.

Mae Woods Bell was 99 years of age when I talked to her in 2018. She knew Sam Ragan well, was a photographer for him, and also contributed to *Southern Accent* on a regular basis. Mae actually met Thomas Wolfe. When she was a child, Wolfe visited her parent's house. Mae remembers well the tall man clutching her in his hands and lifting her high above his head. Of course, he meant no harm, but this scared the wits out of the young girl. So the next time Wolfe came to visit her parents, Mae, upon seeing this huge man walk in the front door, promptly ran out the back door and climbed as high as she could in a tree in the back yard.

Mae has made many contributions to North Carolina over the years. She was given The Long Leaf Pine Award in 2017 by Governor Roy Cooper. She was the driving force behind the creation of the Rocky Mount Children's Museum and is a former president of the Archaeological Society of North Carolina and a former chairwoman of the N.C. Writer's Conference. She was a longtime book reviewer for the *Rocky Mount Telegram* and has written two books of poems and epigrams.

Sam Ragan really enjoyed including some of the short poems and epigrams of Mae Bell's in his column, *Southern Accent*. By 1992, *Southern Accent* had been running for 44 consecutive years, which made it the longest running column of its kind in the United States. It was being read in 43 states and 24 foreign countries. Following are some of Mae Woods Bell's short poems, what she called "WRYmes." These "WRYmes" contained comments on the human condition and social issues.

Responsibility causes some people to grow,
others to swell.

No artificial color can match
the green of nature.

Poetry is the words of nameless thought
that everybody has but only a few can express.

My bank account, I admit,
to my sorrow,
is here today,
drawn tomorrow.

We complain about inflation,
but I question that, more or less,
for my money goes as far as ever,
from me to the IRS.

Qualified women are fighting for ERA,
because when all is said and done,
it's the only way to get a man's wages,
without having to marry one.

Southern Accent remained a popular column in 1992, with Ragan, as usual, writing about varied subjects. One such subject was about porches.

Porches—front or back—have a special meaning for most Southerners, and for most adults there are inextricable ties to a porch, more often than not, now seen in memory. It may be a certain porch where their lives came into focus, where they absorbed the virtues that shaped their lives, where memory was indelibly touched and still remains.

I think it was Thad Stem who wrote most movingly of porches and their meanings.

The front porch, he said, was where neighbors visited, where talk was pleasant, where tales of families were told, where time was passed in a pleasing way. Those long Sunday afternoon tales and after-supper talks were meant to entertain as well as to inform.

If there was really serious discussion or business to transact the head of the household and the visitor would move to the privacy of the back porch. But the back porch was also the workplace for the housewife or farmer who was looking over his account books or when he was helping or lending a hand with fruits and vegetables.

Reynolds Price has written a moving account of a day in July 1942 which he spent with relatives at Macon in Warren County, where he was born, and that special time he and his kinfolks spent on the porch.

On January 20, 1993, Sam Ragan, happy that Bill Clinton was being inaugurated as President after 12 years of Republican control of the White House under Ronald Reagan and George Bush, listened on television as Maya Angelou read a poem at the inauguration ceremonies. That very same day, he wrote to Angelou, telling her "your poem today was great. I was moved by it and I share the pride of all North Carolinians in your splendid performance at the inauguration. I congratulate President Clinton in choosing you to speak for all of us." Angelou sent the poem to Ragan and Ragan published it in *Southern Accent*. In fact, the entire column of January 28 was devoted to quoting the entirety of Angelou's poem, so fond of it that Ragan was. Angelou, after Robert Frost at President Kennedy's in 1961, became just the second poet to read a poem at a presidential inauguration. Angelou was the first black person and the first woman to be so honored. The poem was "On the Pulse of Morning," and the poem's themes were change, inclusion, and responsibility.

Also in 1993, Ragan was named as the winner of the John Tyler Caldwell Award for the Humanities. Fred Chappell, speaking about Ragan on the night of the award, quoted Sally Buckner, who said Ragan's poetry "makes ordinary people special and makes special people ordinary."

The John Tyler Caldwell Award for the Humanities is named for a former chancellor of North Carolina State University, who was the first winner in 1990. John Hope Franklin was the winner in 1991, and Doris Betts in 1992, followed by Sam Ragan in 1993.

An employee of The O'Neal School in Southern Pines was upset with Ragan in October of 1993. So he addressed a letter to Ragan, and Ragan followed up with a sharp reply.

This past Monday, I delivered to *The Pilot* an article and two pictures about our volleyball team winning the Triad Conference Volleyball Tournament last Saturday. The article, and pictures, did not appear in your next issue. I called your office for an explanation and was told that you had so many articles and pictures that you were not able to get them all in. I find it interesting that the article on Pinecrest's soccer team winning their conference appeared on page 18-A when normally all your sports articles appear in section C.

All you need to do is watch the difference in the status you give to public school articles as compared to our articles, such as size of headlines, placement of articles, leaving them out altogether.

*

I have been a friend of The O'Neal School since its beginning, and with all schools I think my record of treating everyone fairly in news coverage is solid and firm. The news coverage received by The O'Neal School surely has been generous and the incident you cited is one faced regularly by every newspaper which makes an effort to provide total news coverage for its community.

In other words, I do not think you have anything to complain about. We will continue to do our job as best we can, and may I suggest you try to do the same.

On the other hand, Ragan wrote a letter to the President of the Sandhills Area Chamber of Commerce on an issue he took umbrage to.

I was shocked and greatly disturbed when the Chamber's Shopping Guide was brought to my attention. It is difficult to believe you and the Chamber would try to undermine one of its own members and supporters by issuing a competing publication. I consider it very un-ethical and a conflict of interests, as well as demeaning for the Chamber to take such action.

As you well know, *The Pilot* provides you and the Chamber with considerable free space every week for your promotional purposes. *The Pilot* has more than 15,000 paid circulation and with 4.2 readers per copy I am sure that our advertisers are well served with our proven record and readership.

I am disturbed that the organization of which *The Pilot* has been a long-time member, to which it pays dues and has given faithful support is seeking to undermine us.

I tried to reach you by telephone but you were not available, and I would appreciate a reply to this letter.

Barton College, what was Atlantic Christian College when Ragan attended and graduated from in the 1930s, was close and dear to Ragan's heart. He had enjoyed his years on campus, really started to learn the craft of writing there, and made many long-lasting relationships. Over the years, he had accepted many invitations to come back to his beloved campus and speak, and he was awarded an honorary doctorate degree from the college in Wilson.

Ragan donated $10,000 to Barton in 1993, which was applied to the Writing Center program. The money was placed in the Endowment Fund so that interest on the amount could be used for the writing program, to help future writers. Today, the Sam and Marjorie Ragan Writing Center is located on the Barton College campus. The annual "Walking into April Poetry day" is held in the Sam and Marjorie Ragan Writing Center. The day is held each year to celebrate the written word in the spirit of Sam Ragan. There are also special lectures held in the writing center throughout the year for authors, along with serving as a place for classes on the writing profession for Barton students.

Ragan kept a picture of him shaking hands with Jimmy Carter on his office wall. Ragan admired President Carter very much, both for his politics and for what he did after leaving office.

We first met Jimmy Carter in Southern Pines at a Governor's Conference held at Pine Needles. He had been elected governor of Georgia but had not taken office and he had been invited to the conference here by N.C. Governor Bob Scott. We had lunch together and his quiet intelligence was quickly obvious. Later we encountered him, quite unexpectedly, when he stopped by an Arts in the Park exhibit in downtown Southern Pines. He had been driving through the Sandhills and saw an item in *The Pilot* about the art exhibition here and quietly walked in to see it. We conversed briefly and he offered an opinion on some paintings. When he became President we were among a group of newspaper editors invited to spend a day with him at the White House.

In all of these encounters we met the same man, a genial but quiet observer with uncommon things to say in a common language.

That's the way his poetry comes across to us. He writes about growing up on a farm three miles from town, of his father and mother and other members of his family, of people he worked with on the farm and in public office, including moments in the White House.

Carter confesses in a foreword to his book, *Always a Reckoning*, that he had nurtured an admiration for poetry over the years and it should be noted that he hosted a poet's reception at the White House in 1980, something which no other president has done.

Ragan loved books and libraries, and often wrote about them.

A few years ago we attended a meeting of state librarians and heard a talk by Isaac Asimov in which he described a wonderful invention.

The invention, he said, could be carried in his coat pocket and he could take it out and use it any time at any place. It could move forward or backward with equal grace and provide delight and enjoyment with every movement. It could be picked up and put down and used whenever he wanted to use it. It did not require any batteries or have to be plugged into a wall socket. As he told it, this was the most marvelous invention in our civilization.

What he was talking about was a book.

We thought about Isaac Asimov's talk the other day when we reread an essay on libraries by the late Richard McKenna, the author of the widely acclaimed novel, *Sand Pebbles*, who lived in Chapel Hill. McKenna wrote about the great pleasure he received in going into a library and looking at the thousands of books on the shelves.

The reverence which these two writers had for books also was revealed in an item we read in the newspapers recently. A woman was reporting on the pleasure she received from reading, and remarked, "The few words created a thousand pictures in my mind." It was the reverse of the old saying about a picture being worth a thousand words, but it was quite true.

There is one thing which the writer and the reader have in common, and that one thing is imagination. Both must bring imagination to their task—the writing and the reading.

We share the esteem these people have for libraries, and long have held the belief that the quality of life in a town is measured in large part by the quality of its library.

One thing Sam Ragan did not like was someone cutting down trees. Just as he fought for John Patrick's walnut trees earlier in his career in Southern Pines, in 1995 he went to bat for more of his beloved trees.

The Pilot has learned that the initiative for cutting down six magnolia trees and one sycamore in front of the Southern Pines Library did not come from Town Manager Kyle Sonnenberg but from the Town Council itself.

Mayor Mike Fields responded to a headline in *The Pilot* which stated "Town Manager Plans To Kill Magnolias," saying that the town manager was merely carrying out the council's directions.

Even so, it's a bad idea and should be rescinded.

It is difficult to believe that the members of the Town Council are unaware of the century old tradition, dedication and unabated affection of Southern Pines citizens for trees. The magnolias along West Broad Street were planted in the early days of the town and cutting any of them down is like destroying a member of one's family—it just isn't done. Given a preference of trees and a sidewalk we daresay that a majority of the people in town would promptly take the trees.

At any rate, repairing the sidewalk in front of the historic library building is not contingent on killing off six magnolia trees and a beautiful sycamore. The sidewalk can be repaired and the trees left to live out their lifespans, and the Town Council should see that this is accomplished.

We well recall other efforts to destroy trees in Southern Pines and how the people rose up to fight it. There was the time when a state highway engineer was ordered by the Governor of the State to stop cutting down trees on Midland Road — the Governor was responding to a plea from a citizen of the town to do something about the early morning destruction then under way. The engineer soon went into retirement.

Hundreds of Southern Pines citizens have fought hard for the trees we have — the town has earned Tree City USA honors for twelve years — and we believe they will fight again to save those trees which officials have marked for destruction.

The magnolia and the sycamore are two of our most beautiful trees and the magnolia especially has a special mystique here. In addition it provides shade in summer and an appealing greenness in winter.

We feel that Southern Pines would be the loser in the loss of these trees. For the sake of an honored tradition, community harmony, the beauty of the town, and an overall aesthetic quality the trees should be saved.

Several short poems come to mind on the subject of Ragan's love for trees.

The Pines

The tall slender pines
Keep reaching for the sky.
Even in moonlight
They cast long shadows,
The wind only sways them.
I walk on the needled softness,
I listen for the murmur
Of the wind.

Preservation

In this September sky
There are silences, and only
A thin sliver of moon lights the dark.
Even the wind is stilled,
And no sound comes from the pines.
This is not a major moment
Of great events or portents
But, somehow, sitting here
In the darkness, I have the feeling
It should be preserved.

Ghost Pines

Two longleaf pines tower
Above all the rest in the woods.
They are ghost pines really—
Simply reflections by the sun
From the large windows,
But I am sure they reflect
The giant pines that long ago
Towered over the South,
And now are almost gone,
Still hovering like ghosts
Over the trees left behind.

Ragan's love of trees, including pine trees, would seem to have been in alignment with the thoughts of Henry David Thoreau, who once wrote about his love of pine trees.

Strange that so few ever came to the woods to see how the pine lives and grows and spires, lifting its evergreen arms to the light—to see its perfect success, but most are content to behold it in the shape of many boards brought to market, and deem that its true success! But the pine is no more lumber than man is, and to be made into boards and houses is no more its true and highest use than the truest use of a man is to be cut down and made into manure. There is a higher law affecting our relations to the pine, as well as to man.

The following poem, in my estimation, tells perhaps most clearly why Ragan never wanted to see trees come down.

My Tree

Every day in October for years
I would drive past the maple tree,
Often slowing down, sometimes stopping,
Reveling in and celebrating
Golden yellow, splashes of red,
A wonderment of colors.
I never knew who owned that house,
They probably thought they owned the tree,
But I knew it was mine—
It was my tree.

LeGette Blythe was a journalist and an author of novels, biographies, and dramas. Blythe was born in Huntersville, and was a classmate at UNC with Thomas Wolfe, Paul Green, and Jonathan Daniels. He wrote for the *Charlotte Observer* from 1927 to 1950. He was the winner of the Mayflower Cup for Nonfiction in 1953 with the publication of his book, *Miracle in the Hills*, and again in 1961 with *Thomas Wolfe and His Family*.

The Mayflower Cup was awarded until 2002, and this award is now called the Ragan Old North State Award Cup for Nonfiction, in honor of Sam Ragan. Blythe passed away in 1993, and Sam Ragan wrote about him in *Southern Accent*.

LeGette Blythe told us the story of the time he was working on his book, *Thomas Wolfe and His Family*, which won a Mayflower Award as the best book published in 1961.

"We went up to Asheville to talk with some of Tom's folks and Tom's mother was sitting on the porch shelling butterbeans," he said.

LeGette and Thomas Wolfe had been classmates at the University of North Carolina at Chapel Hill. They were members of that famous post World War I class which also included Paul Green and Jonathan Daniels — all were literary giants.

LeGette Blythe was one of the best writers of the lot and he and Green published the most books. And he was the last living member of the writers from that famous class at Chapel Hill.

William LeGette Blythe died at the age of 93 Sunday, Oct. 31, and with his passing goes the last of an illustrious group of writers who launched the Southern Literary Renaissance and kept it sustained through the years.

The story he told about visiting the home of Thomas Wolfe is typical of how he worked. LeGette liked the down home touch and he sought out details such as shelling butterbeans to give life and meaning to his writing.

He had learned a lot about the craft of writing while a student at Chapel Hill, but it was honed to a fine point through years as a newspaper reporter, first on the old *Charlotte News* for three years, and then for 25 or 30 years on the *Charlotte Observer*, where he covered just about every type of news story there is and also served in his later years as the newspaper's literary and book editor.

We talked about books a lot — and LeGette wrote and published more than 30 of them, and he had a high regard for both journalism and writing — to him both were a calling, a "high calling" and he had a lifelong respect and reverence for facts.

Last Saturday Tom Bradbury, the associate editor of the *Charlotte Observer*, wrote a three-column long article about LeGette Blythe, and he quoted Jack Claiborne, who had worked years ago with Blythe, that he was "the keeper of the flame." That was the title of Bradbury's signed editorial, and it was in itself a fitting tribute to the North Mecklenburg man from Huntersville who gave so much of himself to Charlotte and Mecklenburg and to North Carolina.

He both "lived and chronicled Mecklenburg's history." We recall when he was working on the drama which was produced for the celebration of Charlotte's bicentennial in 1968 that he wanted a new outdoor theater built near the present campus of the University of North Carolina on NC 49 at Charlotte. He asked us to walk over the site with him, and he told us some of his ideas for the drama. "Paul is the master at this," he said, referring to his old friend and class-mate, Paul Green.

LeGette researched everything at length before he started writing, and there never was a question about his facts. He believed in the Mecklenburg Declaration of Independence and he convinced us with his facts.

LeGette was one of the original members of the North Carolina Writers Conference and we came to know him very well at the annual gatherings of North Carolina writers. He was a genial story teller, and he will be missed, but his legacy to North Carolina literature will be long remembered.

Dixon, Otis, & Co. was hired by Sam Ragan to determine the value of *The Pilot*. By 1995, Ragan was 79 years of age and was experiencing health problems. He had been diagnosed with lung cancer, no doubt due in large part to his lifetime habit of smoking. He had quit by this time, but the damage had been done. Also, Marjorie was having her own health problems, and was no longer able to help at the newspaper like she had done in the past. In fact, she was confined to home care for much of the time, which required more and more of Ragan's time, which meant less time he could devote to *The Pilot*.

The Pilot was one of the most successful small-town newspapers in the entire country, averaging 80 pages per issue, with a paid circulation over 15,000. Ragan received offers to buy the paper on a regular basis. By this time, his two children, Nancy and Talmadge, were established and success-ful in their own careers away from the newspaper business, and so were not considering taking over the business. The Daniels family, including Frank Daniels, former owners of *The News and Observer*, had talked to Ragan about purchasing *The Pilot*.

Dixon, Otis, & Co., in 1995, told Ragan that the "fair market value," which they defined as the "cash or cash equivalent price at which property would change hands between a willing buyer and a willing seller," was $4,324,800. There was almost no debt, only $2,575.

So even though Ragan had not decided to sell *The Pilot*, he was in po-sition to make a big profit, having paid $100,000 for the newspaper when he bought it from Katharine Boyd in 1968.

Betty McCain, the Secretary of the North Carolina Department of Cultural Resources, Sam Ragan's old job, had supported the idea of a North Carolina Literary Hall of Fame. The proposal for the Hall of Fame was initiated by North Carolina State Librarian Howard McGinn and brought before the North Carolina Legislature by Howard Lee and Walker Russell. This cause was championed by Sam Ragan, who eventually led the effort to bring the Hall of Fame into existence in 1996. Its home is now in James Boyd's former study room at the Weymouth Center.

The old Southern Pines Library was originally proposed to be the home of the Hall of Fame. But due to costs of renovation and that the old library building was needed for more pressing needs for Southern Pines, this idea was dropped. The North Carolina Writer's Conference and the North Carolina Poetry Society endorsed the idea for a Hall of Fame. Ragan led the effort to use the old library building, and advocated for the building on West Broad Street in Southern Pines to house the Hall of Fame. But after it was deemed unfeasible, Ragan pushed for Weymouth Center to be the home.

The North Carolina Literary Hall of Fame at the Weymouth Center for the Arts and Humanities now has over 50 writers enshrined there. It is a program of the North Carolina Writers Network. Sam Ragan is considered to be the founder of the Hall of Fame, and justly so. The North Carolina Department of Cultural Resources, led by Betty McCain, had funded the effort with a grant.

Listening for the Wind, another book of Ragan's poems, was published in 1995. The book was dedicated to his wife, daughters, and grandchildren. "To Marjorie, who shared the journey, and Nancy, Talmadge, Robin and Eric, who joined us along the way." In his foreword, Ragan wrote:

After a lifetime of reading great poetry I had concluded that a good poem was the embodiment of all the arts, and indeed I had experienced the physical sensations which Marianne Moore had written about in the reading of poetry as causing the hair to rise and the eyes to dilate.

I seek clarity and conciseness in my poems, and often the writing takes on the characteristics of the search for the Holy Grail. The search never ends but the pursuit goes on. Often a poet can say in twenty lines what it takes a novelist a hundred thousand words to say.

These are frequently short poems which look at the human condition, at people and the world around them, and seek to preserve those glances and the moments in time experienced by human beings.

These are not earth-shaking or historically significant events, but I hope their preservation will provide some insights, perhaps a laugh or appreciative look, and enjoyment.

That, I think, is what poetry is all about.

Ragan wrote a short letter before the book was published to Ron Bayes, of St. Andrews Press, which published *Listening for the Wind*. Bayes was a professor of creative writing at St. Andrews College. He has written many books, including *The Collected Poems of Ronald H. Bayes.*

I am glad you liked the manuscript of *Listening for the Wind*. You see what I am driving at in my poetry more than anyone else, and I am grateful.

I don't know what St. Andrews Press has in mind for the book, but I would hope a thousand copies could be printed, with half of them hardback and half paperback.

Jacob Stephenson is working on a cover, and I will try to push him along.

Ron, I haven't thanked you sufficiently for the splendid luncheon you held for me at Mid Pines. It was, indeed, an overwhelming experience for me.

In an interview from his room at Scotia Village in Laurinburg, where I visited him, Bayes talked about Sam Ragan.

I came from the Pacific Northwest, and I met Sam. He knew North Carolina and the South like few people did. Sam was a very generous man, and he put me in touch with all the literary people in the state that could help me.

He was very helpful at St. Andrews also. He would conduct workshops for students, and he taught there for many years. He would critique students work. We were able to provide a community of interest at St. Andrews, thanks largely to Sam. He was very welcoming as a professor, and encouraged students to open up. He always felt everyone had something to say.

Sam always put what other people were doing ahead of what he was doing. He was a promoter of others, an encourager of others. He was wonderful to be around, he never met a stranger.

As a poet, he was very open, he was accessible. He was not a difficult poet, nor did he want to be. He wanted to be open to the people, and he succeeded in that. He opened up a big audience to poetry for people that way. Sam encouraged people to reach our further than they normally would.

I think he definitely deserves to be called North Carolina's Literary Godfather. I'm so glad you're writing this book. Sam was a close friend for many, many years.

Two of Ragan's poems in *Listening for the Wind* were about his love of reading and writing.

Words

It begins with the word,
With word following word
Music is made
Words make music all their own,
And sometimes there is nothing
More beautiful than words
Marching down a page
…Words marching

Sometimes they dance.

The Man Who Wrote a Book

Paul Green said that when
He left a Harnett County farm
For Chapel Hill he had never met
A man who had written a book.
At the University there was one man
With that distinction, he said,
And they used to point him out to visitors,
Just like a tourist attraction.

One of Ragan's poems was adopted as the official poem of the Kiwanis Club of the Sandhills, the Carolinas, and by Kiwanis International. It was called "We Build." Ragan was very active with the Kiwanis Club for many years. He believed strongly in their mission to help people. Ragan joined in 1969, and became a member of the Legion of Honor, which recognizes members with at least 25 years of service. In 1984 Ragan was awarded The Kiwanis Builders Cup, given annually to a man or woman of Moore County for outstanding contributions to the "upbuilding of the Sandhills Section."

We Build

Building is done
Brick by brick, stone by stone,
Board by board, nail by nail.
It also is done with words,
And by deeds.
Word by word, deed by deed,
We are proud that we build.
We find pride and courage
From our yesterdays,
We celebrate today,
And we look to tomorrow
And the sun of our seasons
Shine on our visions
As builders for people,
And their dreams...
Let us celebrate
Because we build.

Nell Styron, a newspaper writer, poet, and author, wrote Ragan after publication of *Listening for the Wind*.

Certainly "Ice Cream" is for all ages. I especially enjoy your close connection to nature—the earth—the beauty of the seasons—your warm love for life, for your Marjorie—and for the common man. You show in "The Pines" and in "Ghost Pines" the secret of their pull on Southern hearts and our nostalgia for long ago. Several times you

"listen for the wind," your companion as you recall "Old Poems."
And that wonderful poem to Thad Stem, "I Never Saw It That Way
Before." "The Kudzu Man" is delightful irony.

"Old Poems," a poem written by Ragan that Nell Styron mentions, follows.

Old Poems

All night I have listened
To the wind and the rain,
Sometimes coming down hard,
Sometimes softened by a rare quietness
That comes past midnight,
As I seek sleep by quoting
Over and over old and favorite poems.
Sleep finally comes, and
The wind and the rain are gone.
I wake in the dark before dawn
Still remembering the lines
From old poems.

Later in 1995, Ragan received a letter from the father of a young lady
who interned with *The Pilot*. The father was Howard Stacy from Atlanta.

My daughter, Rebecca, came home this weekend and shared with us
her experience as an intern at your paper. She also brought a front
page with a "Rebecca Stacy" by-line. While the by-line was impressive, I was more impressed at how much she seemed to enjoy being
at your paper. You, and your staff, were very kind to my daughter and
I think she learned a great deal about the business of a newspaper.

You are to be commended for your efforts to introduce the next
generation of writers to the daily workings of a newspaper. Becky
will always remember this first newspaper experience; her mother
and I will always treasure the story about the Moore County Beauty
Pageant.

Thank you.

Ragan wrote an editorial in support of a long-standing tradition in Moore County, the Stoneybrook Steeplechase.

Horse lovers and horse race fans are not the only ones grateful and indebted to the Walsh family for continuing the Stoneybrook Races this year.

The town of Southern Pines, the Sandhills and Moore County, along with a lot of people across North Carolina, have looked forward to this annual event—it's almost an essential rite of Spring.

To all of these people it comes as a pleasing recognition that the Southeast Tourism Society ranks Stoneybrook in the Top 20 events in the region for Spring—ranking the steeplechase event here along with the Kentucky Derby and the famed Dogwood Festival of Atlanta.

This will be the 48th running of the Stoneybrook Steeplechase at the farm of the late Mr. and Mrs. Mickey Walsh at Southern Pines, and their daughter, Phoebe Walsh Robertson, who is the race director, says invitations have gone out and responses for parking spaces are beginning to come in. The public at large is invited, of course, and 30,000 or more people are expected to be on hand on Saturday, April 15, for the event.

When famed trainer Mickey Walsh died last year many people had feared that the Stoneybrook Races would no longer be held. Thus the action of the Walsh family in continuing the long honored tradition is welcome news.

Ragan wrote about his good friend who also became North Carolina Poet Laureate, like Ragan, Shelby Stephenson.

It was a record crowd on hand-more than 175 persons for the spring meeting of the North Carolina Poetry Society at the Weymouth Center here on Saturday.

Diana Pinckney, of Charlotte, an award-winning poet, spoke about Stephenson.

"Shelby Stephenson sings a song of southeastern North Carolina with his guitar and his pen. Whether through country songs (often accompanied by friend and fellow editor Steve Smith or his wife,

Linda) or through poetry, Shelby makes a mighty sweet noise himself. His contributions to poetry and the North Carolina Poetry Society are beyond calculating. Across this state and others this troubadour carries his message that 'poetry saves us.'"

Shelby grew up on a farm in Johnston County, where he loved listening to the talk and story-telling. Also raised on hymns and country music, he began writing his own songs in the ninth grade. His poetry reflects these influences, saving the rural culture and its voices before it is altogether gone.

After graduating from Cleveland High School, Shelby was educated, earning a degree in English and studying law, at the University of North Carolina at Chapel Hill, University of Pittsburgh, and the University of Wisconsin at Madison. He is the author of four books [this was written in 1995]: *Middle Creek Poems*, the co-winner of the Zoe Kincaid Brockman Memorial Award in 1980, *Carolina Shout!*, winner of the statewide chapbook competition sponsored by the Playwrights Fund of North Carolina in 1985, *The Persimmon Tree Carol*, and *Finch's Mash*. In Shelby's 1993 book, *Plankhouse*, his poetic vignettes combine with Roger Manley's panoramic camera to give us intense images of the landscape and rural ways that we are rapidly losing.

Since 1979 Shelby has been the editor of *Pembroke Magazine*, a nationally recognized literary journal. Currently teaching literature and creative writing at Pembroke State University, Shelby lives with his two children and his wife, Linda, in Southern Pines where he is a true supporter of the North Carolina Poetry Society.

Ragan had a close relationship with Sandhills Community College for many year, and its president, Dr. John Dempsey. He taught writing classes there after moving to Southern Pines.

Dr. John Dempsey has shown his vision for education with past performances, but his latest announcement exceeds all former plans and programs, and the president of Sandhills Community College is saluted for what he proposes to accomplish.

It is called "Summa 2000" and its aim is to make Sandhills the finest institution of its kind not only in North Carolina and the nation, but the world. Dr. Dempsey wants to move Sandhills to a new level of distinction, a level where graduates can successfully meet the challenges they will have in the 21st century.

Moore County and its region are fortunate to have a first-rate community college such as Sandhills in its midst [it has long been called "the flagship" of the 58-campus community college system in North Carolina] and the Dempsey vision points to new honors ahead.

It must have been a pleasure to work at *The Pilot* while Sam Ragan was running the newspaper. Rebecca Stacy obviously had a good experience, but everyone this author has talked to that worked at *The Pilot* under Ragan's leadership talked of him as a kind man. But Ragan did expect hard work, and he often would pitch in and do any job that was needed on a particular day. The door to his office was always open, he would walk through the building, offer a smile and a kind word, ask about family. Employees of *The Pilot* knew Ragan cared about them as a person, not just a worker.

Bland Simpson taught creative writing at UNC for many years. His writing focuses on North Carolina's coast, with such books as *The Great Dismal: A Carolinian's Swamp Memoir* and *The Coasts of Carolina: Seaside to Sound Country.* Simpson also has written music and lyrics and performed in a number of plays. He is a long-time pianist for The Red Clay Ramblers, a Tony Award winning string band.

He wrote to Ragan in 1995, and expressed his appreciation for his help and encouragement.

I am thrilled to learn of my election to membership in the North Carolina Writers Conference, and would have written you earlier had I not been roaring back and forth from Chapel Hill to New York to put on our North Carolina coastal show, *King Mackerel & The Blues Are Running.*

If The Red Clay Ramblers concert schedule allows, my wife Ann and I would love to come to Southern Pines in July. Stephen Smith asked me to come down and read on April 23, so maybe we'll see you.

In any event, I offer my appreciation to you, who have always encouraged me.

In *The Pilot* each week, Ragan printed many "letters to the editor." In many issues an entire page was devoted to these letters. He printed letters that disagreed with something in the paper, or if the letter was about something on other matters. As he always exhibited in his life, he was perfectly fine if someone disagreed with him. They were welcome to walk in his office and sit down and discuss the matter. But he expected people to be civil, both in personal conversation and in letters to be printed in the paper. An example follows.

> I am returning the enclosed letter to the editor because it violates our policy of not printing personal attacks on an individual. Mrs. Dunlap is a respected teacher and writer, and your violent attack on her is not warranted. Moreover, the courts have held that accusing someone of being a Communist when they are not is libelous.
>
> As you know, *The Pilot* is open for free expressions of opinions. If you care to revise your letter to attack the idea she advanced for consideration, we will be glad to print it.

Weymouth continued to accept writers-in-residence to come and spend a week or two weeks to work in the quiet atmosphere of the big house. One writer wrote to Ragan to thank him for the experience in 1995.

> I'm sorry I didn't get a chance to speak with you when I was at Weymouth last week. I just wanted to thank you again for allowing me the privilege of working in such an inspiring place.
>
> I've written nearly 200 pages there. I've never worked with that kind of speed and creativity before. If the house is haunted, I'm grateful for such friendly spirits.
>
> Mae said we writers owe the existence of the place and the program to you. On behalf of all writers who have benefitted from Weymouth — thank you!

Nina Wicker wrote a book called *Where Pelicans Fly: Fourteen Haiku.* She passed away in Sanford, North Carolina, in 2012. Ragan wrote to her about her book.

Congratulations on your upcoming new book, and I hope the following will be adequate as a jacket comment:

Nina Wicker has used the haiku to invite us into her world and we do so to our betterment. Her short poems are lucid revelations to stir our senses and sensitivities, and the result is a pleasing experience.

I hope all goes well with your book. With best wishes always.

Ragan made another donation to his former college, Atlantic Christian, today called Barton College. He gave $5,000 to the Writing Center on campus. He had previously given $10,000. James Hemby, then president of Barton, wrote to Ragan shortly after the donation was made.

Thank you so much for your recent gift of $5,000. We continue to make significant progress in our efforts to find support for this important enterprise. You did not respond to my suggestion that we call our project the Sam and Marjorie Ragan Writing center. Knowing your modesty, I can imagine why you chose not to respond, But I am really quite serious about the suggestion, and would appreciate your input. Together you have meant much to writing in North Carolina, and I think such a title might be appropriate.

Today, the Sam and Marjorie Ragan Writing Center is located on Whitehead Avenue on the Barton College campus in Wilson, North Carolina. Dr. Rebecca Godwin is the Director, and an annual "Walking into April Poetry Day" is held there to honor Sam and Marjorie Ragan. "Let Us Walk into April" is a well-known poem of Ragan's.

13

"Birth and death, and in between a little living,"
Goodbye to a Southern Gentleman

R agan was continuing to experience health problems. The lung cancer was sapping his energy, but he continued working at *The Pilot*. He had told his family not to let anyone know, as he was a private man in such matters. Even those who suspected something seriously wrong had too much respect for the man to probe too deeply with questions. Those who knew him knew to leave it up to him to divulge any information.

But by late 1995 and into 1996, there were days Ragan simply felt too weak to make it to his office at *The Pilot*. That was a definite sign Ragan was seriously sick to those who worked with him and knew him. This man was in his office each day unless he was speaking somewhere or at a function that required his presence. So people knew, even though he never opened up about the lung cancer that was slowly killing him.

Marjorie Ragan was sick also, with chronic pulmonary disease. Talmadge Ragan and her husband, Worth Keeter, were living in Los Angeles, as was granddaughter Robin Smith. Nancy Ragan, the oldest daughter, was living in Vancouver, as was her son Eric. So no family was around on a daily basis to look after Sam and Marjorie, although Talmadge frequently flew from California to spend time with them. The family arranged for nurses to be with the Ragans in the spacious house on Hill Road in Southern Pines.

The Ragans' longtime housekeeper, Monica, was very helpful also, not only keeping house but watching after Sam and Marjorie too. Marilyn

Bridgeman, who worked at *The Pilot* for many years, and her husband, Melton, also visited the Ragans often and helped out. They were good family friends. Marilyn even taught Robin and Eric, the Ragan grandkids, how to drive. Melton would give Sam Ragan haircuts and shaves when it got to the point Ragan could not do it for himself.

Marilyn Bridgeman went to work at *The Pilot* part-time in 1981 as a file clerk and retired 27 years later working in the advertising department. She recalled those years in an interview with this author.

Sam and Marjorie Ragan were wonderful people to work for. Mr. Ragan was a true Southern Gentleman. I never met anyone that didn't like him, even Republicans. He was such a caring father, and he so loved his grandchildren, Robin and Eric. It was my pleasure to work at *The Pilot* for him. I was good friends with Talmadge. He was a private man and didn't want anyone to know about his illness. After he sold the newspaper, Frank Daniels and David Woronoff came in and they didn't fire people, and now David has made the newspaper one of the best around, in my opinion. Just like it was when Mr. Ragan ran it. Mr. Ragan would be very proud of what *The Pilot* is today, the wonderful job David has done.

Christmas 1995 was a joyous occasion for Sam Ragan, but not so much for his family who could see his deteriorating condition. But the family was together in Southern Pines, as Talmadge and her husband, Worth, came, along with Nancy, Robin, and Eric. It was a very special time, as Sam and Marjorie were very happy to have their family together. Sam Ragan had lost quite a bit of weight due to his illness, but he had a twinkle in his eyes and his smile was as warm as ever. There was gift exchanging, laughter, beautiful decorations inside and outside the house, and a lot of catching up to do. They drove around Southern Pines to look at other houses gaily decorated for Christmas and went to Dairy Queen for ice cream, even though it was a very cold night. Ice cream at Dairy Queen was a family tradition, as Sam Ragan loved his ice cream, and that made all the family love it too. Ever the good storyteller, Ragan regaled the family on Christmas night with stories from the past, as they all sat close to the big Christmas tree in the big house on Hill Road.

When Robin was taken to the airport with her fiancée, who had accompanied her to Southern Pines, she reminded Ragan of her wish to get married on the beautiful grounds of his house on Hill Road. They had talked of this on several occasions before. Ragan listened to Robin, whom he loved dearly, and looked down for some time. Then he looked up and patted Robin's fiancée on the back and said to him, "You take good care of her, you hear?" Ragan knew he was dying. It was at that moment that Robin realized they were perhaps saying goodbye for the last time. But she maintained her composure so Ragan would not realize she knew. When she got on the plane, the tears were allowed out, and they came for most of the long flight back to Los Angeles.

With his advancing age and illness, and knowing that he was being offered a good price for *The Pilot,* Ragan decided to sell to a group of five people, headed by the former publisher of *The News and Observer* in Raleigh, Frank Daniels Jr. The other men were Frank Daniels III, David Woronoff, Jack Andrews, and Lee Dirks. All of these buyers were previously associated with *The News and Observer.* The sale price was $4.8 million. Negotiations had been going on for some time, and Ragan's deteriorating health was the main reason for the sale. He loved *The Pilot,* had nurtured it into one of the leading newspapers in the state, and didn't want to let it go. But he had worked with the Daniels family for many years at *The News and Observer,* respected them as good newspaper people, and considered them friends. He knew the paper would be in good hands.

Today, the Daniels family continues to own and run *The Pilot.* David Woronoff is the publisher, and *The Pilot* has been named Best Community Newspaper in the United States by the National Newspaper Association several times. It is a vital part of the Sandhills region, just as it was under Sam Ragan. Ragan would absolutely be proud of *The Pilot* today.

The North Carolina Literary Hall of Fame, which Sam Ragan had been pushing for years, came to fruition in 1996, as mentioned earlier. The Hall of Fame is housed in the Weymouth Center in Southern Pines. In May fifteen writers were the initial inductees. They were James Boyd, Charles Chesnutt, Jonathan Daniels, Inglis Fletcher, Paul Green, Bernice Kelly Harris, O. Henry, George Horton, Randall Jarrell, Gerald Johnson, Guy Owen, Thad Stem, Richard Walser, Manly Wade Wellman, and Thomas Wolfe.

But an awful damper on the ceremony was the death of Sam Ragan on May 11, one week before the inductions. Lung cancer had taken the life of North Carolina's Literary Godfather before he could see one of his dreams come true. Hundreds came to Weymouth that day, but it was a bittersweet occasion. David Brinkley, the nationally-renown television broadcaster who Ragan mentored at the *Wilmington Star* before World War II, sent a moving video tribute.

"He was a great writer, a great poet and a great friend," Brinkley said, as many of those in attendance wept. "I was just a kid at the time, and he taught me a great deal. I became good friends with Sam and Marjorie and we used to eat and drink together. I came really to love him. We've kept in touch over the years. He's always what I think of as the proper, perfect, historically oriented Southern gentleman and all the positive things that implies. I think of all the time we spent together…when I think of him, I think of the Old South, live oak trees and Spanish moss and dogwood trees and camellias and pine woods, green water, ocean. Sam was always there. And I'll always miss him."

Sam Ragan died in his sleep about 5 a.m. "He was so dreadfully sick," said his wife of 56 years, Marjorie Ragan. Ragan's death, even though he had been sick, took his family and friends by surprise. His death called to mind a stanza from one of his own poems, "The Marked and Unmarked."

I cannot say upon which luminous evening
I shall go out beyond the stars,
To windless spaces and unmarked time,
Turning nights to days and days to nights.

Governor Jim Hunt, who had appointed Ragan North Carolina Poet Laureate, said of his friend, "Sam Ragan was a North Carolina original—poet, newspaperman, gentleman and scholar. He lit up our state and we will greatly miss his creative work." Former Governor Terry Sanford said, "Sam Ragan was one of North Carolina's treasures. He was a crusading editorial force where he fought for the improvement of education, the elimination of racial injustice and the broadening of economic opportunities."

Visitation was held at Powell Funeral Home in Southern Pines, and the funeral was conducted at Brownson Memorial Presbyterian Church in Southern Pines. *The Pilot* offices closed at 1:30 p.m. on the day of the funeral so staff could attend. The funeral was held on May 14, 1996. Burial was at Bethesda Cemetery in Aberdeen. At the time, Ragan was survived by Marjorie, daughter Talmadge Ragan Keeter and her husband, Worth, daughter Nancy Ragan Smith, grandchildren Robin Smith and Eric Smith, a brother, Melvin Ragan, and a sister, Dorothy Jones.

The Ragan family suggested that memorials be sent to The Poet's Garden at the Weymouth Center, Friends of the Southern Pines Library, St. Andrews Press, or the Sam and Marjorie Ragan Writing Center.

In a letter to the editor of *The Pilot*, just a few days after the passing of Ragan, John Foster West, a good friend and professor emeritus of English at Appalachian State University, wrote: "Sam Ragan, Southern gentleman, journalist, poet, scholar, is no longer with us. 'Ask not for whom the bell tolls.' It tolls for the State of North Carolina."

On May 16, five days after Ragan had died, a tribute to Sam Ragan was read on the floor of the United States House of Representatives by North Carolina Representative Eva Clayton. Clayton began her tribute by saying,

> I rise today to pay tribute to a great journalist, a great poet, a great North Carolinian, a great American, Sam Ragan, who died Saturday, May 11, 1996. Born, Samuel Talmadge Ragan, 80 years ago in Granville County, Sam was devoted to his wife of 56 years, Marjorie, their two daughters, Talmadge and Nancy, his two grandchildren, Robin and Eric. Sam's tall frame, flowing white hair, trademark bow tie and fedora hat, made it easy, even for those who did not know him, to pick him out of the crowd. He had an affinity for people that was readily acknowledged and returned by those who met him. As an editor he fashioned a distinguished career of recording and examining newsworthy events. How remarkable, then, that in his poetry he focused on ordinary people, the small incidents of daily life, the quiet unfolding of nature, events that never rated a headline.

Clayton also read one of Ragan's poems and summarized some of his achievements.

After her husband passed away, Marjorie Ragan included this in the masthead of *The Pilot*: "Although Sam Ragan is no longer with us, other editorial voices will follow his lead. I expect the paper to remain the same — a community newspaper of broad interests with an emphasis on the arts. I care about Moore County and the people of the Sandhills and I assure you *The Pilot* will continue to speak for what is right, for what is fair and for what is important to us all."

But shortly after Ragan's death, the sale of *The Pilot* was finalized. Negotiations had been going on before his death. The Daniels family had sold *The News and Observer* in 1995 to McClatchy Newspapers for more than $300 million. Frank Daniels Jr. said, "Sam and I have been talking about this for over a decade, but there was nothing in the world that he enjoyed more than running *The Pilot*. The unfortunate circumstance of his death coincides with my retirement as publisher of *The News and Observer,* so that is why the sale has been made final."

Tributes poured in for Sam Ragan after his death from around the state and country. Excerpts follow:

Sam Ragan's death deprives North Carolina of its greatest practicing Renaissance man. — *Former Governor Bob Scott*

※

Sam Ragan embodied and expressed the spirit of North Carolina. He always was looking for the good in people and believed in the great potential of this state. Because of his vision, his eloquence and his words, I appointed him poet laureate. He spoke of us, and for us, in a way that was always positive and redeeming. I think I speak for all North Carolinians when I express my thankfulness for his life. — *Governor Jim Hunt*

※

Sam Ragan was an outstanding newspaperman who always tried to treat people fairly and with dignity. He held strong beliefs and was willing to use the editorial page to further them, but he strived to keep his beliefs out of the news columns. He fervently believed in community newspapers, their survival depending on covering local news, which *The Pilot* has done so well under his ownership. — *Frank Daniels*

＊

Ragan ran the newsroom of *The News and Observer* for 20 years, nurturing the careers of a multitude of the state's best writers and reporters. Yet in that time, and in the 28 years he was the owner and editor of the Southern Pines *Pilot*, he took time to smell the flowers, issuing several books of poetry and being named to the position of the state's poet laureate. Ragan was genuine, Southern to the marrow, striking in his bowtie and long white hair, and memorable to all with whom he had contact. — The News and Observer *editorial*

＊

Sam Ragan encouraged me to write, to query, to push past the chasms that he recognized would be barriers for me in the same literary circles that embraced, honored, and validated his creativity. So it is not strange that a photo of Sam Ragan prominently sits on my writing desk amongst the many faces of my elders and all the people who support and continue to guide me on my writing journey. His perceptivity to issues of emotion, history, and Southern culture remain soulfully instructive for me.

A long time ago he encouraged me to be steadfast and generous with my writing of poetry. It is my hope that if he were still here he would see that I strive in that spirit of commitment and continue to honor the promise I made to him many years ago…to write about the histories and herstories that bear much truth to endurance.

Knowing Sam Ragan, experiencing his writing world and passions is a blessing that continues to teach me about the integrity of perspective, gratitude, and grace. Like his poems, his persona still echoes the quiet genius of lyric and metaphor. — *Jaki Shelton Green, NC Poet Laureate*

＊

Mr. Ragan, a tall man with flowing white hair, had a fondness for wide-brimmed fedoras and a voice that had been called a whisky baritone. Though Mr. Ragan was courtly, his poetry could be terse and wry.

＊

Sam Ragan was a rare, gentle spirit and kind soul who genuinely believed in the good of human nature and would give anyone and everyone the benefit of a doubt. He might not agree with you and yet he respected your right to your beliefs. My father was generous in encouraging and nurturing people. He genuinely loved to help people and I loved that about him. He believed in strong character, ethics and values. He wanted to make a difference in people's lives. He loved to encourage people, not only in literary arts but in all of the arts. I was so blessed to have someone like him as a father and friend. If you knew him, you know what I mean. If you didn't, I wish you had. — *Talmadge Ragan*

※

Former Governor Terry Sanford said this week, "Sam Ragan was one of North Carolina's treasures." A treasure he was, and his loss is great, but because he passed our way, North Carolina is forever enriched. — *Neal Rattican*

※

It comes as heartening news that Frank Daniels et al won out in their bid for *The Pilot*. The long association between the Daniels and Ragan families bodes well for the continued success of the newspaper. Like many North Carolina writers, I subscribe to *The Pilot* primarily for its book reviews and news of literary and artistic happenings. Every issue, I find myself drawn into the news and feature stories, the regular columns, editorials and letters to the editor. I'm a big fan of Glenn Sides' photography, too. It seems to me his rural scenes capture that timeless quality that is a hallmark of Mr. Ragan's poems. — *Letter to the Editor in* The Pilot

※

The funeral service for Ragan was held in an overflowing Brownson Memorial Presbyterian Church in Southern Pines. After the service, best-selling author Jerry Bledsoe said Ragan's passing marked the end of an era in journalism. "Sam was the last of the great newspaper editors," he said. Speaking of *The Pilot*'s offices, Bledsoe said, "When you walk in that building you can still smell the ink."

In his eulogy, the Rev. Hal Hyde, retired pastor of Brownson, told members of Ragan's family to take comfort in the fact that the words Ragan committed to paper will immortalize his legacy.

Poet Shelby Stephenson read four of Ragan's poems — "Two Butterfles," "Journey into Morning," "The Marked and the Unmarked," and "One Small Singing." — The Pilot

❈

Sam Ragan called up every Southern dream of romance and beauty among the live oaks and pines and the quietly sad longing for a Southern past that none of us now alive ever knew. — David Brinkley

❈

Sam learned to ignore much of the human cacophony and encourage the "one small singing." It is his most apt epitaph that the ideals of community journalism have begun to find their way back into newsrooms once again. — Neil Morgan

❈

Like many North Carolina writers, I owe a very large debt to Sam Ragan. My debt to Sam was very specific. Thirty-two years ago when he was executive news editor of Raleigh's News and Observer and I was languishing in Greensboro, Sam offered me a job on his staff. I jumped at the chance and I never regretted it. As editor, poet and a kind of cheerleader for Tar Heel writers, he left an abiding mark. He was generous with his advice on writing. It boiled down to read, read, read and write, write, write, care deeply about what you are doing, and always seek the truth, then tell it simply. That's pretty good advice. — Guy Munger

❈

Sam Ragan taught writing at N.C. State University for many years, and 76 of those attending his classes went on to become published authors. But perhaps the most important thing Sam Ragan has done was to form "The Friends of Weymouth" to rescue the home of James Boyd from becoming another land development. — Mary Evelyn de Nissoff

❋

In the seven years I have been at Sandhills Community College, our college and the cause it represents have had no greater champion than Sam Ragan. Much of our college's success is due to the excellent reputation it enjoys in this community—a reputation which Sam Ragan had a large part in creating. We will always be grateful to him. To his successors at *The Pilot*: be worthy. You are assuming a trust, as well as a newspaper. —*John R. Dempsey*

❋

He was a man of letters. He was a man of the people. Sam Ragan left more than a legacy of superior literature and dynamic journalistic leadership. He left a legacy of humanity.

As a newspaperman he was adamant in his opposition to secrecy in government, in his support of those programs directed toward the betterment of the needy, the underdog or the afflicted. As a newspaper editor he could be a taskmaster, demanding that reporters dig out every detail of every news story. And he pushed his advertising staff to sell more and better ads.

As for that open door, it was truly open to everyone. Sometimes they came in anger only to be greeted not by a redneck or bigot, but by a soft-spoken Southern gentleman of sensitive demeanor.

He never adapted to new-fangled technology. Sam Ragan eschewed the computer age. The newspaper used computers, but his writing was accomplished either on an old manual typewriter or in pen and ink.

Sam Ragan was passionate about preserving the environment. Never was a tree chopped down that an editorial did not blossom. He early recognized the rich heritage of the longleaf pine ecosystem which supports the Sandhills. —*Florence Williams Gilkeson*

❋

Sam Ragan is not alone, of course, in pushing for recognition of the arts as an influence of improvement in the quality of the lives of North Carolinians. But his have been the most unflagging, the most tellingly effective of efforts. —*Thomas Walters*

✳

Sam Ragan was the giant of North Carolina literature. His generous encouragement and teaching skill inspired novelists, poets, short-story writers and dramatists. As a journalist, he set an example of integrity and devotion to the truth. I have lost a friend, a boss, a mentor. North Carolina has lost a great human treasure. — *Roy Parker*

✳

Sam added a dimension of beauty to the lives of all North Carolinians. He was of course a great journalist and poet, but I will always remember him as one who taught us to reach for the finest and best of what we can achieve. We shall all miss him with that wonderful bow tie and that everlasting smile. — *William Friday*

✳

Sam Ragan was truly North Carolina's Literary Godfather. His wand was his favorite word, "splendid," which propelled writers of all kinds — novelists, journalists and poets — to go forth and do more than they ever thought they could do with the English language. His magic will endure. — *Sally Buckner*

Song for Sam

God bless Sam,
Whose genial eye, true blue,
Sees poems in prosaic men,
The weather, purple plums,
Girls in green bathing suits.
And bless his shock of silver hair,
his senatorial air,
his wicked wit that saves him from
a saccharin saintliness.
Bless his ubiquitous bow ties, blue suit,
His gravelly Granville accents, Tar River taproot.
God bless Sam, a Tar Heel
Gulliver among the Lilliputians
And a damn good newspaperman.
　　— *Kathryn Gurkin*

Mae Woods Bell, a dear friend of Ragan's, wrote a moving poem shortly after he passed away, reflecting on his funeral and a visit to the grave the day after burial. Bell, along with being a poet who sent her "WRYmes" to be published in *The Pilot*, was also more than just a friend to Sam Ragan, but a close companion.

That Day in May

It was your favorite kind of day.
Clear skies, sun shining,
just as you'd choose
for sitting on your terrace
with a book.

We found the church cool,
certain as centuries,
its mullioned glass
fractured light,
filling the silence.

Seeing all your friends
you would have planned a party.
So many people bearing love,
moved slowly, careful not to spill,
brimfilled with tears.

And did you hear your words
take wing among the shadows?
A fitting epitaph
That final accolade
"He was a poet."
"And still is." We murmured
From our pews.

Next day we visited
that place.
Following birdsong
down among carved stones
deep-etched in grief
to fresh-turned earth.

We could not see your name
for flowers,
a cloud of petals
covered sun-warmed soil.

We left you there to sleep.
Walked quietly away
through pines so still
they seemed to hold their breath.
Strong silent witnesses of life
springing from death.

Many poems have been written in tribute to Sam Ragan, such as the one by Mae Woods Bell, both during his life and after his death. I am sure he would be pleased, and although a most modest man, would agree with what Walt Whitman once said after reading a poem about himself. "You see, if I can't write poetry at least I can inspire it."

Epilogue

Marjorie Ragan lived more than five years without the man she loved so dearly since their marriage in 1939. She passed away on June 15, 2001, at her home in Southern Pines. She was not in good health in her last years, and that was coupled with the deep loss she felt from losing her husband. Friends and family visited, and she continued to read, one of the passions of her life, just like Sam.

She and Sam still have the Sam and Marjorie Ragan Writing Center on the campus of Barton College to memorialize them, and at the University of North Carolina at Chapel Hill there is the Marjorie Usher Ragan Scholarship awarded to a student in the UNC School of Media and Journalism. And of course, her two daughters whom she loved with all her heart, Nancy and Talmadge, survive her, as do her granddaughter Robin and grandson Eric.

In 1997, Sam Ragan was inducted posthumously into the North Carolina Literary Hall of Fame. In 1999, the First Health Moore Regional Hospital honored Ragan with the Sam Ragan Memorial Research Library. A commemorative plaque, was placed in the reading room of the Health and Sciences Library in the hospital. The plaque reads:

> As the editor and publisher of *The Pilot*, Sam contributed to the quality of Moore Regional Hospital throughout his life by his support of its services in his editorials and the fair coverage of its development and growth in his news stories. No one person placed a greater value on books and learning and on the health and welfare of the people who live in the community this hospital serves. Remembering this, we dedicate this memorial tribute to the man who is remembered for his love of the printed word, his belief in community journalism and his commitment to the people he served.

Also in 1999, a ceremony was held at Weymouth to honor Ragan, the man most responsible for Weymouth being used today as a center for the arts. A plaque honoring Ragan was placed in a rock garden and planted area near the Connecticut Avenue entrance to Weymouth. On the plaque was this: Sam Ragan 1915–1986, Poet Laureate of North Carolina, Publisher of The Pilot, Founder, Benefactor and Friend of The Weymouth Center. Stephen Smith emceed the ceremonial event. Several people, including Lena Brillhart, shared memories of Ragan, and Jane McPhaul, Stephen Smith, and Shelby Stephenson read some of Ragan's poems. Lois Holt made closing remarks.

A bust of Sam Ragan was unveiled at Weymouth in 2005, and the bust stands near the entrance today. In the last months of his life, Ragan had sat in his office at *The Pilot* to have his likeness sculpted by Gretta Bader, a nationally acclaimed artist. Bader, among many other works, has a statue of famed golf course designer Donald Ross in Pinehurst and an eight-foot statue of United States Senator J. William Fulbright at the University of Arkansas. She said, "From the moment I encountered Sam, I sensed his intensity, the warmth of his voice and manner, the richness of his capacity to listen, his accessibility. In this sculpture, there is something in gesture, smile, and expression that convey the extraordinary man I came to know and love. My hope is that it speaks to all of us that Sam is still ready for a good conversation."

A "Bring Sam Home" campaign had been launched to raise $25,000 for the bust to be placed in Weymouth. Charles Blackburn and Marsha Warren were campaign co-chairs. "Weymouth was close to Sam's heart," Warren said. "He was instrumental in preserving the old Georgian mansion as a cultural center and in creating the N.C. Literary Hall of Fame there, which inducted him posthumously in 1997. So, for many reasons, Weymouth is the ideal home for this remarkable portrait bronze of North Carolina's Literary Godfather."

Elena Ruehr, a Composer-in-Residence at the Massachusetts Institute of Technology at the time, was commissioned by the Coastal Carolina Chamber Music Festival to write a musical work based on Sam Ragan's poetry. Ragan had seen his poetry danced to, painted, and now it was sung and played to. Ruehr's work was titled "Exodus," and debuted in 2006. Scored for soprano, violin, viola, cello, and harp, "Exodus" presented musical ideas derived directly from Ragan's poetry.

Commentary on
Sam Ragan

I can say about Sam is that he is North Carolina literature. He exemplifies what is best in all of us, what every writer aspires to: he's generous yet rigorous, forever young. — *Lee Smith*

⁂

Whatever else, his existence, what he is as much as what he does, gives the state's writers heart to fight. — *John Herbert Roper*

⁂

What Sam Ragan does best is embrace the mystery of the commonplace. Like Robert Frost, he takes his cues from nature and enlarges them into a map of the senses. Ragan possesses what Eudora Welty terms "the lyrical impulse," the impulse to praise, to love, to call up, to prophesy. What notches the eye of Sam Ragan again and again is the ordinary, but the ordinary, the daily, is his most elegant and persuasive muse. It's also his most precious commodity. — *Joseph Bathanti*

⁂

Many of Ragan's poems mark time, the changing seasons. But the hard edge of life is not ignored; there is no glossing over human shortcomings — poverty, hypocrisy, deceit — the inevitable fall from innocence into knowledge. — *Stephen E. Smith*

⁂

His poetry has given me permission to write about the everyday things that touch me. And his graciousness has taught me that being a poet is not all hunching lonely in the corner with a pen and a note-

333

book. It is something to be celebrated, opened up, and given freely. — *Marjorie Hudson*

※

I've been trying to figure out what it is exactly that makes Ragan's poetry so vibrant, so pulsing it jumps off the page. He isn't choosing shocking subjects — or even titillating ones. He is writing about sitting in traffic jams and admiring a river. Sometimes he writes about the experience of writing — a mystery that baffles, confuses and eludes those of us who aspire to worship at its shrine. Yet his writing is so compelling. It is the active, hard-working verbs he wrestles into service, and the truly spare and focused painting he does on the page. — *Gwenyfar Rohler*

※

Tall and slender with expressive blue eyes and a ready smile, his silvery hair overflows onto his collar. Sam is the epitome of solidity, honesty and strength. Unpretentious, readily accessible and tolerant, he is also a marvelous raconteur. He wears hand-tied bow ties, Panama straw hats and linen jackets in summer. He sports tweedy jackets and soft fedoras in winter.

He gave me the boundless joy of being published for the first time. When I thanked him for the honor, he simply said, "It was a good poem." — *Frances Outhwaite*

※

The persona is as rugged and enduring as a ridgeline along the flank of old Mount Mitchell, with his handsome chiseled features, the lank gray hair, the cigarette, the bow tie, the big ol' straw hat, he is a sight for sore eyes. His graciousness, his quiet, strong diction, his magnificent smile, and the quick, ebullient way he flicks his ash when he is really excited about an idea, these things stand out in your recollections. — *Roy Parker*

※

I always feel the world is going to be all right when I see Sam Ragan's bow tie. — *Terry Sanford*

Whether it's a writers' conference, *The Lost Colony*, The Cultural Resources Division of Government, *The News and Observer*, or his beloved *Pilot*, he is always offering a congratulatory word here, picking up or telling a story there, and always urging us to be our best. To me he is North Carolina's Renaissance Man. — *William Friday*

⁕

We are a better people and our state is a better place because of his many and varied contributions. With apologies to Tennyson and Sam Ragan, I humbly submit my simple lines:

> Sam Ragan is a friend of mine,
> Who's noted for his skill with rhyme;
> With a twinkle in his eye
> And his trademark bow tie,
> He is truly one of a kind!

— *Bob Scott*

⁕

The very first review I ever received by anyone was written by Sam Ragan, editor of *The News and Observer*, a man I did not know. He chose my poem as an example of the quality the new quarterly (*Carolina Quarterly*) contained and published the poem in his column, *Southern Accent*. I will never forget Sam Ragan's compliment nor my first review. — *John Foster West*

⁕

I think of Daddy singing "Hello my baby, Hello my honey, Hello my ragtime girl" and his dancing about the room trying to cheer up a kid who needs to find a smile. At night, he'd sing "Summertime" while he pointed out the moon and the constellations through the trees, quoting poetry — others as well as his own — to a little girl barely old enough to read.

Although we didn't always agree, I know he supported that right he taught me was mine, to make my own choices and to decide what is right for my own life.

I love that he wrote a birthday poem for my mother each year. I love that he wrote a poem for me. — *Talmadge Ragan*

❋

Since founding St. Andrews Press, with a lot of help from friends, it has been a profound pleasure to "utter forth" three of Sam's finest, including his multi-prizewinning *Collected Poems*. You will find the man there, if you do not yet know him. Warm, generous, funny, analytic, by turns. Always the hand extended in personal and intellectual friendship—to the newly met as certainly as to the cherished companion. — *Ron Bayes*

Index